Demeter and Persephone

Demeter and Persephone

Lessons from a Myth

TAMARA AGHA-JAFFAR

McFarland & Company, Inc., Publishers
Jefferson, North Carolina, and London

Library of Congress Cataloguing-in-Publication Data

Agha-Jaffar, Tamara, 1952–
    Demeter and Persephone : lessons from a myth /
Tamara Agha-Jaffar.
        p.   cm.
    Includes bibliographical references and index.

    ISBN 0-7864-1343-3 (softcover : 50# alkaline paper) ∞

    1. Demeter (Greek deity)   2. Persephone (Greek deity)   I. Title.
BL820.C5A44   2002
292.2'114—dc21   2002009912

British Library cataloguing data are available

Cover photograph ©2002 PhotoSpin

Manufactured in the United States of America

McFarland & Company, Inc., Publishers
  Box 611, Jefferson, North Carolina 28640
  www.mcfarlandpub.com

To my beloved parents,
Najla Chalabi and
Abdul Latif Agha-Jaffar
in loving memory

Acknowledgments

I owe this book to the support and encouragement of a great many individuals, beginning with my colleagues on the sabbatical committee, the administration, and the Board of Trustees at Kansas City Kansas Community College—all of whom were instrumental in awarding me a sabbatical in Fall 1999 that made much of this research possible. Without this respite from my teaching responsibilities, *Demeter and Persephone: Lessons from a Myth* may not have been born.

To past and present employees at Kansas City Kansas Community College whose support of my work may have been nonspecific but immeasurable, I owe a sincere debt of gratitude. Prominent among them are Morteza Ardebili, Jim Brown, Tom Burke, Andrea Chastain, Bill Chennault, Ken Clark, Deb Clough, Cindy Coleman, Steve Collins, Antonio Cutolo-Ring, Mary Fenlon, Amy Fugate, Lisa Gammon, Ben Hayes, Evelyn Huffman, Melanie Jackson-Scott, Michael Kimbrough, Cindy Lahmann, Pat Lawson, Pat Lipsey, Kim Lutgen, Denise McDowell, Hira Nair, Joann Nelson, Deloris Pinkard, Becky Pinter, Sumitra Rattan, Anita Reach, Jerry Reid, Charles Reitz, John Ryan, Patty Schmaus, Marilee Shrader, Steve Spartan, Jerry Toney, Kaye Walter, Valerie Webb, Charles Wilson, and Valdenia Winn.

I am indebted to my friends in the Department of English. Specifically, I am thankful to Adam Hadley, Phil Miller, Mike Pettengell, Gregg Ventello, Rob Vuturo, and Tom Weis for their advice and support as well as for their delightful banter and a delicious sense of irony that continues to enrich my mind.

With heartfelt gratitude, I acknowledge the contributions of Guillermo Barreto-Vega, Charles Cowdrick, and Jennifer Gieschen. They read preliminary drafts of this manuscript and provided insights, suggestions, editorial comments, and unflagging encouragement.

The staff at Kansas City Kansas Community College Library has been invaluable. A special thank you goes to Teri Hunter for her uncanny ability to ferret out books and research materials even if the only clue I was able to provide her with was half a name and a smidgen of a title. She performed each search with grace, good humor, punctuality, and success.

My thanks extend to my many students throughout the years who have enriched my life and work in ways that cannot be measured. Their remarkable stories of resilience and strength in the face of adversity have educated me, encouraged me, challenged me, humbled me, and inspired me.

Thanks also go to Princeton University Press for giving me permission to reproduce the Helene P. Foley translation of the Homeric *Hymn to Demeter* in its entirety.

A special thanks goes out to my three sisters, Zaynab, Sara, and Besma, and to my brother, Jaffar. I am indebted to my father, Abdul Latif Agha-Jaffar, for teaching me the importance of structure, discipline, and organization in any endeavor, and for instilling in me a thirst for intellectual development and a passion for books. I am indebted to my mother, Najla Chalabi, for demonstrating the importance of voice and for showing me how to channel fierce dedication, commitment, and compassion to the service of others. It is to my beloved parents that this book is humbly dedicated.

To my dear friend, Leslie Overfelt, I say thank you for your kindness, generosity, compassion, and gentleness of spirit. Leslie has been a source of comfort and support during the good times and the bad times in the nearly two decades that I have known her. She listens to my whiny phone calls and hears my interminable narratives of successes, failures, frustrations, joys, and sorrows, and she embraces each of these stories as if it were her own.

Finally, I want to thank the three most important people in my life: my husband of nearly 25 years, Samih Staitieh, and our two sons, Bashar and Reshad. My words of thanks emerge out of my sense of how much I owe these three people and of how much I love them. They have helped to shape my perspectives, my work, and my life. Without their support and faith in my abilities, I may never have embarked on this project or been able to complete it.

To Bashar and Reshad, I say thank you for filling my life with joy; for showing me the meaning of goodness, empathy, and compassion; for reminding me of priorities; for reeling me in whenever I veer too far in any one direction either in word or in deed; for forcing me to try to be a better human being than I might otherwise have been; and for continuously reaffirming my belief in the goodness of human kind. Nothing I have ever done in my life or will ever do in the future will bring me as much pride or as much joy as the two of you have brought to me.

To Samih Staitieh, my mentor, guide, partner, and husband for the better part of my life, I am deeply indebted. He keeps me watered, fed, sheltered, and clothed. He demonstrates infinite patience in listening to my stories and reading my words. He nurtures my every growth spurt. He bolsters my confidence when it sags. He replenishes my spirit. He challenges me to do better. Best of all, he continues to indulge my insatiable appetite for jewelry, shoes, and fast cars. And he does all of this with an infectious humor, a generous spirit, and a gentle heart.

Kansas
Summer 2002

Contents

For I think your beloved Athens has brought to birth, and contributed to human life, many outstanding and divine creations, and nothing better than those mysteries. Thanks to them we have become mild and cultivated, moving from a rough and savage life to a state of civilization; we have learned from so-called "initiations" things which are in fact the first principles of life, and we have been taught a way of living happily and also of dying with brighter hopes.

Cicero, The Laws 2:36, *referring to the Eleusinian Mysteries*

Cast of Characters

Demeter

Granddaughter of Gaia and Uranos; daughter of Kronos and Rheia; sister to Zeus; mother of Persephone; known as the goddess of the grain; presided over bountiful harvests. Romans knew her as Ceres (cereal). Worshiped as a mother goddess, specifically as mother of the grain and as mother of Persephone. Her myth with Persephone became the basis for the Eleusinian Mysteries.

Demophoon

Infant son of Metaneira and Keleos; brother to Kallidike, Kleisidike, Demo, Kallithoe.

Hades

Grandson of Gaia and Uranos; son of Kronos and Rheia; brother of Zeus and Demeter; uncle and abductor of Persephone; god of the underworld, also known as Erebos or the chthonic realm (Chthonia is the Greek word for in or under the earth, i.e. the land of the dead). Hades is also known as Pluto (derived from *plautos*, which means wealth) i.e. god of wealth.

Hekate

Sometimes referred to as "three-faced"; perhaps once identical with three-headed Cerberus, the dog who guards the entrance to Hades. She is the goddess of the threshold between the underworld and earth; also the goddess of the crossroad. Her image stands at the entrance to every house and at intersections; the key is her emblem. Hekate represents the seriousness and precariousness of all transitions. As guardian of the entrance to the inner world, Hekate is present at times of transition and at those moments when souls connect with and leave bodies, at childbirth and at death.

Helios

Lord of the sun; observed the abduction of Persephone from his chariot as he traveled across the sky.

Hermes

Son of Zeus; also known as the Slayer of Argos; messenger of the gods; sent by Zeus to the underworld to tell Hades to release Persephone from captivity.

Iambe/Baubo

A post-menopausal female who lives and works in the palace at Eleusis.

Kallidike, Kleisidike, Demo, Kallithoe

The four daughters of Metaneira and Keleos; sisters to Demophoon.

Keleos

King of Eleusis; husband of Metaneira; father of Kallidike, Kleisidike, Demo, Kallithoe (females) and Demophoon (male).

Kore/Persephone

Daughter of Zeus and Demeter; granddaughter of Kronos and Rheia; niece of Hades; known as the Grain Maiden, the new crop—her presence in the overworld signifies the coming of spring. She is Kore in her maiden aspect and Persephone after she has been violated; becomes wife of Hades and queen of the underworld.

Metaneira

Queen of Eleusis; wife of Keleos; mother of Kallidike, Kleisidike, Demo, Kallithoe (females) and Demophoon (male).

Rheia

Wife of Kronos; mother of Zeus and Demeter; grandmother of Kore/Persephone.

Zeus

Grandson of Gaia and Uranos; son of Kronos and Rheia; head of the Olympian gods; brother to Demeter; father of Persephone.

Introduction

This is a book about a very old story of a forced separation between a mother and her daughter, the mother's successful struggle to regain access to her daughter, their joyful reunion, and an ancient ritual that re-enacts and commemorates their story. For over one thousand years, the ritual quenched the spiritual thirst of our ancestors and claimed to bestow blessings and happiness on any who were initiated into its mysteries. Demeter is the mother; Persephone is her daughter. Theirs is a story that continues to speak to us on a profound level even after all these years.

My appreciation for the story of Demeter and Persephone grew through a circuitous route. I have a vague recollection of first being introduced to the myth in an undergraduate humanities class. We had been assigned Edith Hamilton's *Mythology*.[1] But like much of what I had been exposed to as an undergraduate, this myth left little or no impact on me. I dismissed it as a quaint attempt on the part of the ancient Greeks to explain the agrarian cycle of nature. So I dutifully filed it away in the murky recesses of my brain along with all the other inconsequential raw material that I could call upon when needed for interpreting a work of literature. But the myth itself failed to speak to me personally—a young undergraduate who believed she had the world figured out and who knew exactly where she was heading in life. Or so she thought at the time.

It wasn't until many years later that I stumbled into an appreciation of this myth. I had been a faculty member at Kansas City Kansas Community College for several years. My graduate degrees are in English literature. My training and background had taught me to value the writing of male

Europeans, and, with very few exceptions, to dismiss the writing about women and by women as peripheral to the serious business of literature. So I plodded on, immersing myself in teaching the obligatory undergraduate composition classes and a smattering of one or two literature classes a semester to help me maintain my sanity.

But then something happened. My personal readings had led me down a winding path to the discovery of pre-patriarchal goddess figures. This material totally captivated me. It also angered me. I was angry with my professors—male and female alike—who had failed to expose me in a serious manner to any of these empowering stories. But I was primarily angry with myself for absorbing without question what I later came to identify as values, perspectives, and choices that reeked of misogyny. How could I have been so stupid? I berated myself.

My appreciation for mythology deepened, and I gradually developed an understanding that myths should not—and could not—simply be dismissed as mere curiosities. A myth will hold little relevance for us today if we approach it as a vestige of an ancient time when a people fabricated make-believe stories in order to satisfy their craving for an affirmation of the existence of a sequential cause and effect on what must have appeared to be a chaotic, incomprehensible universe. If myth is restricted to this etiological approach, it becomes inert matter that is hardly worth the effort it takes to resuscitate it. Eventually, I arrived at the awareness that a myth's function in claiming to impose an order on the natural world is one of its least significant aspects.

Myths perform a number of functions: they provide us with ways of perceiving and understanding reality; they provide us with examples of human actions that we are to emulate or to repudiate; they provide us with guidelines for what is acceptable and what is unacceptable human behavior; and they provide us with moral, spiritual, and ethical frameworks—frameworks that, in many ways, are able to transcend their temporal and cultural inflections since they speak to the perennial concerns of humanity. In short, a culture's mythology reflects, reproduces, as well transcends the attitudes, aspirations, and perceptions of its people in much the same way that the stories we tell our children reflect, reproduce, and transcend their attitudes, aspirations, and perceptions of themselves and of the world around them.

A myth becomes a breathing entity only when we strip it of its superficial covering and allow it to reveal its many layers of meaning and interpretation. It is only by penetrating to its hidden depths can we begin to decipher the ways in which the myth continues to address the perennial concerns of humankind. My teachings and discussions of myths and ancient stories have very little to do with the explanation they offer of natural phenomenon and everything to do with what they reveal to us about what it means to be human ... our relationships, our successes and failures, our defeats and victories, our weaknesses and strengths, our position in and our connection with the world we inhabit.

My exposure to pre-patriarchal mythology served to increase my determination to provide my students—the majority of whom are females—with mythology and literature that is gender-inclusive and gender-empowering. I wanted them to read about powerful female role models: strong, assertive females who performed the multiple roles of healers, nurturers, creators, saviors, and spiritual guides. So I decided to offer a course in which I explore the mythology depicting these pre-patriarchal goddesses as archetypes and then use those archetypes to discuss and analyze the contemporary literature about women and by women. Hence, my Women in Literature course was born—as far removed from the phallocentric literature I had been trained to value as anything could possibly be.

The development and subsequent revisions of my Women in Literature course corresponded with what grew to become my increasing fascination with mythology. Included in my Women in Literature course was the story of Demeter and Persephone. Gradually, I came to recognize that this myth was not just about the agrarian cycle. In fact, the etiological aspect of the myth receded into the background. What slowly emerged in its place was a recognition that this story has something significant to say to me as a woman, a mother, and a daughter. By extension, it has something to say to all women: about who we are, about our roles as mothers and daughters, about the nature of our interactions, about our subordinate status in a patriarchal society, about fighting back, about refusing to submit, and about personal growth. It has a message that extends even beyond women to include men, since it touches a universal chord in all of us about the meaning of loss, grief, healing, insight, initiation, and a return to mother. Furthermore, through its acknowledgement of the primacy of the female experience, the myth has come to represent an attempt to restore a much-needed balance to the skewed, hierarchical, phallocentric, and damaging masculinist forces that have dominated society for many centuries and that continue to saturate it with destructive consequences.

My reading of the myth of Demeter and Persephone has been further enriched by my immersion in feminist literature that I undertook when I decided to initiate the Women's Studies program at the college several years ago. Nowadays, it seems as if much of what I read reveals deeper layers of meaning and subtle nuances, breathing more life into this preeminent myth that I had once dismissed in such a perfunctory manner.

I am convinced that the myth of Demeter and Persephone speaks to us in significant and complex ways—a complexity that may never be fully revealed or exhausted. It resonates on so many different levels with the experience of being human. Kore/Persephone, Demeter, or all three have fascinated me simultaneously at different times in my life. I have been intrigued by the different episodes of the myth: Demeter's meeting with Helios, her stay at Eleusis, her anger at Metaneira, her veiling, and her penance. I have been no less intrigued by the image of the young Kore, innocently picking flowers only to be brutally initiated into womanhood through abduction and rape. And what of Persephone in the underworld? What does her journey to and from the chthonic realm reveal to us about our own journeys to that dark and fearful vicinity which, paradoxically, may be the only space where we can experience genuine growth spurts in our own psyche?

With each reading of the myth, I find myself increasingly drawn to the characters and what they have to say to us. I seek to understand the perspectives of Zeus and Helios, recognizing their limitations while at the same time acknowledging their genuine contributions. I embrace Hades as a figure who seems to experience growth in that he moves beyond rigidly constructed gender roles and adopts a perspective that is inclusive and holistic. I listen carefully to the words of Demeter, Persephone, Metaneira, Hekate, and Rheia trying to decipher their insights and guidance on what it means to be a female living in a society that has attempted to strip me of choice, agency, and control over my body and my life. I celebrate the youth, enthusiasm, and boundless energy of the four daughters of Metaneira, remembering a time when I was once that young and eager to experience life with breathless anticipation. And now that I have become increasingly conscious of my aging body, I revel in the raucous belly laugh of the ostensibly minor figure of Iambe/Baubo, a figure who has much to teach me about the freedom, autonomy, and exuberance that can characterize those impending crone years.

This work is an attempt to explore these issues. My exploration is based on my own readings of the myth, my readings of the written and oral contributions of others concerning the myth, my life experiences, the life experiences of my students, my friends, my colleagues, my family, and others I have interacted with.

There are many variations and many versions of the story of Demeter and Persephone, some that are as ancient as Hesiod's *Theogony* and Ovid's *Metamorphoses*, and some that are as recent as the feminist retellings and renditions of the story that are included in, for example, Christine Downing's *The Long Journey Home: Re-Visioning the Myth of Demeter and Persephone for Our Time*.[2] However, for the purpose of this work, my focus and analysis will be based on the Homeric *Hymn to Demeter*.[3] Homer's poem consists of a beautiful, lengthy, and complete rendition of the story from ancient Greece. It is a rendition that reveals a multiplicity of layers and lends itself to in-depth analysis. The complete work, translated by Helene P. Foley, is included in the Appendix of this book.

Demeter and Persephone: Lessons from a Myth begins with a summary of the story of Demeter and Persephone as told in the Homeric *Hymn to Demeter*. Chapter 2 examines the story from the perspective of Demeter and explores the lessons we glean from her experience. Chapter 3 performs the same task, but from the perspective of Persephone. Chapter 4 explores the symbolism of the narcissus, the veil, and the pomegranate—three objects that play a pivotal role in the story. Chapter 5 discusses Demeter, Hekate, the four daughters of Metaneira, Iambe, Metaneira, and Rheia in terms of female mentoring. This is set in contrast with the masculinist perspective as presented by Zeus and Helios and discussed in Chapter 6. Chapter 7 examines the meaning of the underworld or chthonic realm and the role of Hades. Chapter 8 explores the subject of rape—its literal as well as its metaphorical meaning in the story. Chapter 9 unlocks the mysteries by providing a summary of the guidelines for healing and knowledge that we have gleaned from our analysis. And the Afterword demonstrates the profound impact that the story continues to hold for a contemporary audience.

A myth is an attempt to invest regularity and order in an otherwise apparently chaotic world. As Bettina L. Knapp has argued in *Women, Myth, and the Feminine Principle*, a myth is an attempt to render comprehensible what would otherwise be incomprehensible, and by its very richness and depth, it lends itself to a variety of interpretations.[4] As with any work of literature, a myth can support a wide range of interpretations as long as each interpretation is grounded in the words of the text.

I do not claim to have a definitive meaning of the myth of Demeter and Persephone. For me, understanding the story of Demeter and Persephone in all its complexity is a lifelong work in progress. I fervently believe that this myth is no different from any other ancient myth in that it has much to teach us if we take the time and effort to probe deeply into its meaning. The effort is well worth it because once we penetrate beneath the superficial level of its story line through to a reading of the myth as metaphor, we begin to discover layers of truths and insights that are as relevant to us today as they were to audiences two thousand years ago.

My aim is to render the Homeric *Hymn to Demeter* accessible to a modern sensibility. I am attempting to share some of the insights I have gleaned through deconstructing an ancient myth in the hope that this will propel others on their own odysseys to growth and self-discovery. I invite my readers to make connections between the interpretations and lessons gleaned from this myth to their own deeds, their own thoughts, and their own lives. I invite my readers to explore the different dynamics through which the individual and the collective interact and relate to each other as can be evidenced by this myth. And I invite my readers to use this myth as a catalyst for increasing their understandings of their inner and outer dimensions, of themselves and of the world around them.

Join me on a journey as I share with you a very old story that continues to talk to us after all these years.

CHAPTER 1

The Story

Briefly, the story of Demeter and Persephone as told in the Homeric *Hymn to Demeter* is as follows.

Kore, the maiden daughter of Demeter, the goddess of the grain, is picking flowers with her friends when she sees a narcissus. Enticed by its beauty, she bends over and plucks it from the earth. As soon as she does so, the earth opens up and Hades, her uncle, lord of the dead and god of the underworld, emerges in his chariot, abducts her to his deathly realm (Erebos), rapes her, and claims her as his bride.

Meanwhile, Demeter has heard her daughter scream but does not know her whereabouts. For nine days, she frantically searches the surface of the earth for her missing daughter, after which time she is joined by Hekate. Together, they go to Helios, the sun god, to seek information. Helios informs Demeter that her daughter has been kidnapped by Hades to be his bride, and that all this has happened with the knowledge and blessings of Persephone's father and king of the gods, Zeus. Infuriated by her daughter's abduction to the land of the dead, Demeter disguises herself as an old woman, leaves Olympus, and wanders over the earth, eventually ending up in Eleusis, a city west of Athens. There she sits by the Maiden's Well until she meets the four daughters of Metaneira. She fabricates a story about being kidnapped from her homeland and raped by pirates, claiming that she made her eventual escape while the men were busy eating. She feigns ignorance of her whereabouts, and after asking the gods to bless the young girls with husbands and children, she solicits their help in finding employment suitable for an elderly woman. The daughters of Metaneira invite her

7

back to their father's palace to nurse their infant brother, Demophoon. Demeter agrees.

Maintaining her disguise as an elderly woman, Demeter enters the palace at Eleusis and is greeted by Metaneira, the mother of Demophoon. Initially, Demeter, aloof and still grief-stricken over the loss of her daughter, is reluctant to accept Metaneira's hospitality. But after watching the playful antics of Iambe, her sorrow diminishes somewhat and she joins in the laughter. She becomes Demophoon's nurse. Under her care, Demophoon flourishes—but in a highly unusual manner. Instead of feeding him, Demeter places him in the fire at night in order to "purge" him of his mortality and make of him a god. One night, Metaneira interrupts her in this ritual. The mother is horrified to see her son in the fire and cries out in panic. It is at this point that Demeter reveals her identity as the goddess of the grain, and she lashes out at Metaneira and, by extension, at all mortals, for their ignorance and stupidity in challenging the gods.

Demeter then instructs the people of Eleusis to build a temple in her honor in order to mollify her anger. Once the temple is completed, Demeter takes her place within it and stays there for one year, mourning for her daughter. As goddess of the grain, she withholds her bounty from the earth, which then experiences a corresponding period of mourning precipitated by the absence of fertility and new life. The gods panic because of the paucity of sacrifices and offerings in their honor. Zeus sends an entourage of immortals to cajole Demeter to abandon her mourning and release the earth from its strangulation, but she refuses to do so until her daughter is released from the underworld. Finally, Zeus is forced to submit to her demands and sends Hermes down to the underworld to inform Hades that he has to release the girl.

In this way, Kore, whose name has been changed to Persephone to signify her altered status since she is no longer a virgin, is eventually released from captivity in the underworld—but not before she has eaten the pomegranate seed given to her by Hades. This seed ensures her return to the underworld for four months of the year. Persephone's annual return to the underworld for four months triggers Demeter's mourning and the corresponding seasonal death of the earth. Persephone's release from the underworld at the end of four months signals the coming of spring. Not coincidentally, the name Persephone means spring.

Persephone, now queen of the underworld and the bride of Hades, is reunited with her mother, and after some gentle persuasion from her own mother, Rheia, Demeter agrees to release the earth from its strangulation. She then hastens to Eleusis to initiate the people into her mysteries. The *Hymn* concludes with praise of the two goddesses and of the two blessings conferred by Demeter: the inner blessing of happiness and regeneration in life and in death as experienced and transmitted through her mysteries and the outer blessing of wealth.

The earliest known account of the myth is the Homeric *Hymn to Demeter*. Composed at approximately 650 B.C.E., the hymn was part of an oral tradition that celebrated the gods and goddesses of the Greek pantheon. As Edward F. Edinger has observed in *The Eternal Drama: The Inner Meaning of Greek Mythology*, the hymn commemorates the Eleusinian Mysteries, sacred rites that were performed on an annual basis and that survived for nearly twelve hundred years until the church fathers suppressed them at the end of the fourth century C.E.[1]

Those who were initiated into the mysteries were sworn to secrecy. Anyone who breached the injunction was subject to the penalty of death. Consequently, we are left with scant information about what actually transpired during the ritual, and much of the little information we do have has been transmitted through the unsympathetic lens of the Christian church.[2] But, as Barry B. Powell tells us in *Classical Myth*, we do know that there were two principal phases to initiation: the Lesser Mysteries, which were held once a year in spring in Athens; and the Greater Mysteries, which were held in fall at Eleusis.[3]

Scholars are in general agreement that the Lesser Mysteries consisted primarily of purification and instruction and were a necessary prerequisite for initiation into the Greater Mysteries. The Greater Mysteries, which lasted nine days (symbolic of the nine months of pregnancy and reminiscent of Demeter's search for her daughter before learning of her abduction to the underworld), also consisted of purifications and sacrifices, concluding in a final, visionary experience. However, scholars can only speculate as to what actually transpired in the rituals because no participant's description has surfaced. Sarah Pomeroy in *Goddesses, Whores, Wives, and Slaves: Women in Classical Antiquity* informs us that purification, fasting, prayers, sacrifices, and the drinking of a barley potion, kykeon, were involved.[4] Christine Downing in *The Long Journey Home* concurs with others that all participants, including the men, were given names with feminine endings.[5] Scholars speculate that some sort of reenactment of the myth occurred, that the initiate probably played the role of Demeter, that the final vision involved the reunification of mother and daughter, and that the hierophant or chief priest emerged at the conclusion of the ritual carrying a single ear of grain, symbolizing new life. In *Eleusis: Archetypal Image of Mother and Daughter*, Carl Kerenyi argues that although the grain was nothing more than grain, it may possibly have come to represent the gifts that Demeter and Persephone had bestowed on mankind. Demeter provided food and wealth; Persephone presented the possibility of birth under the earth.[6]

Obviously, the myth also has a connection with the agrarian cycle. As the goddess of the grain, Demeter taught mortals how to cultivate corn, wheat, and barley. The abduction of her daughter by death precipitates her mourning and the corresponding death of the earth. But what is equally obvious is that the Eleusinian Mysteries must have offered more to its participants than a simple reenactment of the seasonal death and rebirth of nature. Why else would it have captivated women and men for over one thousand years?

As the center of religious life for over a thousand years, the Eleusinian Mysteries filled a spiritual need that was lacking in people's lives. Repeated annually and with the participation of a large assembly of people, practice of the rites continued well into Christianity. In his landmark study of the myth and its ritual, *Eleusis: Archetypal Image of Mother and Daughter*, Carl Kerenyi concludes that the totality of the experience coupled with the concluding vision gave it a unique position in the Greek and Roman world.[7] The experience of loss, suffering, death, transformation, renewal, and hope that it ritualized embodies a universal appeal that transcends time and space and that continues to address perennial human concerns.

At the outset, the mysteries were open only to female participants. We can only speculate as to why men were initially excluded. Deborah Lyons observes in *Gender and Immortality: Heroines in Ancient Greek Myth and Cult* that when women exclusively perform the rituals, it is because the deity being honored is female.[8] Another possible reason for the initial exclusion of males may have something to do with the fact that this is a story that speaks to women in a very unique and powerful way. The two possible reasons are not unrelated. A myth that honors a female deity or deities will present alternatives for action, models of behavior, and ways of being that resonate with the experience of being female. By locating the female at its center instead of on the margin, the Homeric *Hymn to Demeter* is unique in Greek mythology since it does not concern itself with the traditional subject matter of the heroic—and, sometimes, thoroughly unheroic—exploits of the male hero or the male gods. If women have a place in these more traditional myths, their location is peripheral to the action, and, more often than not, they are situated as objects to be raped, bartered, impregnated, repudiated, used, abused, and abandoned.

Eventually, however, all Greek-speaking women and men who were not guilty of homicide were allowed to participate in the mysteries. So the experience was ultimately recognized as being relevant to both women and men. Tanya Wilkinson in *Persephone Returns: Victims, Heroes, and the Journey from the Underworld* argues that the appeal of the myth lies in its depiction of a fundamental human experience that transcends gender, class, and ethnicity: that of having our innocence, our Kore, experience betrayal and transformation through abduction to the underworld.[9] Edward F. Edinger shares a similar observation. In *The Eternal Drama: The Inner Meaning of Greek Mythology*, Edinger argues that since the Greater Mystery took place in fall, the emphasis seems to be on the experience of the descent into the underworld and not on the reemergence.[10] In other words, the initiation and transformation that took place in the underworld through separation and loss was the key that unlocked the whole experience. The mysteries provided an opportunity for all participants to experience pain and mourning for whatever part of themselves they had lost. Initiates were put through the process of grieving for and then reconnecting with their abducted selves—those parts of their psyches that had been ravaged and that were identified with the young and innocent Kore.

In *Eleusis: Archetypal Image of Mother and Daughter*, Carl Kerenyi claims that the focal point of the myth, namely, the separation of mother and daughter, transcends the exclusive destiny of women. According to Kerenyi, the separation of mother and daughter and the yearning of the mother for her daughter is characteristic of the yearning of both men and women for an undivided human existence. However, Kerenyi concedes that men and women experience the separation and yearning differently.[11] He argues that the split between mother and daughter is a split from the source of our origin. It is a split that is universally experienced by men and women, but the nature of the experience differs according to one's gender. Kerenyi interprets the division of mother into mother and daughter as opening up to a vision of the feminine source of life—a source that men and women have in common. He sees this vision as symbolized by the ear of corn since it, too, opens up to reveal the seed contained within its own abyss.[12]

Kerenyi understands the ritual performed during the Eleusinian Mysteries to be a vehicle for providing access to the goddess Demeter and, through her, to experience reunification with the feminine. By adopting the role of Demeter, the initiates experience the possibility of moving beyond grief towards understanding and acceptance. His interpretation is supported by the fact that, as Christine Downing observes in *The Long Journey Home*, all who were being initiated into the mysteries, regardless of their gender, adopted names with feminine endings—as if to suggest that the new understanding of human relationships and death that the mysteries provided necessarily entailed an embrace of the feminine perspectives and feminine concerns on the part of all participants.[13]

Similarly, Beatrice Bruteau in "The Unknown Goddess" argues that the Eleusinian Mysteries enabled men and women to reunite with the feminine source of life. The experience represents a return to unity. The rite constitutes a process of moving from partiality to wholeness, from fragmentation to completeness, from separation to reunification, from alienation to reintegration. According to Bruteau, this wholeness or return to mother is the root meaning of femininity. The feminine principle in the form of Kore is abducted underground by the masculine principle. There it merges with and integrates the masculine principle within its own being, and it emerges from the ordeal with new life. This process is cyclical and ongoing, with each succeeding synthesis incorporating the riches garnered through the preceding abduction. This movement towards a higher consciousness and integration is vital for women and men alike if we are ever to be reunited with ourselves, with each other, and with the planet.[14]

The impact of the mysteries was apparently profound. Homer tells us:

> Blessed is the mortal on earth who has seen these rites,
> but the uninitiated who has no share in them never
> has the same lot once dead in the dreary darkness.[15]

(Lines 480–482)

Initiation into the mysteries constituted a means for addressing the perennial concerns of humanity: the meaning of life, loss, grief, suffering, death, and renewal. The mysteries provided insight, hope, and transcendence. As Kerenyi has argued, they offered the participants confidence in the face of death, a guarantee of life without the concomitant fear of death.[16] The *Hymn to Demeter* tells us that blessedness was achieved through participation in the rite—a blessedness conferred on the individual not only in the hereafter but also from the moment in this life when she/he beheld the vision. According to the *Hymn*, the ensuing impact was profound. It is not coincidental that, as Kerenyi points out, "Eleusis" means "the place of happy arrival."[17] Furthermore, the Eleusinian Mysteries also provided a means of validating the importance of and the reconnection with the feminine source of life—a source that patriarchy has tried to suppress.

In *Persephone Returns: Victims, Heroes, and the Journey from the Underworld*, Tanya Wilkinson claims that the Eleusinian Mysteries reconciled the binary designation of the universe as established by Zeus in which the upper world (the land of the living) and the underworld (the land of the dead) are split into two separate realms with no link between them. Through her annual ascents and descents, Persephone becomes the vehicle that links the two realms.[18] Furthermore, through participation in the rites, the initiate is provided with a means to reconcile with the split or "lost" part of her/his own psyche and thereby become reconnected or "whole." In that sense, Persephone also becomes our link to the lost selves that we have had to discard in the underworld.

The Homeric *Hymn to Demeter* is unique because unlike many of the stories we read in Greek mythology, the *Hymn* privileges the female position. The story of Demeter and Persephone unfolds from the perspective of the grieving mother as she reacts and eventually comes to terms with the abduction and rape of her daughter. The *Hymn* explores the dynamics of the primary relationship between any two human beings: that of the mother and her child. And it does so through the lens of the female. Although male characters are present and serve as catalysts to the action, their presence is marginal to the central concerns of the narrative—female dilemmas of female protagonists as they are articulated in a female sphere of influence. Furthermore, through the initiation of the mysteries themselves, the *Hymn* renders these female concerns and perspectives in a very public way to influence the individual as well as the collective spiritual well being of the community at large.

Until very recent times, stories that privileged the female position and articulated the female experience were permitted to surface only in the dusty nooks and crannies of the domestic sphere. But this story—focusing as it does on the mother/daughter bond; the severing of that bond; the violation of the bodily and psychic integrity of the female; the separation, loss, and reconciliation between the grieving mother and her child—gained entrance to the public sphere and became the center of a profound religious experience for over one thousand years. In "The 'Theology' of the Mysteries," Helene P. Foley argues that the Eleusinian cult was unique in that it offered a promise of a better life and afterlife to the worshipper through an encounter with the experience of a divine mother and daughter, in contrast to Christianity which offers the same promise through the experience of a divine father and son.[19] The Eleusinian Mysteries led the initiate from ignorance to enlightenment and from alienation to connection by entrance into the female experience and cultivation of female values through the vehicle of the two goddesses.

From the time of our physical birth to the time of our physical death, we experience many psychological births and deaths. Life and circumstances leave us with little other choice. We change; we grow; we die a little; we are born anew. One of the conditions of living is that we are constantly losing bits and pieces of our psychological selves as we journey to the underworld, and we give birth to new bits and pieces of ourselves as we emerge from the underworld. Participation in the ritual at Eleusis provided ancient Greeks with the opportunity to reconnect with their lost selves and to become whole. For a modern audience who no longer has the option of participating in the Eleusinian Mysteries, the opportunity presents itself in the reading, analysis, and unraveling of this very ancient myth. The relevance of the story of Demeter and Persephone, then as now, lies in its ability to pave the way for health, healing, and reconciliation. It allows for a new way of perceiving life and death and all that goes on in between. Just how it does that we will see as we begin our discussion with Demeter and her lessons on grieving and reconciliation.

CHAPTER 2

Demeter: Grieving, Retaliation, and Reconciliation

As the goddess of the grain, Demeter presided over the harvest. From her union with Zeus emerged Kore/Persephone. Demeter was worshipped as the goddess of the grain (food for the body) and as the mother of Persephone. After she had established the Eleusinian Mysteries, she was also worshipped as the goddess of spiritual nourishment (food for the spirit). Demeter has been characterized as the most nurturing and most generous of all the goddesses.

Demeter's most significant relationship, as far as a contemporary audience is concerned, is her relationship with her daughter, Kore/Persephone. Demeter has a lot to teach us about mother / daughter relationships. Furthermore, she teaches us, women and men alike, about coping with the loss of a beloved, whether that loss be in the form of death, divorce, or estrangement; about grieving; about displacement; about anger; about fighting back; about transcending grief; about knowing when to let go; about knowing when to reconcile; and about personal growth and transformation.

Demeter's bond with Kore is unlike Zeus' bond with his daughter. This is illustrated by the fact that Zeus blithely handed over his daughter to Hades without consulting with her or her mother. Furthermore, we are told that as Kore was being abducted, she called out to her father: "She screamed with a shrill voice/calling on her father, the son of Kronos high-est and best" (lines 20–21). Zeus does not respond to his daughter's cry:

> But he [Zeus] sat apart
> from the gods, aloof in a temple ringing with prayers,
> and received choice offerings from humankind.
>
> (Lines 27–29)

It is possible that Zeus both heard and ignored Kore's cry for help. Or, per-haps he didn't hear it at all. But he knew what was happening because he had asked Gaia (Earth), his grandmother, to grow the narcissus for the sole purpose of entrapping Kore and delivering her to his brother. Whether he heard her or not, it is obvious Zeus showed an apparent indifference to the plight of his child. Not so her mother.

By way of contrast, the poem describes Demeter's reaction when she hears her daughter's cry:

> Sharp grief seized her heart, and she tore the veil
> on her ambrosial hair with her own hands.
> She cast a dark cloak on her shoulders
> and sped like a bird over dry land and sea,
> searching.
>
> (Lines 40–44)

Demeter behaves like a frantic mother who is grief-stricken and distraught over the disappearance of her daughter.

In "Rape, Marriage, or Death? Gender Perspectives in the *Hymn to Demeter*," Nanci DeBloois argues that the status of women in ancient Greece creates complications in arriving at possible interpretations of the *Hymn*. In those times, young women did not have the right to choose their own bridegrooms. However, we do not know if they had the right to refuse their father's choice of a bridegroom for them.[1] Consequently, we do not know if Kore, had her opinion even been solicited, would have been able to exer-cise the option of refusing her father's choice of a husband for her.

Since women (daughters as well as mothers) were perceived as the prop-erty of males, the probability is high that a young girl had to accept her father's choice of a spouse for her and that her mother had no say in the matter whatsoever. If that is the case, then it opens up the possibility that what Zeus and his male counterparts in ancient Greece perceived as a per-fectly reasonable way of marrying off one's daughter could be interpreted by women in a totally different way: as a violation and an abomination. Of course, ordinary women may have been powerless to prevent such marriages since they had no legal recourse or social sanction to defy the father or hus-band.

Unfortunately, this situation of forced marriages still holds true today in some parts of the world where ordinary women and young girls are powerless to prevent such compulsory unions. However, in this case, Demeter is no ordinary woman. She is a goddess, and as a goddess, she retaliates. Although mortal women cannot duplicate her precise actions of inflicting blight and famine on the earth until we get justice (much as some of us may like to!), Demeter, nevertheless, holds out the possibility for all women to find their own ways of asserting their rights as women, as mothers, and as daughters. Her example urges us to cultivate what is inherently strong in our own nature. We do so by tapping into our own inner strength, by channeling our internal power to fight for what we believe is our right, and by advocating for the rights of others who are powerless to fight for themselves.

Demeter searches for nine days for Persephone. These nine days symbolize the nine months of pregnancy, indicating that Demeter has embarked on a journey that will culminate in birthing her daughter anew as well as birthing herself anew. Both Demeter and Persephone will experience parallel journeys of death, growth, and transformation. In effect, the former Demeter will shed her old skin by experiencing a death of sorts, and a new Demeter will emerge to take her place. Although well worth the effort, this process of birthing oneself is fraught with difficulties and pain. Demeter's behavior reflects the magnitude of the undertaking through her refusal to eat, drink, or bathe herself because of her grief over the loss of her daughter, and, correspondingly, grief over the death of her old self and her yet-to-be born new self.

Demeter's grief contrasts dramatically with the behavior of Zeus, back on the home front and stuffing himself with "choice offerings from humankind" (line 29). On the tenth day of her grieving and searching, Demeter is joined by Hekate. Together they visit Helios to solicit his assistance in determining the whereabouts of Persephone. Helios has observed the abduction in his capacity as the sun god who sees all that transpires on the surface of the earth in the daylight. Demeter's appeal to Helios for information carries with it the heavy burden of a mother's anguish:

> "Helios, respect me as a god does a goddess, if ever
> with word or deed I pleased your heart and spirit.
> The daughter I bore, a sweet offshoot noble in form—
> I heard her voice throbbing through the barren air
> as if she were suffering violence. But I did not see her with my eyes.
> With your rays you look down through the bright air
> on the whole of the earth and the sea.
> Tell me the truth about my child. Have you somewhere
> seen who of gods or mortal men took her
> by force from me against her will and went away?"
>
> (Lines 64–73)

Helios breaks the news to Demeter: Kore has been abducted to the underworld by Hades and is now his bride. He encourages Demeter to be reasonable and accept the fate that has befallen her daughter. He even has the unmitigated gall to urge her to perceive her daughter's violation as a blessing since Hades is not an unsuitable bridegroom for the girl: "Among the gods Aidoneus [Hades] is not an unsuitable bridegroom/ Commander-to-Many and Zeus's own brother of the same stock" (lines 84–85).

Far from accepting the situation, Demeter is seized with "brutal grief" at the loss of her daughter and anger at Zeus for causing it. Her anger eventually translates into violence against others. But she does not channel that anger directly towards the gods at this point in the story. Instead, she takes us through a circuitous but necessary detour in which she learns and, through her example, teaches us about the process of grieving and healing. She withdraws from the assembly of the gods, disguises herself as an elderly woman, and wanders among cities and fields until she arrives at Eleusis.

Demeter's flight away from Olympus to Eleusis suggests that she is not yet prepared to seek direct retaliation from the gods. Her act of fleeing from the source of the problem indicates avoidance. She does not have the self-confidence or self-knowledge that is needed to confront the aggressor head-on because she has yet to recognize her own inner strength or the manner in which she can utilize that inner strength to force the gods to do her bidding. These are lessons she will learn as the story unfolds.

Demeter's flight away from Olympus further reveals the powerful impact of an emotion that can render us completely immobile: guilt. Any human being can experience guilt, but probably no one is more adept at internalizing the blame for an injury done to a child than the child's mother. As women and as mothers, we have an uncanny knack for blaming ourselves for whatever misfortune or failures we experience in our lives or in the lives of our loved ones. For many of us, motherhood is synonymous with guilt. Somehow, somewhere, we will find a way to berate ourselves and lay the blame firmly where we believe it belongs: on our own shoulders. And if we even attempt to lay the blame for misfortune or failure elsewhere, society is sure to step in and do its part by wagging the finger of disapproval in our direction and reminding us of our ostensible culpability.

One doesn't have to be a goddess in ancient Greece to understand the extent of Demeter's feelings of guilt. As mothers, we are all too familiar with the little voices we have internalized in our heads, voices that echo society's condemnation: "What kind of a mother are you, letting your daughter play in the fields, unprotected? Didn't you know that it is dangerous out there? She relied on you to protect her from harm. And you betrayed her. You let her down. You have violated the most sacred promise we make to our children: to nurture them and to protect them from harm. You ought to be ashamed of yourself! And you call yourself a mother!"

An individual has to be made of more than just flesh and bones to withstand this barrage of self-condemnation and guilt. But withstand it we must because guilt serves little purpose other than to reinforce feelings of inadequacy, powerlessness, and self-hate. Guilt is all-consuming and leaves little energy for channeling our anger in the appropriate direction: outward where it belongs. Instead, guilt forces us to channel our anger inward, against ourselves, causing us to feel helpless, powerless, and immobile. Eventually, Demeter does channel her anger in the appropriate direction. But for the time being, she limps away from Olympus, a broken-hearted mother racked with guilt and self-blame.

At the Maiden's Well in Eleusis, Demeter meets the daughters of Metaneira. Since fetching water was typically a feminine task, presumably Demeter goes to the well intentionally in order to encounter females and solicit their help. After fabricating a story about who she is and why she is there, she asks the daughters of Metaneira if they know of a home where she can be employed to perform the household tasks befitting a woman her age:

> "Now pity me, maidens,
> and tell me, dear children, with eager goodwill,
> whose house I might come to, a man's
> or a woman's, there to do for them gladly
> such tasks as are done by an elderly woman.
> I could nurse well a newborn child, embracing it
> in my arms, or watch over a house. I could
> spread out the master's bed in a recess
> of the well-built chamber and teach women their work."
>
> (Lines 137–144)

The daughters of Metaneira arrange for her to be a nurse for their brother, Demophoon. Demeter agrees. This poses an interesting question. Why would a female who is mourning the death or loss of a loved one seek shelter in someone else's home and become a nurse to another woman's newborn infant? What insight about grief or turmoil does Demeter provide for us through these actions?

We can glean some understanding for Demeter's actions by analyzing some of our own actions in times of chaos, turmoil, or grief. Frequently, when a woman is troubled, she can find solace and comfort in performing daily, household tasks: cleaning, doing laundry, preparing dinner, washing dishes, taking care of the children. There is something very comforting about the performance of such routine chores. Somehow, the habitual tasks that women perform to keep their homes in order have the added benefit of setting their minds in order. The execution of these activities helps to ground us in reality and helps to restore a sense of balance and perspective to our lives—as if by setting our physical house in order, we are setting our psychological house in order. Daily rituals become invested with significance; habitual gestures provide a refreshing refuge.

This performance of ordinary but productive tasks coupled with the routine of engaging in the same activity over and over again function as a reprieve from mental turmoil. Occupying both one's mind and body with the performance of essential household chores provides a much-needed break—analogous to the pit stop that the race car driver must make in order to service the needs of his/her car. Such psychological "pit stops" act as punctuation marks in a sentence: they provide a few, precious seconds to pause and catch one's breath. In times of crisis and tumult, if we temporarily shelter ourselves in the protective and reassuring atmosphere of domesticity, we allow ourselves the time and space to breathe. Furthermore, we are able to brace ourselves for the next hurdle that will inevitably thrust itself in our pathway.

Perhaps Demeter's actions reflect the same need. Perhaps she, too, is seeking the comfort and solace that the performance of routine household tasks can bring. Perhaps, by embracing domesticity in this way, by doing what has been designated as female work in female space, Demeter is showing us that in order to seek refuge from our own grief and turmoil, we need to perform meaningful, repetitive tasks in a non-threatening and nurturing atmosphere in order to restore a sense of balance and perspective to our lives. And, in the case of women, the arena for performing these tasks is typically the domestic sphere.

In *Tapestries of Life: Women's Work, Women's Consciousness, and the Meaning of Daily Experience*, Bettina Aptheker attributes an additional value to women's work. She argues that women are not essentially more nurturing or more loving or more caring than men but that the very nature of women's labors cultivates an ability to nurture, to care about life, and to develop an awareness on how best to sustain it.[2] If Aptheker is correct in her assessment (and we have no reason to dispute her), then it follows that anyone, male or female, can cultivate a consciousness that is sensitive to the sustenance of life, relationships, and community through engaging in the daily, routine tasks that are essential for maintenance and survival.

Elisabeth Badinter in *The Myth of Motherhood: An Historical View of the Maternal Instinct* draws a similar conclusion. Through her analysis of familial patterns of behavior in late-eighteenth-century Paris whereby the overwhelming majority of infants born to the middle class and the less privileged aristocracy were parceled off to live under appalling conditions in foster homes in the countryside, she concludes that maternal instinct and maternal love is not innate in women's nature but is a learned behavior and the result of social conditioning.[3] Again, that opens up the possibility that "maternal" love can be cultivated by anyone—male and female alike—who is willing to invest the time and energy it takes to nurture and care for an infant. Perhaps if we restructured society in order to allow greater opportunities for men to participate in child care and to engage in behaviors that are designed to nurture life instead of destroying it, we would see a corresponding decline in violence, aggression, and oppressive behaviors.

So Demeter becomes Demophoon's nurse. And here the story takes an interesting turn. We are told that at night, Demeter places the infant Demophoon in the fire in order to purge him of his mortality, that is to say, to turn him into an immortal. Again, the question is why? Why would a goddess seek to immortalize a human?

We know that Demeter is grief-stricken over the loss of her daughter. Instead of confronting the powers that have caused her grief, instead of trying to mourn her loss, Demeter takes a detour. She turns away from the gods on Mount Olympus and directs her attention on filling the gnawing void that she feels for her daughter. She focuses on someone else's child. Is she seeking a substitute because she cannot come to terms with her own loss? Does her attempt to immortalize Demophoon constitute displacement? Polly Young-Eisendrath suggests this is the case. In "Demeter's Folly: Experiencing Loss in Middle Life," Young-Eisendrath argues that by trying to abduct Demophoon from his mother, Demeter replicates the role of the aggressor, the role her brother Hades has played with her. According to Young-Eisendrath, the unconscious repetition towards another of an aggressive action that was initially directed at oneself constitutes an ironic defense against grief.[4] In effect, Demeter reacts to aggression by behaving aggressively. Furthermore, she makes the same mistake that many of us make when we are on the rebound: we desperately seek alternatives or substitutes to pacify the gaping emptiness we feel at the loss of a beloved. And, like Demeter, we do so without thinking of the ramifications or the long-term consequences to ourselves and others.

Demeter's actions shed light on the behavior of all groups that experience marginalization, discrimination, and institutionalized oppression because of their race, class, ethnicity, gender, sexual orientation, or ability. All too often, when people who have experienced such oppression are put in positions of authority, they adopt the role of the oppressor by turning against their own kind. In aligning themselves with the oppressor, they are attempting to align themselves with the power structure. Furthermore, when the oppressed adopt the roles and attitudes of the oppressor, they frequently take these roles and attitudes to the extreme—as if they are trying to demonstrate their own legitimacy by outdoing the oppressor in their ability to oppress others.

A related explanation for Demeter's actions is suggested by Germaine Greer in *The Change: Women, Aging, and the Menopause*. Greer discusses anaphobia, a term that she coins to refer to a hatred of older women. This phenomenon, more prevalent in developed countries than in developing countries, can be exhibited by women as well as men, and, in the case of women, it considerably complicates their process of aging. In her discussion of this topic, Greer makes the following observation about oppression: "It is a permanent aspect of all kinds of oppression among human groups that the oppressed are forced to act out institutionalized oppression and exert pressure on those immediately beneath them in the power structure."[5] In other words, the nature of oppression is such that those who have been or continue to be oppressed frequently react by oppressing their subordinates in the hierarchy. Sometimes those who have experienced oppression internalize the oppression to such a degree that they lash out against members of their own race, class, gender, or, in the case of domestic violence, against members of their own family. They feel powerless to combat their oppressors, so they vent their frustrations on those who are in a weaker position than themselves—those who are powerless to retaliate. A pecking order is established whereby men beat up on women and children, and children, situated at the bottom of the hierarchical totem pole, are abused and assaulted by adults.

In *Pedagogy of the Oppressed*, Paulo Friere's perceptive analysis on the nature of oppression, the oppressor, and the oppressed, Friere argues that revolutionary change consists not only of transforming the nature of oppressive situations but also of expunging that piece of the oppressor that has embedded itself deeply in our psyche. Friere argues that at certain times the oppressed can feel an irresistible attraction towards the oppressor and attempt to emulate oppressive behaviors, adopt oppressive values, and share in a lifestyle that oppresses others.[6]

Perhaps this is what has occurred with Demeter. Having not yet formulated a course of action that will challenge Zeus and the male hegemonic structure he represents, she internalizes her own oppression and vents her anger and frustration by appropriating what does not belong to her. When interrupted by Metaneira while performing her nightly ritual with Demophoon, Demeter lashes out at those who are like her in the sense of being female (Metaneira and her daughters) but who are also beneath her in the hierarchy. Fortunately for Metaneira and the people of Eleusis, Demeter's abusive behaviors are short-lived because it is immediately after she has chastised them for their ignorance that she provides them with a means to mollify her spirit: building the temple. Later, she rewards them with the gift of her mysteries.

Kathie Carlson in *Life's Daughter/Death's Bride* offers yet another interesting insight into Demeter's words and actions. When Demeter lashes out at Metaneira for her concern at seeing Demophoon in the fire, she characterizes human beings as stupid and ignorant. According to Carlson, Demeter is actually commenting on a limited human perspective on death: what appears to be certain death to humans is, in the hands of a deity, a transformation and new life.[7] In other words, Demophoon in the fire is not Demophoon facing imminent death; it is Demophoon being granted new life. Carlson sees a parallel between Metaneira's reaction to the "death" of her son with Demeter's reaction to the "death" of her daughter. In both cases, what appears to be death when viewed through a restricted or human lens is actually the harbinger of new life when viewed from a "divine" or transcendent lens.[7]

By disguising herself as a mortal, Demeter temporarily disconnects from her real nature and engages in human pettiness and vindictiveness. Furthermore, the loss of her daughter so traumatizes her that she temporarily separates from her real identity and she subscribes to the human perspective on the finality of death. Metaneira's erroneous assumptions concerning the "death" of her child shock Demeter into a nascent recognition that perhaps she has made the same erroneous assumptions concerning the fate of her daughter: she has perceived death from a human perspective. She tells Metaneira:

> "Mortals are ignorant and foolish, unable to foresee
> destiny, the good and the bad coming on them.
> You are incurably misled by your folly."
>
> (Lines 256–258)

But this accusation can be leveled against Demeter in much the same way that it can be leveled against Metaneira or other mortals.

Once Demeter reveals her true identity—an identity she had submerged while assuming the guise of a mortal—she regains the transcendent knowledge that from death new life can emerge. In other words, Demeter reconnects with her goddess nature. She derives sustenance, strength, and purpose by tapping into her authentic self, and through the insight she has gained, she propels herself one step further on the path towards individuation or wholeness.

What other insights can we glean from this incident with Demophoon? Perhaps what we learn from this is the same lesson that Demeter has apparently learned: although grief and loss can be mollified temporarily, they cannot be avoided indefinitely. They must be dealt with appropriately in order to be transcended. It is psychologically unhealthy to stay in denial and to search frantically for substitutes in order to satiate an aching need. The rebound makes us susceptible to looking for an alternative—any alternative.

What we can also glean from this incident is that dealing with grief can be a matter of timing: we deal with grief only when we are ready to do so. Sometimes our egos are so fragile that we are unable to confront the emptiness right away. We are afraid of being alone. We seek the company of others. We engage in denial as a temporary refuge until our emotions are strong enough to face our loss and experience the healing power of the grieving process.

After being admonished in no uncertain terms, Metaneira realizes her appalling error of mistaking a goddess for a mortal. Obviously, no mortal in his or her right mind would deliberately provoke a goddess in this way. So the people at Eleusis build a temple in honor of Demeter with the intention of performing the rites to "propitiate" her spirit.

Once the temple is built, Demeter positions herself. She now becomes more focused and deliberate in her actions. She has connected with her authentic self. She withdraws to the temple and consciously embraces her grief instead of trying to avoid it. By doing so, she indicates her need—and the need common to all humanity—to have space and time to grieve.

> Then golden-haired Demeter
> remained sitting apart from all the immortals,
> wasting with desire for her deep-girt daughter.
> (Lines 302–304)

And in the process of grieving for her daughter, she formulates a plan of action. She decrees a "terrible and brutal year" on the earth, wreaking havoc on all that lives. Demeter's legacy survives in many parts of the world where a year of mourning is still designated as the appropriate period to grieve for the loss of a loved one. Because of her actions, because she uses her powers as the goddess of the grain to serve her purpose, Demeter forces the powers of patriarchy to acknowledge her right as a mother, and she wins the release of her daughter.

Demeter's unbreakable bond with her daughter illuminates the nature of the oldest social unit: that of mother and child. As Kathryn Rabuzzi informs us in *Motherself: A Mythic Analysis of Motherhood*, long before human beings had recognized that there was a role for the male in procreation, it was assumed that the female created life out of her own being. In other words, the female was parthenogenetic.[8] Hence, for the longest period in human history, communities held the female in awe and worshiped female deities since it was readily apparent that the female—and not the male— gives birth to living things. Perceived as vehicles of magic and new life, women not only had the ability to birth creatures like themselves (females), but they could also birth creatures unlike themselves (males). The female naturally perceived her newborn infant as an extension of her own body and bonded with the child accordingly. Even after women had discovered that the male had a role in procreation through observing animal behavior, the mother/child bond continued to be the primary bond between human beings since the paternity of the infant was not always readily apparent and was a matter of little consequence for our ancient ancestors.

Patriarchy maintains somewhat of a schizophrenic attitude towards the institution of motherhood. On the one hand, motherhood is presented as patriarchy's highest reward for women. Even nowadays, women continue to be castigated to varying degrees in many parts of the world for their refusal or inability to assume the mantle of motherhood. Motherhood is one of the few roles in which women can achieve legitimate access to status and power. Historically, women have used this to their advantage. In fact, they initially earned the right to education by arguing that it would make them better mothers.

On the other hand, patriarchy has attempted to discredit the institution of motherhood and to sever the mother/child unit by designating the female as merely the receptacle and incubator of the offspring of males. Primacy is allocated to the father of the child. (Some might argue that this is still true today.)

This ambivalent attitude towards motherhood is reflected in evidence from the field of anthropology. Henrietta Moore in *Feminism and Anthropology* maintains that in small-scale societies, women's status and cultural value seem to improve when they are not defined exclusively as mothers and child rearers.[9] However, she cautions us against assuming that women's status is a function of their roles in any given society. What it means to be a woman and how much value is assigned to that has been and continues to be culturally defined.

Stephanie Golden reinforces the point that the appropriate roles and behavior for women are culturally defined. In her work *Slaying the Mermaid: Women and the Culture of Sacrifice*, Golden traces the historical development and transformation of the concept of sacrifice from its religious origins to a secular ideology that urges women to continuously disregard their own needs in the service of others, primarily by assuming the mantle of motherhood. According to Golden, this culture of self-sacrifice leads women to engage in self-destructive behaviors. Golden's deconstruction of the culture of sacrifice distinguishes between the nature and attitude towards sacrifice of black women and white women. Golden claims that one form inverts the other due to distinctions in class.[10] For middle-class white women, the domestic ideal and the culture of motherhood were frequently perceived as traps that denied females the right to self-expression and self-fulfillment and required of them interminable sacrifices. For the African-American female struggling economically to hold her universe together, the domestic ideal was, indeed, an ideal that she longed to achieve but could only hope for. Golden postulates that unlike their white counterparts, black women perceive motherhood to be a source of power, providing them with emotional satisfaction, high self-esteem, and a positive identity.[11]

In patriarchy as a whole, women continue to be afforded subordinate status. As an ideology, patriarchy is predicated upon control and domination of those designated as "others," specifically, women, children, and all people of color. The ideology can—and does—assume different manifestations, guises, and fronts. We see this battle raging today through the legal, political, and religious institutions that continue to seek control of a woman's most private and intimate space—her body.

Just like her modern feminist counterparts, Demeter reacts with anger at patriarchal norms. Unlike guilt—which immobilizes—anger, when it is properly focused and channeled, can catapult a constructive response to oppression and injustice. It can motivate people to action. Anger is not traditionally considered a feminine trait. Men are permitted to express their anger; women are expected to control or repress it. In this poem, Demeter's anger is an expression of a deep, emotional response to her situation. She personifies the anger of all politically conscious and self-aware women in all patriarchal cultures, women who defiantly repudiate patriarchal dictates on their behavior and who decide to do something about it. Her plight reflects the plight of all women who struggle to achieve self-definition in a world that attempts to thwart their success at every turn. She refuses to behave with the meekness and subservience that is expected of her as a female in a patriarchal society. She refuses to silence her voice. She refuses to be nice and just play along as if nothing outrageous has happened. Instead, she speaks the language of anger, which, unfortunately, is the only language that can be heard in this oppressive situation.

Demeter's actions threaten the patriarchal order through her obstinate insistence of her rights as a mother. She uses her power to subvert authority. She will not submit to male hegemony. She will not allow the most powerful of the gods to deny her a voice in the welfare of her child. By insisting on the primacy of her relationship to her daughter, Demeter challenges Zeus' self-proclaimed position as the center of her universe. As Carol Christ has argued in *Laughter of Aphrodite: Reflections on a Journey to the Goddess,* the story of Demeter and Persephone celebrates the mother/daughter bond, affirms the heritage passed from mother to daughter, and rejects the patriarchal pattern which posits that the primary loyalties of mother and daughter are to men instead of to each other.[12]

Demeter affirms mother-right through actions as well as through dialogue. When she first meets the daughters of Metaneira at the well in Eleusis, she identifies herself through her mother and places her origin in Crete—the last surviving culture of goddess-worshipping communities.

> "Doso's my name, which my honored mother gave me.
> On the broad back of the sea I have come now from Crete,
> by no wish of my own. By force and necessity pirate men
> led me off against my desire."
>
> (Lines 122–125)

The name "Doso," according to Kathie Carlson in *Life's Daughter/Death's Bride*, means "giver" and is also an epithet for "earth."[13] So as earth-giver, Demeter grounds herself in the feminine—the goddess responsible for the fecundity of the earth. Furthermore, flagrantly disregarding the role of the father, she credits her mother with naming her, signifying a time when communities were matrilineal and descent was traced through the line of the mothers instead of the fathers. She places her origin in Crete, the last culture to keep alive goddess worship until its ultimate demise at the hands of the patriarchs. She claims to have been abducted by "pirate men"—patriarchal ideology that usurped her role as mother, that denied the legitimacy of her mother-right, and that disconnected her from her history and place of origin. She manages to escape from her captors before she is sold into slavery—a patriarchal institution that originated with the enslavement of captive females of a defeated army. And she seeks employment as a nurse and homemaker—employment that has traditionally been assigned to the female. So in word as well as deed, Demeter is firmly grounding herself in the feminine sphere and asserting the role of the female in defiance of an ideology that seeks to denigrate and subordinate all things female and feminine.

Fiercely determined not to relinquish her daughter, Demeter challenges patriarchal ideology that designates women and children as the property of males to dispense with as they see fit. As Cheryl Exum demonstrates in *Plotted, Shot, and Painted: Cultural Representation of Biblical Women*, patriarchy depends on women's complicity to maintain and perpetuate itself.[14] It shares this in common with other oppressive ideologies since the survival of such ideology is contingent upon the ability and willingness of an oppressed group to internalize and participate in its own oppression. By adamantly refusing to perpetuate the dominant order, by refusing to play along, by refusing to be nice, Demeter is challenging patriarchy and asserting her right as a mother and as a female—and, by extension, asserting the rights of all mothers and all females—to have a voice in the welfare of children and of future generations. In effect, what Demeter is saying to the forces of oppression is this: "If anyone thinks I will cower down and permit my inviolable rights as a female and as a mother to be subjugated, think again."

Demeter demonstrates the importance of tapping into one's own internal power. We all have internal power. If we do not recognize our own power, or if we do not allow that power to materialize, our growth is stunted and we remain psychologically subjugated and oppressed. And psychological or internal oppression can be more permanently damaging than physical oppression. Through tapping into her internal power, through using her power to fight power, Demeter successfully brings patriarchy to its knees: she forces the powers-that-be to acknowledge her rights as a female and mother and to submit to her demands. Her fierce refusal to cower down to oppression is inspirational. We have a lot to learn from Demeter.

How does Demeter accomplish this? What can we learn from her successful challenge to patriarchy? Confrontation is always difficult, and, in this case, it is even more so because the adversary is not an individual but a whole power structure. In the Homeric *Hymn to Demeter*, we are told that Demeter intentionally situates herself apart from all the immortals when she occupies the temple at Eleusis. She willfully positions herself outside of the male-centered, male-dominated symbolic order that they represent. And by doing so, she threatens it. She defiantly declares her "otherness" for all to see. She challenges the gods and their way of conducting business. Until now, the gods of Olympus have paid little heed to Demeter, her anguish, or her antics. Firmly entrenched in her position outside of their androcentric order, she now hits them where it hurts: for one year she wreaks havoc and famine on the earth:

> The ground released
> no seed, for bright-crowned Demeter kept it buried.
> In vain the oxen dragged many curved plows down
> the furrows.
>
> (Lines 306–309)

Earth is dying. Animals are dying. Humans are dying. Demeter waxes ruthless in her grief and anger. She is determined to persevere in her struggle for justice. The poem tells us that she is prepared to destroy the whole human race by famine.

On the one hand, Demeter's actions lead to chaos and calamity; on the other hand, her actions provide an outlet for moving beyond the androcentric constructs imposed on women living in a patriarchy. Demeter challenges Zeus' assumption that, as a male, he is entitled to be the most important beneficiary of her energies, and she refutes his presumed right to channel her energies in any way he sees fit. She deviates from the patriarchal norms that dictate that women are supposed to be in constant service to others by providing them with an endless supply of nourishment, care, and support. As Kathie Carlson observes in her book *In Her Image*:

The Unhealed Daughter's Search for Her Mother, women in patriarchal society are expected to flow out all the time, to "...use their magic to be of service to others, especially children and men."[15] In this instance, Demeter withholds her services and her magic. She refuses to feed the forces of patriarchy. Instead, she taps into her own internal source of power and wields it against patriarchy as would a ruthless warrior on the battlefield. And that is when—and only when—she gets the attention of the gods.

The Greek gods are notorious for caring little about the fate of human beings. Greek mythology is littered with examples of the gods manipulating humans and wreaking havoc on their lives in order to further their own selfish needs. So why should they care now? Quite simply, Demeter makes it in their self-interest to care. Because there is famine and death, humans are unable to offer their usual inventory of sacrifices to the gods. So the gods themselves begin to suffer from hunger and deprivation. We already know how much Zeus enjoys receiving his "choice offerings from humankind." Hence his concern.

Zeus sends Iris to plead with Demeter, but to no avail. Then he sends her an entourage of the immortals, one by one, all of whom beg, plead, and even resort to bribery. Again, nothing doing:

> Never, she said, would she mount up to fragrant
> Olympus nor release the seed from the earth,
> until she saw with her eyes her own fair-faced child.
>
> (Lines 331–333)

Finally, Zeus is forced to submit to her demands. He sends Hermes down to inform Hades that he has to release the girl. And so Persephone is released. Zeus ignores Demeter's anger. He ignores her futile attempt to substitute Demophoon for her daughter. He ignores her anguish and her grief. But he does not ignore what is in his own self-interest. And that is how Demeter triumphs.

What can we learn from Demeter's triumphant tactics? What are the lessons for warfare that Demeter teaches us as we hear her story? First of all, in any confrontation or battle, it serves no purpose to appeal to our opponent's sense of sympathy and compassion because that won't get us very far. Unfortunately, a raging war leaves little room for sympathy and compassion. Demeter engages in harsh and brutal tactics to achieve the release of her daughter. By preventing the seeds from growing, by denying earth its fertility, she inflicts pain and suffering on humanity as well as the gods. However, her tactics are not necessarily aimed at human beings since human beings are powerless to give her what she wants. Her goal is to force the gods—those in the position of power—to submit to her demands. Unfortunately, the only way she has of achieving this goal is by causing a corresponding injury to humanity. Ultimately, she succeeds in her goal, but she does so only because the gods themselves begin to experience the pain of deprivation and sanctions and are, therefore, forced to capitulate.

Demeter's action teaches us an important lesson about the success and failure of sanctions. Sanctions will fail if they have little or no impact on the intended group—those who have the position and authority to grant us what we want. If Demeter's actions increased the misery of human beings exclusively and had no impact on the gods—the group that can exercise the authority to release her daughter and against which the sanctions are aimed—Demeter would still be waiting for Persephone to emerge from the underworld. As Demeter shows us, sanctions succeed only if and when they begin to influence those who have the authority to meet our demands. If it becomes apparent that only the powerless are suffering as a result of the imposition of sanctions, then sanctions have failed and we need to explore alternative methods for achieving our goal. The prolonging of sanctions under such circumstances amounts to cruelty beyond belief since all we will be doing is increasing human misery without having the corresponding desired impact on the power structure.

Secondly, Demeter's actions demonstrate that it serves no purpose to deny our grief, to frantically seek for a substitute, or to engage in behaviors that are self-destructive. In the end, we will be the ones who suffer. Thirdly, we learn that it is counterproductive to channel the anger that we feel for our opponent towards innocent bystanders or ourselves. All we will succeed in doing is spreading misery.

So how do we triumph? What strategies do we follow in order to defeat the enemy? We begin by channeling the anger towards constructing an effective course of action. We need to determine how to turn the tables around on our opponent to make it in his or her self-interest to agree to our terms. Anything short of that will not succeed. But there is a catch, which leads us to our third strategy. Once we have determined our course of action, we must not waver in our resolve. Any hesitation on our part will be interpreted as weakness and could lead to disaster.

This is not as easy as it might sound. The tendency is usually to make excuses, to hesitate, to try to find an alternative, to hope against hope that things will improve. Life provides us with many examples of how difficult it can be to hold fast to our goal—even if we can recognize that it is ultimately in our best interest to do so. Any volunteer at a shelter for battered women, any counselor who deals with victims of psychological and physical trauma on a daily basis, or even any faculty member whose students pour out their tales of horror and abuse suffered at the hands of relatives or significant others—any of these individuals can attest to the difficulty victims experience in holding fast to their goals in the face of abuse.

Although the specifics of each situation may vary, the common denominators are the same: "He is a good person if only he didn't drink. He really does love me. He feels so bad about beating me up. He didn't mean to hurt me. He has promised he will never do it again. He brought me such beautiful flowers/jewelry/clothes to show me how truly sorry he was. He'll change. And anyway, it was my fault. I shouldn't have done/said/thought what I did. I'll do better next time." And the litany goes on.

Many of these victims internalize the anger and experience self-blame, self-hate, shame, and guilt. Instead of spiraling on this downward path of self-destruction, let us take our cue from Demeter. In order to change a person's behavior, we have to make it in his or her self-interest to do so. Quite simply, we have to tap into our inner strength and exercise agency by taking control of our lives and setting the agenda. In this case, the abuser must be made to understand that it is in his or her self-interest to seek help in order to change behaviors. Otherwise, we walk out.

It bears repeating that this course of action is not easy. Even under the best of circumstances, it requires a great deal of strength, courage, and a well-defined sense of identity for a woman to confront an adversary and emerge relatively unscathed. In these circumstances, the risks are multiplied many times over. The situation can be dangerous. However, unless we force the issue, abusive behaviors will only escalate. Leaving an abuser requires a great deal of pre-planning and preparation so that we are ready to exit at a moment's notice. If family and friends are unwilling to offer support, social service agencies and organizations are there to help. But once we have made the decision to leave, like Demeter, we should not waver in our resolve. And if ever we decide to reconcile, like Demeter, we should not do so unless our demands have been met.

There is another interesting parallel in cases of domestic violence and in the story of Demeter and Persephone. In situations of domestic violence, the main reason that women finally agree to leave their abusers is because of concern for the welfare of their children. This concern seems to be the catalyst that precipitates action. Many women may tolerate personal insult and injury. They may experience denial, self-hate, self-blame, and depression. They may internalize guilt. But more often than not, those same women will fight back once they recognize that now it is their children who are in jeopardy. They adopt a fierce, unwavering determination to protect their children at all costs, just like Demeter.

As we saw earlier, the anguish Demeter experiences at the loss of her daughter is evident in the words she speaks to Helios early in the poem:

> "The daughter I bore, a sweet offshoot noble in form—
> I heard her voice throbbing through the barren air

as if she were suffering violence. But I did not see her with my eyes."

(Lines 66–68)

The circumstances may vary, but Demeter's words, fraught with panic, fear, and heart-wrenching anxiety for the well-being of her child, strike a universal chord that reverberates with all who want to protect children from violence.

And what of reconciliation? What lessons does Demeter teach us about reconciliation? Following the instructions he has received from Hermes, Hades (Aidoneus) puts Persephone in his chariot and Hermes delivers her to Demeter at the temple of Eleusis. The passage describing the reunification of mother and daughter is one of the most beautiful and moving passages in the poem:

> With one look she [Demeter] darted
> like a maenad down a mountain shaded with woods.
> On her side Persephone, [seeing] her mother's [radiant face],
> [left chariot and horses,] and leapt down to run
> [and fall on her neck in passionate embrace].

(Lines 385–389)

Immediately, Demeter senses a trick. She asks Persephone if she has eaten anything in the underworld and reminds her that if she has done so, she will have to return there for a third of the year. And here she prompts Persephone in such a way as to provide her daughter with a possible explanation that will absolve her of guilt: 'By what guile did the mighty Host-to-Many deceive you?'" (line 404). No longer the young, innocent, and naïve Kore, Persephone takes the hint. She suggests that her excitement at the thought of seeing her mother again and of gaining release from the underworld made her vulnerable to trickery:

> "Then I leapt up for joy, but he [Hades] stealthily
> put in my mouth a food honey-sweet, a pomegranate seed,
> and compelled me against my will and by force to taste it."

(Lines 411–413)

Well, with all due respect to Persephone, someone may be able to put food "stealthily" in your mouth, but how on earth can he or she force you to eat it? All you would have to do is spit it out. But as we shall see later, perhaps Persephone was not as gullible as she tries to appear. Perhaps she knew exactly what she was doing when she ate the pomegranate seed.

Immediately after Persephone has narrated the story of her abduction, we are told that mother and daughter spend the day together:

> Then all day long, their minds at one, they soothed
> each other's heart and soul in many ways,
> embracing fondly, and their spirits abandoned grief,
> as they gave and received joy between them.
>
> (Lines 434–437)

In other words, Demeter does not pursue the matter any further. As soon
as she hears that Persephone has eaten the food of death, she says no more
on the subject. She recognizes that this is a loss she cannot undo.

This is an important point to consider because it demonstrates that
not only has Demeter become reconciled to her loss, but she also assists
Persephone on her path to healing and reconciliation. Demeter knows full
well the consequences of eating food from the land of the dead. She has
already told Persephone:

> "My child, tell me, you [did not taste] food [while below?]
> Speak out [and hide nothing, so we both may know.]
> [For if not], ascending [from miserable Hades],
> you will dwell with me and your father, the
> dark-clouded [son of Kronos], honored by all the gods.
> But if [you tasted food], returning beneath [the earth,]
> you will stay a third part of the seasons [each year],
> but two parts with myself and the other immortals."
>
> (Lines 393–400)

When Persephone admits to eating the pomegranate seed, Demeter has the
option of turning on her daughter and venting blame and recrimination.
How many of us would have been tempted to insert a lecture at this point
on the foolhardiness and gullibility of youth? How many of us ask for total
honesty from our children but then proceed to chastise them for revealing
the truth? Such negative behaviors serve only to diminish a child's self-
worth and instill guilt. Fortunately, Demeter does not engage in these behaviors. Instead, she says no more on the subject. She treats Persephone with
understanding—a quality that entails intimacy and equality between the
self and the subject being understood. By choosing not to chastise Persephone, Demeter is, in effect, reinforcing her daughter's right to make her
own choices. She validates Persephone's transformation from girl to woman
by affirming and celebrating her daughter's agency, autonomy, individual-
ity, and choice. In other words, Demeter gives Persephone the respect that
is her due, thereby facilitating the healing and reconciliation that are a necessary part of the growth process.

In *The Eternal Drama: The Inner Meaning of Greek Mythology*, Edward F.
Edinger argues that the nourishing mother, as personified by Demeter, has
a double image. On the one hand, she can be the benevolent caretaker who

provides much needed nourishment to her child; on the other hand, she can be the devouring mother who insists on feeding her child long after the child is able to feed herself or himself. The devouring mother limits her offspring's potential for growth and autonomy in order to satisfy her own compulsion to be needed and depended upon. [16] Fortunately, Demeter does not succumb to the temptations of the devouring mother. She recognizes that Persephone has evolved into a powerful, autonomous female independently of her. And rather than trying to make her daughter feel guilty about her burgeoning independence or forcing her to regress into a state of infantile dependency, Demeter allows her daughter to flourish. She says no more on the subject.

In *Motherself: A Mythic Analysis of Motherhood*, Kathryn Rabuzzi provides further insight on the nature of motherhood. Rabuzzi defines motherself as a desirable state involving a complicated balancing act between the woman's own self and the self of her child. She argues that once a woman becomes a mother, she no longer experiences selfhood as a single, separate unit. Instead, her concept of selfhood becomes inextricably interwoven with the self of her child—a concept that Rabuzzi terms "binary-unity" to indicate the bringing together as one the two separate selves of mother and child.

According to Rabuzzi, if a woman fails to mother herself but is, instead, swallowed up by the demands entailed in the mothering of those around her, she will lose all sense of self. If, on the other hand, she neglects to mother others but operates as if she were still a single, separate unit, her mode of operation is equally skewed but for the opposite reason. Neither the mother nor the child benefits from this imbalance. What is required of mothers is to negotiate a balance between the demands of the self and the demands of others. The concept of the "I" that emerges as a result of this balancing act is characterized by a combination of unity (maintaining a space for the self) and multiplicity (maintaining a space for others). Rabuzzi argues that motherself is badly needed by women who become mothers because it enables them to mother themselves while simultaneously mothering the child to whom they physically gave birth.[17] Using Rabuzzi's terms and definitions, one can see that in the process of birthing herself, Demeter has learned to mother and nurture herself while simultaneously mothering and nurturing her child. She has negotiated a balance and embodies Rabuzzi's concept of motherself.

Through the intercession of Rheia (her own mother), Demeter learns that Zeus has agreed to let Persephone spend two-thirds of the year with her and one-third with Hades. Furthermore, he has promised to give her whatever honors she chooses from among the gods. So Demeter relinquishes her strangulation of the earth:

At once she set forth fruit from the fertile fields
and the whole wide earth burgeoned with leaves
and flowers.

(Lines 471–473)

She then returns to Eleusis to teach the residents her mysteries: "Holy rights that are not to be transgressed, nor pried into / Nor divulged" (lines 477–478). Demeter, therefore, channels her energy towards a creative activity: the institution of the Eleusinian Mysteries, designed to teach the initiate a different understanding of life, death, and loss. Demeter herself is the first initiate.

In one sense, Demeter does not get everything she wants because Persephone still has to return to the underworld for four months of every year. But in another sense, the fact that Demeter does not insist on her daughter's release for all twelve months of the year perhaps suggests that she has learned the importance of compromise in resolving any conflict. It is also quite possible that she is not at all unhappy with this solution. After all, her daughter is now wife of Hades and queen of the underworld. She is no longer the young, innocent Kore she once was. She is no longer tied to her mother's apron string. Demeter may have come to a recognition that her daughter is not simply an extension of herself but that she has become a powerful and autonomous being in her own right. Furthermore, Helios' words early in the poem about the suitability of Hades as a bridegroom for Persephone may be registering with her. In fact, in many ways, Demeter has undergone her own journey to the underworld and emerged from her ordeal with greater strength and wisdom.

From the time that she first hears her daughter's screams to her final reconciliation, Demeter experiences a metamorphosis. She "dies" a little—sheds her old skin and births herself anew. She learns and grows. And, by extension and example, she teaches us. As Tanya Wilkinson in *Persephone Returns: Victims, Heroes, and the Journey from the Underworld* observes, Persephone's initiation is that of the victim who experiences the abduction and betrayal; Demeter, on the other hand, is initiated to the underworld of loss and grief because of her daughter's abduction.[18] However, both Demeter and Persephone undergo a fundamentally similar experience: the death of an old self and the birth of a new one.

Demeter takes us through the stages of grief, mourning, and reconciliation. Furthermore, she teaches us the importance of tapping into our internal power and using that power to force our opponent to acquiesce to our demands. First, we learn that we cannot avoid dealing with grief if ever we hope to transcend it. We must come to terms with our loss and then move forward. Second, we learn that we need to enter into ourselves and allow time and space for mourning. Third, we learn that grief makes us susceptible to seeking "the quick fix"—alternatives that are temporary and short-term solutions, alternatives that will invariably fire back on us. Fourth, we learn that when we want something from an adversary, we must make it in his or her self-interest to do our bidding. Fifth, we learn that we must be unwavering and firm in our resolve when we decide to pursue a course of action. Sixth, we learn the importance of knowing when to let go and when to compromise in bringing a conflict to a successful resolution. If Demeter had wavered while Persephone was still in the underworld, Persephone would never have been released. If Demeter had remained obstinate after Persephone's release, she would not only be violating her part of the bargain with Zeus, she would have risked losing everything. Seventh, we learn that in life, although there are some losses we can recover from, there are others that we have to endure. Eighth, we learn that without death, there can be no life; without life, there can be no death. Life and death are different stages in what constitutes an ongoing cycle, a rhythmic process in which each stage should be celebrated for its uniqueness and for what it has to offer us in terms of knowledge and insight. And, finally, as Christine Downing tells us in "Persephone in Hades," as women, we also learn the additional lesson of just how much of motherhood is characterized by loss.[19] These are valuable lessons to learn—both for Demeter and for ourselves— when we experience our own journeys to the chthonic realm.

But our lessons aren't over yet, for we have more to learn about journeys to the chthonic realm—as we shall see when we visit with Persephone and share her experience with loss and rebirth in the underworld.

CHAPTER 3

Persephone: Moving Beyond Victimization

The Homeric *Hymn to Demeter* begins with the following lines:

> Demeter I begin to sing, the fair-tressed awesome goddess,
> herself and her slim-ankled daughter whom Aidoneus
> seized...

> (Lines 1–3)

The poem is dedicated to Demeter and her "slim-ankled daughter." It is interesting to note that Kore is referred to as Demeter's daughter and not as someone who has an identity in her own right. In the beginning of the poem, she is presented merely as an extension of her mother. In fact, the word "kore" simply means a young girl, a maiden, a virgin. Tanya Wilkinson in *Persephone Returns: Victims, Heroes, and the Journey from the Underworld* argues that, as a maiden picking flowers, Kore is emblematic of the kind of innocence that deserves protection in so far as she unites the qualities of potential and unblemished grace, qualities that are evident in young children and that Western culture tends to associate with virginal girls.[1]

Kore is generic. The word can refer to any young girl or maiden. It can even signify any one of us, male or female, who is "young" in the sense of being gullible, naïve, virginal, and innocent. Kore gains—or earns—her identity, her right to assume a proper name, only after her abduction and rape.

36

She is then identified as Persephone, queen of the underworld. In other words, as a result of her experiences in the underworld, Kore traverses the path from being Anyone to being Someone.

Kore's youth, innocence, and generic quality are emphasized in the next few lines of the poem. She is engaging in the frivolous and pleasurable activity of picking flowers. Upon seeing the narcissus, Kore "...marveled and stretched out both hands at once / To take the lovely toy" (lines 15–16). Her youth and innocence reflect the sense of wonder and marvel that characterize young people before they have become jaded by life. This is one of the most endearing qualities of youth. But it is also a quality that can increase their susceptibility to making foolish, gullible mistakes.

Homer captures the enthusiasm, vibrancy, innocence, beauty, and boundless energy of youth in his eloquent description of the daughters of Metaneira, who, like the young Kore, are still maidens. As the young girls rush back to the Maiden's Well to invite Demeter to their home, Homer describes them in words that echo the innocence and playfulness of the young Kore.

> Just as hinds or heifers in the season of spring
> bound through the meadow sated with fodder,
> so they, lifting the folds of their shimmering robes,
> darted down the hollow wagon-track, and their hair
> danced on their shoulders like a crocus blossom.
>
> (Lines 174–178)

But unlike the daughters of Metaneira, Kore's innocence comes to a screeching halt. Captivated by the narcissus, she stretches out both hands to take the "toy." She perceives it as a new play object, something that is hers to appropriate. She doesn't question her right to take it. She doesn't approach it with suspicion. She has yet to learn the potential hazards that can come of being too trusting. She assumes, as do all young people, that the world revolves around her and that any object or person she perceives in her path is there for her benefit and to do her bidding. Part of our maturation process involves shedding this self-centered perspective and learning that, in life, not everything—or everyone—is there for our benefit; and not everything—or everyone—is as innocent as we would like to think. This is a lesson that Kore has yet to learn.

Having plucked the narcissus, Kore precipitates a series of events that lead to her abduction and rape. The earth opens up and Hades, god of the underworld and lord of death, emerges from his chariot. He snatches the young girl and abducts her to Erebos, his deathly realm. Kore screams to her father for help. We are told that Hekate and Helios hear her scream.

> She screamed with a shrill voice,
> calling on her father, the son of Kronos highest and best.
> Not one of the immortals or humankind
> heard her voice, nor the olives bright with fruit,
> except the daughter of Persaios; tender of heart
> she heard it from her cave, Hekate of the delicate veil.
> And lord Helios, brilliant son of Hyperion, heard
> the maid calling her father.
>
> (Lines 20–27)

There is no mention of Kore calling out to her mother. It is interesting to note that although Kore calls to her father for help, it is actually her mother who comes to her aid.

Zeus, the grand, old patriarch, has agreed to his daughter's abduction and rape. Kore turns to him for help, but none is forthcoming because, unbeknownst to her, Zeus has been in on the scheme all along:

> Against her will Hades took her by the design of Zeus
> with his immortal horses—her father's brother,
> Commander- and Host-to-Many, the many-named son of Kronos.
>
> (Lines 30–32)

Why does Kore call to her father and not to her mother for help? Perhaps it is because the young girl has already absorbed one of the lessons of patriarchy: the father has power and the mother does not. As Shulamith Firestone argues in *The Dialectic of Sex*, children sense at an early age that the father is in total control and the mother is halfway between authority and helplessness.[2] Although this is generally the case in families within a patriarchy, it is not the case in this story. Demeter is anything but helpless in her insistence on the integrity of the mother/child bond.

What does Kore's cry suggest to a contemporary audience? And what does her father's refusal to help suggest? A possible interpretation of her plea to father is that women constantly seek help from the very forces that are actively opposed to helping them. As women, we seek validation and support from those we perceive to be higher up in the hierarchy, those individuals who have power. And since we live in a patriarchy, those individuals who have power and who have a vested interest in maintaining the existing power structure are primarily males. As women, we put our trust in male figures in positions of authority—only to have our hopes severely dashed, more often than not. According to Jean Shinoda Bolen in *Goddesses in Older Women*, sometimes it is this very betrayal of a daughter of patriarchy by the patriarchy that initiates a woman into feminism.[3] In the case of Kore, recognition of her betrayal by the father acts as the catalyst that triggers the development of her feminist consciousness.

As an oppressed group, women have yet to forge links and create a common identity with other women to the same degree that members of other oppressed groups have succeeded in doing. The situation is exacerbated by the fact that heterosexual women tend to identify with the interests of the males they associate with as opposed to identifying with other females across racial and economic divides. For example, white, heterosexual females, since they are the indirect beneficiaries of a system that privileges white, heterosexual males, may find great difficulty in locating commonalities with women of different races and from different economic classes. In the short term, it is probably easier for such women not to challenge a system that gives them access to power—even though that access is indirect—than to call for a transformation to a new system in which all members have equal access, equal rights, and equal privileges, regardless of their race, class, ethnicity, or gender.

The feminist movement has done much to raise consciousness about the global oppression of women and to articulate the commonalities of women's oppression. Furthermore, Women's Studies and Gender Studies programs, the academic arms of the feminist movement, are making their presence felt through curriculum transformation and feminist pedagogy in educational institutions throughout the world. Consequently, the plight of women is improving. However, we still have a long way to go. For until we recognize the inherent unfairness of a system that privileges the few and excludes the many; until we recognize that as long as one group is oppressed, we are all oppressed; until we recognize that we are performing a serious disservice to ourselves and to our own economic empowerment by relying primarily on the men in our lives for support as opposed to relying on ourselves and each other; and until, as women, we recognize that it is only by forging coalitions with our sisters across racial, ethnic, economic, and geographical boundaries; we can never hope to transform a system that privileges the few and excludes the many. Instead, we will be perpetuating a system designed to keep us weak, dependent, and powerless. In the long run, such a system is not to anyone's advantage.

In *Gyn/Ecology: The Metaethics of Radical Feminism*, Mary Daly refers to women's tendency to seek confirmation and endorsement from the men in our lives as the M.A.D. syndrome (an acronym for Male Approval Desire). Daly claims that women who look for validation and support from males are doomed to disappointment. In her inimitable fashion, Daly refers to this syndrome as "clearheaded M-A-Dness."[4] Women need to learn to seek support from forces that are not opposed to them. What is true for women is true for all oppressed groups: we need to work together to overcome the circumstances of our oppression. We need to know where our true source of validation lies. For Kore, help does not come from the grand, old patriarch; help comes from her mother—a female who holds fast in her refusal to abandon her child to the throes of a patriarchal system that objectifies women and dispenses with them at the behest of a male hegemonic power structure.

Kim Chernin in *Reinventing Eve: Modern Woman in Search of Herself* offers a similar perspective. She argues that when a young girl is at a crossroads in her life and is about to depart from the safety and security of the private, domestic sphere as represented by the world of the mother, she idealizes the power of the father. She does this partly because she believes that the father will assist her in her own self-development as she enters the public sphere, but also because she experiences guilt and terror at abandoning the world of the mother.[5]

Zeus refuses to come to the aid of his daughter because he has already given permission for her abduction and rape. By giving his blessing to her marriage, he is acting well within the social and cultural constructs of his time, a time in which rape was not considered a crime against the bodily integrity of the female. Instead, if it was perceived as a crime at all, it was considered a crime of property, the injured party being the father of the girl or her spouse. Hades, therefore, had no choice but to seek permission from the father before carting the young girl off to be his bride by claiming his right over her through rape. Otherwise, he would have risked incurring the wrath of her powerful father by inflicting damage on his property.

Being the majestic patriarch that he is, Zeus operates under the assumption that Kore is his property to do with as he pleases. He is simply exercising his privilege as a male: that of dispensing with the women in his life in any way that he sees fit. He would no more consider asking Kore for her opinion on the matter than he would consider asking Demeter, her mother. From his perspective, these are, after all, only women, and women in a patriarchy are voiceless and powerless and should remain so. In fact, so comfortable is Zeus in his right to dispense with his daughter that he is somewhat unnerved and baffled by Demeter's challenge to his authority.

After her abduction and rape, Kore can no longer be referred to as Kore since she has lost her maiden status. Instead, she is referred to as Persephone—a word signifying spring and reflecting the cyclical rebirth of nature that occurs with Demeter's release of the earth from its strangulation. Kore's change in name indicates her change in status. It also brings up the important issue of naming and re-naming.

As Gerda Lerner has demonstrated in *The Creation of Patriarchy*, the belief system of ancient Mesopotamia ascribed a profound significance to the power of naming, a belief that has survived the centuries.[6] In *Genesis* 2: 19–23, for example, Adam is given the power to name the animals. This reflects his sovereignty over them: "These he brought to the man to see what he would call them; each one was to bear the name the man would give it. The man gave names to all the cattle, all the birds of heaven and all the wild beasts."[7] A few lines later, in *Genesis* 2: 23–24, after Yahweh has created the female from Adam's rib, Adam is given the authority to name her: "This is to be called Woman, for this was taken from Man." In other words, through this unique act of reversing the natural order of creation, a reversal that had never before or since been duplicated, a male not only "gives birth" to a female—thereby establishing his precedence over her— but he has sovereignty over her by virtue of the fact that he is given the authority to name her.

This reversal of the natural birthing process establishes the female's subordinate status in relationship to the male: she is created *for* man to be his help mate; she is created *from* man's rib, a part of him that was not essential for his survival; and she is *named* by man, an act which reinforces her subordination. After the Fall, Adam re-names the woman. He calls her Eve: "The man named his wife 'Eve' because she was the mother of all those who live" (*Genesis* 3: 20–21). Woman's change in name indicates an alteration in her status.

The significance of naming and re-naming continues to be experienced today in many traditional communities in which the female adopts her husband's name in marriage, an indication that she is no longer under the control of the father but is now under the control of the spouse. Whatever individual identity she was permitted to have while living in her father's house becomes subsumed under the honorific title of "Mrs. So-and-So." It bears mentioning that Mr. So-and-So does not experience a corresponding name change even though there is a change in his status as a result of marriage. He remains Mr. So-and-So throughout his life, a vocal declaration of his autonomy and personhood for the entire world to acknowledge.

Kore and the biblical Woman share a change in status and a parallel fate: they both "fall" and, as a consequence, not only lose their innocence but are also given new names to reflect their altered state. However, there is a significant difference between the two: in the case of Eve, it is clearly Adam who endows her with both her first and second name. In the case of Kore, the change in name occurs without any indication as to who decreed it. All we know is that Kore in the underworld is now addressed as Persephone. So whereas Eve's subordination to Adam is reinforced through his re-naming of her, Kore's re-naming does not carry the same bitter taste of a double subjugation to male hegemony.

In *The Creation of Patriarchy*, Gerda Lerner deconstructs the issue of naming even further by distinguishing between naming and re-naming: whereas naming and re-naming indicates sovereignty over the person or object being named by the person doing the naming, re-naming has an

added significance. According to Lerner, re-naming "...signifies the assumption of a new and powerful role for the person so re-named."[8] Lerner cites
the examples of the re-naming of the god Marduk (with fifty names, no
less!) after his defeat of Tiamat and the solidification of his power in the
ancient Mesopotamian *Enuma Elish*. She also cites God's re-naming of
Abram to Abraham to signify the latter's altered status after receiving the
covenant.[8]

Utilizing Lerner's discussion, we can see that Kore experiences a similar fate. Her change in name to Persephone indicates not only has she experienced an altered change in status, but she has also experienced an elevation
in status: as Persephone, she has assumed a new and powerful role as queen
of the underworld, a position that affords her the authority and respect that
was denied her when she was merely Kore, the "slim-ankled daughter" of
Demeter.

After her abduction and rape, we do not encounter Kore again until
we see her in the underworld as Persephone. Upon receiving his instructions from Zeus to retrieve her, Hermes heads to the underworld. He
encounters Persephone, reclining on a bed with Hades.

> Hermes did not disobey. At once he left Olympus's height
> and plunged swiftly into the depths of the earth.
> He met lord Hades inside his dwelling,
> reclining on a bed with his shy spouse, strongly reluctant
> through desire for her mother.
>
> (Lines 340–344)

Persephone has obviously been miserable in the underworld and has spent
her time pining away for her mother. She has also yet to eat anything in the
underworld.

Hermes makes his case:

> "Dark-haired Hades, ruler of the dead, Father Zeus
> bids me lead noble Persephone up from Erebos [underworld]
> to join us, so that her mother might see her with her eyes
> and cease from anger and dread wrath against the gods.
> For she is devising a great scheme to destroy
> the helpless race of mortals born on earth,
> burying the seed beneath the ground and obliterating
> divine honors."
>
> (Lines 347–354)

It is interesting to note that Hermes accuses Demeter of "burying the seed
beneath the ground." In one sense, he is correct since Demeter has stricken
the land with drought and has obstinately refused to allow any seed to grow

until the release of her daughter from the underworld. In another sense, Hermes simply doesn't seem to get it. Persephone, is, after all, the offshoot of Demeter, her seed. Demeter didn't initiate the burial of her seed underground. The male power structure brought this catastrophe upon itself: Zeus acting in compliance with the wish of his brother, Hades. Since they have chosen to bury her seed underground, it seems only fitting that Demeter retaliates by denying the growth of all seed from the underground. But the logic and poetic justice of her action seems to escape Hermes and the rest of the gods.

This isn't the first time, nor will it be the last, that a patriarchy has been unwilling or unable to situate a course of action in its context and evaluate it accordingly as a form of retributive justice. Instead, the patriarchy views it as an isolated act and treats it as if it were a totally unreasonable, irrational, and emotional course of action to pursue. In short, Demeter's behavior is labeled a "scheme," the implication being that her mode of conduct constitutes stereotypically hysterical "female" behavior.

As he is about to set her free, Hades tries to mollify Persephone's anger:

> "Go, Persephone, to the side of your dark-robed mother,
> keeping the spirit and temper in your breast benign,
> do not be so sad and angry beyond the rest;
> in no way among immortals will I be an unsuitable spouse,
> myself a brother of father Zeus."
>
> (Lines 360–364)

Until now, Persephone has been unable to sever the psychological umbilical cord with her mother, perceiving herself simply as her mother's extension. Occupying the liminal state—the in-between stage that is the necessary prerequisite for transformation—Persephone has lost one status, has the potential to replace it with another, but has yet to do so. She is trapped between two worlds. Caught in limbo between these two worlds or stages, Persephone has yet to recognize the full impact of what has happened to her, namely, that now she has the ability and the potential to be a powerful, autonomous figure in her own right, inspiring fear and dread in all that lives. She has not yet tapped into her inner power. So, before he releases her, Hades obligingly reminds her of the magnitude of her powers and of her high status among the gods:

> "You will have power over all that lives and moves,
> and you will possess the greatest honors among the gods.
> There will be punishment forevermore for those wrongdoers
> who fail to appease your power with sacrifices,
> performing proper rites and making due offerings."
>
> (Lines 364–369)

We are told that Persephone greets these words with joy and exuberance: "Thus he spoke and thoughtful Persephone rejoiced / Eagerly she leapt up for joy" (lines 370–371). What specifically is Persephone rejoicing about? Is she overjoyed at the thought of seeing her mother again? If that is the case, then why didn't she leap for joy as soon as the heard the news from Hermes that her father has ordered her release? After all, she was present when Hermes delivered the news to Hades. Or is her joy caused by more than just her impending release? And why does the word "thoughtful" precede her act of rejoicing? What exactly is Persephone thinking about? The poem leaves these questions open to interpretation.

Persephone doesn't leap for joy immediately after Hermes informs Hades that Zeus has ordered her release even though she knows Hades has no choice but to obey the father of the gods. Nor does she leap for joy immediately after Hades tells her that she is going to be reunited with her mother. She leaps for joy at the end of his speech—after he has expounded on her new status and newly found power. The fact that these two pieces of information are juxtaposed so closely together suggests a causal relationship between the two. Her leap for joy is directly connected to the fact that she has been made conscious of the extent of her power. Is Persephone now realizing, for the first time, that she has assumed a powerful identity that is all her own, one separate from mother? Is that what she is thinking about? And if this is the case, has Hades, in effect, performed a service to her by severing her apron strings to mother while, at the same time, absolving her of the guilt that frequently characterizes such separation?

As many of us know, the mother/daughter dyad is fraught with conflict and tensions. This is not to deny the complexity of father/son or mother /son or father/daughter relationships. However, the mother/daughter relationships are unique because of the nature of the socialization of women. Carol Gilligan's study *In a Different Voice: Psychological Theory and Women's Development* demonstrates that from very early on, embedded within girls' socialization lies a heavy value placed on connection and attachment. Boys' socialization, on the other hand, places a heavy value on separation and autonomy.[9] Girls are socialized to be care-givers; boys are socialized to be care-receivers. So a girl's attempt to sever the primal bond with her mother is complicated by her desire to maintain her connection with mother while, at the same time, seeking to experience freedom and autonomy apart from mother.

In "Family Structure and Feminine Personality," Nancy Chodorow argues that mothers and women tend to identify more closely with their daughters than they do with their sons.[10] This close identification can render it more difficult for a girl to separate from mother and move in the direction of realizing an autonomous identity for herself. According to

Chodorow, because mothers identify less with their sons, they tend to thrust them forward on the path to individuation.[10] Chodorow reinforces her point by arguing that evidence suggests that establishing an identity independent from mother remains a difficult psychological issue for many Western middle-class women.[11]

The situation is further complicated by the fact that a girl's primary role model is her mother. We can see evidence of this even in the language and behavior of the daughters of Metaneira when they first encounter Demeter. The eldest, Kallidike, begins by informing Demeter that mortals have to endure the gifts of the gods—however much it may hurt them to do so (lines 147–148). She then acknowledges Demeter's godlike stature (line 159). Then she reassures Demeter that should she agree to be the nurse and caregiver for their infant brother, their mother will reward her to such a degree that other women would feel envious (lines 166–168). Later, when Metaneira meets Demeter, she echoes her daughter's words, almost verbatim.

> "Hail, lady, for I suppose your parents are not lowborn,
> but noble. Your eyes are marked by modesty
> and grace, even as those of justice-dealing kings.
> We mortals are forced, though it may hurt us, to bear
> the gifts of the gods. For the yoke lies on our necks.
> But now you have come here, all that's mine will be yours.
> Raise this child for me, whom the gods provided
> late-born and unexpected, much-prayed for by me.
> If you raise him and he comes to the threshold of youth,
> any woman who saw you would feel envy at once,
> such rewards for his rearing would I give you."
>
> (Lines 213–223)

Even allowing for the possibility that the parallel sentiments expressed in almost identical words constitute a mnemonic device for the poet, Kallidike's words, modeled on the words and sentiments that she has already assimilated from her mother, reflect the significant imprint a mother can make on her daughter's development and world view.

Kathie Carlson makes a similar observation. In *In Her Image: The Unhealed Daughter's Search for Her Mother*, Carlson argues that a woman receives her first impression of what it means to be a woman from her mother.[12] She identifies with her mother very early in life and she continues to do so for a longer period than does her male sibling. Little boys learn very early in their development that they are dependent on mother but that they are different from mother. So their separation from mother takes place early in life and is not plagued with the same tensions, anxieties, and guilt that characterize the separation for their female counterparts. A female finds it difficult to separate from someone who is like her, who gave birth to her, who nurtured and nourished her, and who is her most significant role model. Vera Bushe in "Cycles of Becoming" laments that one of the greatest tragedies of our culture is the absence of rituals to support movement away from mothers, or to support mothers in letting go of their daughters, or to support mothers and daughters as they seek to define themselves independently of each other.[13]

Women connect to the past through their mothers and to the future through their daughters. The bond is unique. Separation from the source of one's life is invariably fraught with feelings of guilt. To separate means to sever, to reject, to cut off. How can a woman separate from her mother, the woman who gave birth to her, and do so without being plagued with guilt? How can she do so without making her mother feel rejected? Well, it isn't easy. According to Kathie Carlson's *In Her Image: The Unhealed Daughter's Search for Her Mother*, the situation can be further exacerbated by the fact that some women are afraid to sever the connection with mother because it means giving up what feels familiar and, therefore, safe.[14] However, the reality is that unless we do separate from mother, unless we cut that umbilical cord and fly free, we will never have the opportunity to actualize our potential and to discover who we are and what we are capable of doing. As Carlson argues, in addition to intimacy and closeness, a daughter needs permission and support to separate from her mother, to venture on her own, to make her own mistakes and triumphs, and to find her own path in life.[15]

Carol Gilligan's influential work, *In a Different Voice: Psychological Theory and Women's Development*, discusses the different paths that males and females pursue in the process of development. According to Gilligan, masculinity is defined by separation and autonomy and is threatened by intimacy; femininity is defined by connection and attachment and is threatened by separation.[16] This emphasis on social interaction and personal relationships that characterize a young girl's life and development become a liability in terms of her own psychological development as she struggles to maturity. According to Gilligan, women, since they have been socialized to connect, feel severely threatened by separation. But their failure to separate results in a corresponding failure to develop.[16]

The process of individuation (the process by which a person experiences internal transformation and moves towards developing an independent, authentic identity) is predicated upon psychological separation from mother. To remain under the influence of mother indicates immaturity for male and female alike. But the problem for women, as Kathryn Rabuzzi argues in *Motherself: A Mythic Analysis of Motherhood*, is complicated in that it places them in an untenable situation by putting them in conflict with an upbringing and socialization that stresses the value of community and relationships.[17] In order to become autonomous, therefore, a woman either has to repudiate a value system that has become ingrained in her, or she has to reject the value of autonomy and remain entirely dependent on community and relationships. If she chooses the former, she risks incurring the condemnation of a society that labels her selfish since she chooses to pursue autonomy and independence instead of cultivating community and relationships—her gender-prescribed role as a female in a patriarchy. If she chooses the latter, she risks incurring the condemnation of a society that does not place such a high value on community and relationships but views dependence with contempt and derision. In other words, the process of individuation for women is more complex than it is for men because women appear to be damned if they do and damned if they don't. However, that does not deny the essential role that separation plays in the process of individuation for all of us—male and female alike.

A woman's journey to autonomy, power, and selfhood, therefore, entails the difficult process of severing the connection to mother. The mother's hold must be broken in order to prepare the way for rebirth. And if mother is comfortable in her own identity, if mother does not live her life vicariously through her daughter, if mother does not want to control and dominate every aspect of her daughter's life, if mother does not tie herself to her daughter and attempt to interfere or prevent her daughter's movement towards self-sufficiency, she will assist her daughter in the transition from girlhood to womanhood by encouraging and supporting her faltering steps towards freedom and autonomy. Failure to do so results in what Carlson refers to as the "binding mother"—mothers who are unwilling to let their daughters separate by thwarting any movement on their part towards independence.[18] Successful mothering results from the activities of an individual with a strong sense of her self, her worth, her boundaries, and one who makes a conscious decision to mother and who enjoys the connection and responsibility involved in this very serious undertaking.

Persephone is assisted in her transition from girl to woman by her uncle/spouse, Hades. Hades plays a unique role in this story, as we shall see later. He offers Persephone a way out of the quandary that all women face: how to separate from mother and how to do so without making mother feel rejected and hurt? Hades posits himself between Persephone and her mother and forcibly severs the connection between the two. He causes Persephone's metamorphosis from Kore to Persephone, the powerful queen of the underworld. And he enables Persephone to undergo this metamorphosis—one that could only have taken place as a result of separation from mother—while absolving her of guilt and blame. Persephone is not riddled with the guilt that continues to plague many women throughout their adult years as they examine their relationships with their mothers. In effect, Persephone has been able to reap all the benefits of separation without having to endure the cost—a bit like eating chocolate cake without all the calories.

After her leap for joy and before her departure from the underworld, Persephone eats the pomegranate seed given to her by Hades. The fact that she has eaten food from the land of the dead means that she will have to return to it for a certain period every year. The significance of the pomegranate will be discussed in a later chapter. First, however, we need to examine the text for clues as to whether Persephone's eating of the pomegranate seed was due to ignorance of the consequences of her action or with the full knowledge that, by doing so, she was guaranteeing her return to the underworld. The text does not provide a clear indication one way or another:

> But he [Hades] gave her to eat
> a honey-sweet pomegranate seed, stealthily passing it
> around her, lest she once more stay forever
> by the side of revered Demeter of the dark robe.
>
> (Lines 371–374)

How does one "stealthily" pass food around another in such a way as to force a person to eat it? Later, after Persephone is reunited with her mother, she describes the incident in the following terms:

> "Then I leapt for joy, but he stealthily
> put in my mouth a food honey-sweet, a pomegranate seed,
> and compelled me against my will and by force to taste it."
>
> (Lines 411–413)

Is Persephone merely succumbing to the human tendency to blame others for one's mistakes? She makes it sound as if Hades took advantage of her moment of weakness, her leap for joy, tricked her into putting the pomegranate seed in her mouth, and then coerced her into swallowing it.

The problem is that one activity does not necessarily lead to another. Persephone seems to be committing a logical fallacy here by confusing chronology with causality. Just because one thing occurred before another, it does not mean that it caused the subsequent event. You can leap for joy and open your mouth in the process; you can be caught unawares by having someone surreptitiously sneak food in your mouth; however, you cannot be tricked or forced into swallowing the food. Even an infant knows enough to spit and splatter food that he or she refuses to eat—as anyone who has ever tried to feed a baby will confirm. So was Persephone tricked into swallowing the pomegranate seed? Was she coerced? Or did she do it voluntarily, knowing full well the consequences of her actions? Once again, the poem leaves that open to interpretation. However, the sequence of events suggests that Persephone was fully cognizant of her actions. Persephone was no fool. Homer himself describes her on several occasions throughout the poem as "thoughtful Persephone." As Helen Luke in *Woman, Earth, and Spirit: The Feminine in Symbol and Myth* argues, in spite of her protestations, Persephone has absolutely no intention of regressing to identification with her mother again.[19] She knew exactly what she was doing when she swallowed the pomegranate seed. And more power to her.

Let us retrace the sequence of events. First, Hades reminds her of her new status and power as the queen of the underworld. She leaps for joy upon hearing this. Then he "stealthily" puts a pomegranate seed in her mouth. She swallows it. By doing so, she is eating food from the land of the dead and cementing her return to the underworld. If she did this knowing full well the consequences of her action, we need to ask ourselves the following question: why would Persephone want to return to the underworld? In order to answer that question, we have to determine Persephone's status before and after her visit to the underworld.

Who is Persephone before she is abducted to the underworld? She is Kore, a young, virginal non-entity tied to her mother's apron string whose only claim to fame is that she is her mother's daughter. Who is she when she is in the underworld? She is Persephone, the wife of Hades. But she is also queen of underworld. She is powerful, autonomous, feared, and respected. How can Persephone maintain her status as this powerful goddess whom even the immortals fear? And how can she take advantage of this status not only while she is in the underworld but also while she is in the over-world, visiting her mother? In other words, how can Persephone have her cake (in this case, the pomegranate seed) and eat it, too? By doing one thing and one thing alone: she must cement her return to the underworld periodically to renew her status as queen of that realm. And in order to do that, she must eat the food of death that is, ironically, the source of her power. She has to eat the pomegranate seed. So she does.

Until she eats the pomegranate seed, Persephone is a victim. Her youth and innocence cause her to pluck the narcissus that precipitates her abduction to the underworld. However, we cannot—and should not—fault her for being young and innocent. While she is in the underworld, she remains a victim. She is overpowered by Hades and has no means of escape. Again, we cannot fault her for that. However, once she is presented with a choice, Persephone exercises it and, by doing so, she assumes responsibility for her transformation from victim status to survivor. She seizes the opening to transform loss into an opportunity for growth and development. "Thoughtful Persephone" confirms that she is no longer the young, innocent, naïve girl she once was. She has transcended her original status of being a powerless victim of abduction and rape.

All too frequently in society, we tend to blame the victim of rape for her victimization. What was she wearing at the time? Did she ask for it? What was she doing in that neighborhood/apartment/dorm room anyway? Why did she go that party in the first place? What was she thinking? The underlying assumption is that if the victim had sense enough, or if her will had been strong enough, or if her legs had run fast enough, or if she had fought hard enough, she would not have been raped. Such statements constitute victim blaming, and they are ugly, vicious, and cruel. They are also premised on the lie that a woman can always escape from her would-be assailant. In some cases, a woman is lucky enough to escape with her life. Additionally, victim blaming is sadistic because not only is a woman expected to deal with the trauma of her rape, she is also expected to take some measure of responsibility for the heinous and barbaric act that was done unto her. Society is very adept at finding any excuse to wag the stern finger of admonition towards a female victimized by rape.

Victims are not responsible for their victimization; however, they are responsible for turning that victimization into something constructive that can strengthen and empower them and empower others by example. By eating the pomegranate seed, Persephone does just that. She exercises agency. She defines herself. She moves beyond her abduction, betrayal, and rape. She transcends her victim status and becomes the powerful and empowered queen of the underworld—a "kick ass" survivor.

Victims who traverse the path from victim status to survivor status are to be applauded—especially because to do so requires a giant leap forward in terms of accepting responsibility for their subsequent actions and decisions. Victim status can lull an individual into a comfort zone of evading accountability. It absolves the individual of responsibility for her or his behavior. It can be consoling for victims to believe that they continue to be powerless and that they are not responsible for what happens to them or for the decisions that are made on their behalf because they have been victimized and therefore relieved of all accountability. To reject that self-abrogating but comforting perspective requires a great deal of courage since it involves an assertion of agency coupled with a determination to accept responsibility for one's own decisions and behaviors—regardless of their outcomes. Individuals who take even the most rudimentary, faltering steps to move from self-identification as victims to self-identification as survivors should be encouraged, nurtured, assisted, and applauded.

Kathryn Rabbuzzi in *Motherself: A Mythic Analysis of Motherhood* argues that because Persephone does not reject Hades, she demonstrates that a woman does not have to reject men altogether in order to become her own person. Furthermore, because Persephone does not totally immerse herself in Hades and the underworld, she demonstrates that a woman does not have to submerge her identity to that of the male and the allure of sexuality and power he represents.[20] Instead, Persephone maintains a balance between the two worlds of the underworld and the over-world and all they represent, alternating from one to the other. In the process of doing so, she is able to negotiate a woman-centered space for herself in which she can nurture her growth towards autonomy and selfhood. And she does it on her own terms, independent of mother or the man in her life.

Neither Demeter nor Hades can exert any control of Persephone once she has made the decision to traverse both worlds since she no longer belongs to either world exclusively and, therefore, is not subject to the authority of either force. In many ways, Persephone has created a third world for herself, one that partakes of both the underworld and the over-world, but one that is not exclusively the one or the other. It is a world that has transcended the limitations of both. And because she has created such a unique space for herself, Persephone becomes her own person, one who is free of domination by either her mother or her spouse.

In *Woman's Mysteries: Ancient and Modern*, Esther Harding defines the psychological stance in which a woman acts to please herself, independently of what others may think, as a virgin, a woman who is one-in-herself.[21] Harding's definition of virgin has nothing to do with the modern association of sexual chastity. Instead, Harding defines virgin as a woman who acts independently of others, who refuses to conform to the demands of others, and who does not try to seek the approval of or exert power over others. According to Harding, a virgin does not allow herself to be influenced by the considerations that cause a non-virgin woman—whether married or single—to shape herself into conformity.[21] Using Harding's definition, we can argue that Persephone has assumed a virgin status. She has become one-unto-herself. She is no longer dependent on mother or on the male in her life but has negotiated a psychological stance and separate space for herself independent of external influences. She is powerful and autonomous. By heeding her inner voice and tapping into her inner strength, Persephone has become true to herself. Ironically, Persephone achieves her virginal status through abduction and rape.

Persephone's voice is closely connected with her transition from victim to survivor. Until she emerges from the underworld, Persephone has no voice. We hear her shrill cry for her father as she is being abducted to the underworld. However, this cry for her father is presented in the indirect voice, emphasizing the point that Persephone has been deprived both of voice and agency during her abduction. She doesn't speak while she is in the underworld. Instead, she demonstrates her frame of mind through non-verbal communication: "strongly reluctant / through desire for her mother" (lines 343–344). And later, when Hades informs her of her new status as his bride, we are told, "Eagerly she leapt for joy" (line 371). But still she doesn't speak. It is only after she emerges from the underworld that Persephone finds her voice. She speaks to her mother in direct dialogue, providing a fairly lengthy summary of the events that led up to her abduction and her release from the underworld.

In *Waking Sleeping Beauty: Feminist Voices in Children's Novels*, Roberta Trites argues that voice frequently serves as a metaphor of female agency.[22] Trites observes that in children's novels, female characters tend to become increasingly inarticulate as they learn to conform to society's constraining expectations. In other words, their loss of voice indicates their loss of agency and vice versa. In contrast, a feminist protagonist becomes increasingly articulate as the novel progresses, indicating a burgeoning sense of self and agency.[22]

Persephone traverses the path of the feminist protagonist. At the beginning of the poem, she is denied both voice and agency. She is inarticulate and relies exclusively on non-verbal means to communicate. When she emerges from the underworld, she is articulate, fluent, clear, and confident in her speech. This reflects her new identity and her awareness of the woman she has become. She speaks in direct dialogue, with a clarity and confidence that was absent in her communication and behavior before and during her abduction. By capitalizing on her experiences in the underworld, Persephone has not only found her voice, she has begun to exercise agency for the first time in her life. Voice and agency are inextricably intertwined.

Persephone proceeds to narrate to Demeter, in elaborate detail, the sequence of events that led to her abduction: how she was picking flowers with her friends; how she saw the narcissus, and "joyously plucked it"; how the earth opened up; and how Hades emerged in his chariot and kidnapped her. In the process of telling her story, Persephone is fulfilling two functions. First of all, as Polly Young-Eisendrath argues in "Demeter's Folly," her storytelling marks the establishment of a new order: one in which she is enthroned as queen of the underworld; one which marks the return of her mother to Mount Olympus; one which marks the inauguration of the Eleusinian Mysteries; and one in which Demeter is identified as the first initiate.[23]

Persephone's storytelling performs an equally important second function: it helps her to become reconciled with the trauma she has experienced. Through reconstructing the events, Persephone transforms the memory of the trauma and integrates it into her life—an activity that Judith Lewis Herman identifies in *Trauma and Recovery* as the second stage of recovery for victims of trauma.[24] According to Herman, recovery for victims of rape and trauma unfolds in three stages: establishment and safety; remembrance and mourning; reconnection with ordinary life.[25] By negotiating a separate, safe, and autonomous space for herself, by integrating and claiming her experiences through the retelling of the events, and by reconnecting with the ordinary life of the over-world, Persephone succeeds in establishing a safe haven in which she exercises agency and is mistress of her own fate.

Through the in-depth and detailed telling of her story to her mother, Persephone reconstructs the trauma in such a way as to make it more accessible to her and, therefore, easier to integrate into her life. As Judith Herman argues, the goal of the second stage of recovery, the recounting of the trauma, is integration not exorcism.[26] Persephone can never exorcise the trauma. She can never undo what has happened to her. But she can—and does—transform the trauma through narrating the sequence of events in such a way that she appropriates it into her being and thereby exerts control over it. The healing power of re-creating the trauma through the telling of it helps Persephone—and other victims of trauma—to reconnect with ordinary life on new terms. The underlying principle of the healing process is empowerment of the victim and a corresponding ability to exercise agency and control over her own life.

In *Writing a Woman's Life*, Carolyn Heilbrun makes a very strong case for the importance of oral exchanges among women as a source of empowerment. She argues that as long as women remain isolated from one another, as long as they do not share the most personal accounts of their lives with other women, they will not be actors in their own stories.[27] Heilbrun contends that the exchange of stories among women is so crucial that, in her estimation, its absence condemns women to lives of isolation and reliance on others to invent and control their own destiny.[27] In *Teaching to Transcend: Educating Women Against Violence*, Cheryl Sattler similarly locates women's storytelling at the epicenter of the teaching and learning and healing that occur in shelters for battered women.[28]

A woman's narrative, articulated in her own way and in her own voice, enables her to connect with other women and dissolves her sense of isolation—all of which leads to her empowerment. It is important to note, however, that women's voices are generally muffled or marginalized by society. And if that female voice happens to be speaking of abuse, society is particularly adept at sanctioning it. We simply do not want to hear that problems of sexual assault or domestic violence exist in our own communities. So we muffle the voices of abuse and engage in victim blaming to make it even harder for women to speak up.

Girls are socialized to be good and quiet and not to call attention to themselves. If they speak up about their abuse, more often than not, they have to contend with a community that reacts with disbelief. Society orchestrates obstacles that impede the victim's ability to heal through the telling of her story. All of these factors contribute to the continued abuse and victimization of young girls and women. It is significant, therefore, that Persephone is given the space to tell her story because only by doing so is she able to appropriate it, integrate it into her life, and move on.

Persephone concludes her narrative by telling her mother, "I cried out at the top of my voice / I speak the whole truth, though I grieve to tell it" (lines 432–433). Well, not exactly. Persephone does not speak the "whole truth." There is one little detail that she conveniently omits to tell her mother. When she cries out at the top of her voice, she cries out only for her father, Zeus—not for her mother, Demeter. Why does she opt to withhold this significant little detail from her mother? Perhaps because while she is in the underworld, Persephone gains some valuable insights and experiences growth and transformation, in addition to a burgeoning sense of self.

Going into the underworld, Persephone is young, innocent, naïve, and virginal. While in the underworld, she is raped. One way of understanding the rape, as we shall see in a later chapter, is that it represents a forced intrusion into our psychic integrity—a psychological penetration that irrevocably transforms us from the beings we once were to the beings we have now become. Emerging from the underworld, Persephone is strong, powerful, autonomous, and experienced. Through her experience in the underworld, she learns about herself. And she also gains other valuable insights. She learns that things are not necessarily as innocent or as harmless as they appear to be. She learns that her father is not nurturing and loving since he sanctioned her abduction and rape. She learns the meaning of betrayal. She learns that her mother is a power to be reckoned with because it is due to her mother's intransigence that she has been released from the underworld. She learns that her mother is capable of serious retaliation if she feels slighted. She also learns that there are some things in life that are best kept hidden from mother because mother doesn't need—or, necessarily want—to know all the minute details of her daughter's life. She learns that even though she had acted out of innocence and was, therefore, not responsible for her abduction and betrayal, through no fault of her own, she has been irrevocably transformed. And, finally, she learns that she can transcend her victim status by tapping into her inner power, exercising agency, and assuming responsibility for her own healing and transformation towards becoming an empowered, autonomous being in her own right.

No more is said about the subject of the pomegranate seed or about Persephone's inevitable return to the underworld. Instead, we are told that Persephone and Demeter spend the day together:

> Then all day long, their minds at one, they soothed
> each other's heart and souls in many ways,

> embracing fondly, and their spirits abandoned grief,
> as they gave and received joy between them.

(Lines 434–437)

There is a real sense here that Demeter and Persephone are embracing each other as equals. The rank and hierarchy that is associated with the mother/child bond seems to have been obliterated. Demeter and Persephone are engaging in a mutually reciprocal relationship where each one gives and receives simultaneously. This is in marked contrast with the seemingly endless one-way giving that frequently characterizes the relationship a mother has with her child. Demeter may have lost her little girl, but she has apparently gained a friend, a soul mate, and a sister.

Through the intercession of her own mother, Demeter reconciles with the gods and releases the earth from its drought. The poem ends with an address to Demeter and Persephone:

> But come, you goddesses, dwelling in the town of
> fragrant Eleusis, and seagirt Paros, and rocky Antron,
> revered Deo, mighty giver of seasons and glorious gifts,
> you and your very fair daughter Persephone,
> for my song grant gladly a living that warms the heart.
> And I shall remember you and a new song as well.

(Lines 490–495)

Kore is no longer referred to as the "slim-ankled daughter" that she was at the beginning of the poem. She is now Persephone, a powerful goddess in her own right, one who demands—and enjoys—respect. She has had her pomegranate and eaten it, too.

The underworld can teach us valuable lessons, but only if we are strong, open, and receptive to its potentials. Persephone shows us that trauma does not have to immobilize us permanently. Persephone shows us that we can use trauma to strengthen our voice, increase our autonomy, and gain insight and knowledge about ourselves and about the world around us. Persephone shows us that we can tap into our inner strength, exercise agency, and become empowered. Persephone shows us that even though things may be done unto us, we have choices in life, and how we exercise those choices will determine whether we will be rulers in our domain by exercising agency or end up as yet another statistic by relinquishing our agency to others. Persephone shows us that it is possible to overcome our victimization. And she also shows us how to do it.

Persephone has, indeed, come along way. And like her mother, she is assisted in her journey to the underworld by, of all things, the captivating narcissus, the veil of introspection, and the succulent pomegranate, as we shall see in the next chapter.

CHAPTER 4

A Narcissus, a Veil, and a Pomegranate

A Narcissus

In the Homeric *Hymn to Demeter*, Kore is enticed into the underworld by a narcissus. She is playing in the fields with her friends, picking flowers, when she spies a narcissus and plucks it from the ground. Her action precipitates a chain of events that lead to her abduction, rape, and new identity as the bride of Hades and queen of the underworld. What is the significance of this narcissus that acts as an instrument for Kore's abduction and rape?

First of all, we are told this is no ordinary narcissus. It is described as an amazing flower with one hundred stems and an intoxicating fragrance. The narcissus has been deliberately placed there to entrap Kore:

> ... and the narcissus,
> which Earth grew as a snare for the flower-faced maiden
> in order to gratify by Zeus's design the Host-to-Many,
> a flower wondrous and bright, awesome for all to see,
> for the immortals above and for mortals below.
> From its root a hundredfold bloom sprang up and smelled
> so sweet that the whole vast heaven above
> and the whole earth laughed, and the salty swell of the sea.
>
> (Lines 7–14)

In order to fully appreciate the significance of the narcissus, we need to embark on a small and temporary detour: the deconstruction of another story in Greek mythology, the story of an attractive, young male named Narcissus.

Narcissus is described as young and beautiful—so beautiful, in fact, that all the females who see him immediately fall in love with him. They throw themselves at his feet, but he spurns their advances. He exhibits no compassion for them or their plight since he deems them unworthy of his attention. One of these love-stricken females prays to the gods to punish him for his cruelty and arrogance. The great goddess Nemesis answers her prayer. She decrees that Narcissus should suffer from the pangs of self-love. Accordingly, as Narcissus is bending over a clear pool for a drink one day, he sees his reflection in the water and immediately falls passionately in love with himself, so much so, in fact, that he cannot bear to part from his own reflection. And so he spends the rest of his days by leaning over the pool and gazing longingly at his own image. Unable to forgo the sight of his beloved, he eventually wastes away and dies.

From this story, it would be safe to conclude that the narcissus symbolizes unhealthy self-absorption and self-love, the kind of love that ultimately leads to self-destruction. It is sterile and unhealthy because it does not acknowledge the existence or the needs of others. It denies community. It is unremittingly self-focused. It strips a human being of compassion and selflessness. And, ultimately, it leads to starvation and death.

As a young girl, Kore exhibits the tendencies of most young people— that of self-absorption. She is sauntering merrily through life, when, all of a sudden, she is enticed by an object, a path, a decision, or a person that fuels her self-love. Focusing only on herself and her needs, she pursues the object, the path, the decision, or the person, thinking, as she plucks the narcissus, that this will bring her joy. Abandoning her companions and spurning the security that comes with collective action, she performs her deed in isolation. And, just as in the case of Narcissus who suffers death as a result of his self-absorption to the exclusion of all others, Kore suffers a death of sorts when she surrenders to her self-absorption and plucks the flower from the earth. By the time she realizes her mistake and screams for help, it is too late: the earth has opened up and Kore is plummeted to the underworld to be swallowed in its entrails without a trace.

Like Kore, many times we go through life making decisions that we think will bring us happiness. We fuel our self-love by taking actions that, unbeknownst to us at the time, are motivated by an unhealthy and destructive self-absorption. We abandon all else and all others in the pursuit of gratifying our needs. We indulge our self-absorption at the expense of community. We follow that path and pluck the treacherous narcissus. And by the time we have understood the nature of our mistake, it is too late. We find ourselves, like Kore, plummeting downward, groping in the darkness, and looking desperately for the Exit sign.

This temptation to give in to the seductive powers of the narcissus can happen many times in our lives. In many ways, it is inevitable because the loss of innocence can seldom be avoided. Each time, the narcissus can assume a different manifestation, a different choice, a different path, or a different guise. But no matter what form it assumes, the common denominator that weaves its way through the variety of possible manifestations is all too apparent: the narcissus comes to represent a goal that we pursue with a vengeance in order to gratify our unhealthy self-absorption. We pursue this goal, fully anticipating that it will lead to our happiness, when, instead, it leads us tumbling on a downward spiral to the underworld.

In *The Curse: A Cultural History of Menstruation*, Delaney, Lupton, and Toth argue that a flower is a rich and important symbol for female menstruation.[1] They remind us that in *Leviticus* 15:24, the flower means menstrual blood: "If any man lie with her at all, and her flowers be upon him, he shall be unclean seven days." So Kore's self-seduction while she is gathering flowers may also symbolize her flowing menstrual blood, a sign of the loss of her innocence and imminent entrance into womanhood. When interpreted in this way, the plucked narcissus serves as an omen of the impending loss of her hymen. This loss can be a disaster, but it can also signify the potential for a burgeoning fertility and new life. Just as a female has to lose her virginity before she can reproduce, so Kore has to lose her innocence before she can give birth to herself. Kore's fall, therefore, differs from the fall of Narcissus in that it opens up the possibility of movement away from isolation to community, from sterility to fertility, from death to regeneration, and from incomplete being to wholeness. The narcissus, therefore, comes to symbolize those energies that cause us to experience a profound loss while simultaneously holding out the possibility for our growth and transformation.

In an interesting twist, we are told that Zeus solicited the assistance of Gaia (Earth), his grandmother, to grow the narcissus that would be used to tempt Kore. If that is the case, then Gaia must have known that this narcissus would be used as an instrument for the abduction and rape of her great granddaughter. The question then becomes how could Gaia agree to be an accomplice to such a heinous crime perpetrated on her great granddaughter? Her participation suggests that Gaia already knew something that Demeter would eventually come to understand, specifically, that Kore's abduction and rape in the underworld would not portend catastrophe for the young girl. Rather, it would propel her on a path of self-knowledge, autonomy, and empowerment, and a path that would not have been possible had she not gained entrance to the underworld through succumbing to the seductive powers of the narcissus.

If interpreted in this way, the narcissus becomes a necessary agent for greater self-awareness. As a result of her experiences in the chthonic realm, Kore moves from the young, innocent maiden that she once was to Persephone, the queen of the underworld—a role that brings her power and autonomy in her own right and quite independently of her mother. In other words, Kore makes the journey from self-absorption (which kills Narcissus) to self-awareness (which brings full life). The narcissus, therefore, serves the same function as the fruit in the Garden of Eden which, according to Eve, held the promise of nourishment and provided aesthetic pleasure, knowledge, and insight: "The woman saw that the tree was good to eat and pleasing to the eye, and that it was desirable for the knowledge that it could give" (*Genesis* 3:6). Persephone's plucking of the narcissus parallels Eve's fortunate fall. Like the fruit in the Garden of Eden, the narcissus nourished her self-awareness, pleased her eye, and provided her with knowledge and insight. As a result of her action and her tenure in the underworld, Persephone gains insight on who she is, what she is, what she can become, what her limitations are, and how she fits into the grand scheme of things. And, surely, like the fruit in the Garden of Eden, any instrument that leads to a greater self-awareness cannot be totally unwelcome.

Finally, the narcissus serves another important function: once it has been plucked, the void created by its absence causes a huge, momentary gap in the earth. This fissure enables Hades to emerge from the underworld and kidnap Kore. Hades would not have been able to emerge and snatch the young girl without resorting to this ruse. As god of the underworld, Hades does not have direct and easy access to the over-world any more than Demeter or other gods and goddesses of the over-world have direct and easy access to his realm. Hence his reliance on subterfuge to create a gap in the earth which provides him with the temporary access he needs to the over-world. Similarly, Demeter knows that her capacity as an earth goddess restricts her mobility to the heavens and to the earth exclusively. Once she learns the whereabouts of her daughter in the underworld, she makes no attempt to retrieve her from the abyss herself. She knows she cannot cross the boundary that leads to the underworld. It is off limits to an earth goddess.

In order to relay messages back and forth from the realms of earth, sky, sea, and underworld, the gods rely on Hermes. As their messenger, Hermes can traverse the different realms undeterred by the boundaries that restrict the other gods and goddesses to their specific sphere of influence. Iris has a similar role. And at the conclusion of the mysteries, Persephone performs the same function by acting as the vehicle that links the two realms of over-world and underworld.

Through her journeys back and forth between the over-world and underworld, Persephone provides Hades with direct and regular connection to the over-world. More importantly, through her mother's inauguration of the mysteries, Persephone provides human beings with recurring access to Hades and the underworld. Before the inauguration of the mysteries, the most humans could hope for was to improve their lot in this life through appeals and sacrifices to the gods of the over-world, all of whom situated themselves on Mount Olympus. But they had no means for accessing Hades, influencing his actions, or determining the nature of their tenure in the underworld since nothing they did in the over-world could penetrate the barrier to the underworld. But now, through the divine mediation of Persephone, they not only had a means of improving their lot in this life but also of influencing their lot in the afterlife. And they could do so while they were still alive and before they crossed the border to the underworld. It was Persephone, with the assistance of her mother and Hades, who provided humans with this much-needed access to both realms concurrently. And it was the seductive power of the narcissus that made all of these very important connections, transformations, and border crossings possible.

A Veil

Like the narcissus, the veil in the Homeric *Hymn to Demeter* comes to signify something more than itself. Demeter throws off the veil or deliberately puts it back on at significant points in the poem.

The first mention of the veil occurs at the beginning of the poem when Demeter hears her daughter's scream:

> Sharp grief seized her heart, and she tore the veil
> on her ambrosial hair with her own hands.
> She cast a dark cloak on her shoulders
> and sped like a bird on dry land and sea,
> searching.
>
> (Lines 40–44)

The veil is mentioned again when Demeter makes her initial entrance at the palace in Eleusis and sits on the stool offered by Iambe. Homer tells us: "Seated there, the goddess drew the veil before her face" (line 197). This action reflects her reluctance to interact with the community around her. She deliberately positions herself outside of that community and designates herself as "Other." Her action signals a self-established psychological, emotional, and spatial boundary beyond which no one will be allowed to transgress without her tacit permission. Initially, Demeter shows her reluctance to enter the palace and to sit in the chair offered by Metaneira. She even refuses offers of food and drink until Iambe penetrates Demeter's self-imposed boundary by establishing a connection with her through laughter.

Maintaining her disguise as an old woman, Demeter becomes the caregiver of young Demophoon. She anoints him with ambrosia, the food of the gods, and she secretly places him in the fire at night to strip him of his mortality. Demeter wants to turn Demophoon into a god. The agony of coming to terms with the loss of her daughter is so great that Demeter does what many of us do when faced with the painful situation of loss and grief: she looks for a substitute, a quick fix that will ease the gaping emptiness she feels inside. Her action constitutes a futile attempt to make time stand still coupled with a refusal to accept that what is gone is gone.

Her attempt to immortalize Demophoon, to substitute him for her daughter, is met with disaster. Metaneira interrupts their ritual, and seeing her son in the fire, she reacts with a mother's rage and concern. Perhaps this scene serves to remind Demeter that the loss of her child does not justify stealing another woman's child. Perhaps she recognizes that in attempting to transform Demophoon, she is "abducting" him from his mother and playing the role that Hades has played with her in regards to her own daughter. Although she lashes out at Metaneira and the people of Eleusis for interrupting her attempt to immortalize Demophoon, she also gives them a boon. She orders them to build a temple at Eleusis in her honor. She will be the first initiate and will lay down the rites so that the people can perform those rites and, as she says, "propitiate" her spirit.

So the temple is built. Demeter enters the temple at Eleusis, and in some versions of the myth, she veils herself, and sits in mourning and contemplation. She sits in the temple for one year, fiercely defiant and fiercely determined. It is here that she finally gets the attention of the gods. Zeus sends her messengers to try to convince her to abandon her mourning:

> Then the father sent in turn all the blessed immortals;
> one by one they kept coming and pleading
> and offered her many glorious gifts and whatever
> honors she might choose among the immortal gods.
>
> (Lines 325–328)

But Demeter is intransigent. She remains uncompromising. And she remains veiled. It is curious that we are provided with the interesting detail that Demeter veils herself at this juncture, which subsequently turns out to be a turning point in her confrontation with the male-centered, male-dominated power structure. What is the significance of this veil?

In *The Creation of Patriarchy*, Gerda Lerner provides us with some historical perspective on the practice of veiling. Lerner analyzes the Middle

Assyrian Law that regulated the veiling of women.[2] The law legislated which women were entitled to wear the veil when entering the public sphere and which were not. According to Lerner, the distinction is based on the sexual activities of the women. For example, women who served only one man and were under his protection, that is to say, virgin daughters, wives or concubines, indicated their respectable status by veiling themselves in public. Women who were not under one man's protection designated their sexual availability, their status as "public women," by walking the streets unveiled.[3] Any female who tried to pass herself off either by veiling herself under false pretense or removing her veil when she had no right to do so had to face the full consequence of violating the law. The law was taken very seriously and enforcement was mandatory. Violators were punished severely, with brutality, and in full view of the public.[4] Lerner concludes that the intent of the law was to regulate the sexual availability of women, namely, to distinguish between respectable women and prostitutes.[5]

Lerner's discussion sheds light on Demeter's action of veiling herself. Since, as Lerner has argued, in ancient Mesopotamia a veiled woman was visibly identifiable as belonging to one man and under his sexual authority and protection, she could appear in public and expect to be treated with the respect that her status afforded her. No man would consider approaching her since to do so would be considered an egregious offense to another man's property. An unveiled woman, on the other hand, was fair game and free to sell her sexual favors for the right price. However, she was also declaring her unprotected status. Therefore, she could be approached, harassed, taunted, propositioned, and coerced by any man who fancied her.

Demeter continues the legacy established in ancient Mesopotamia. By insisting on her right to remain at the temple at Eleusis, her right to mourn her daughter, and her right to remain veiled, Demeter is insisting on her right to be treated with the respect that her veiled status affords her. Like the veiled women who appeared in the public domain in ancient Mesopotamia, Demeter is appearing in public in a manner which makes her unapproachable and unassailable. But her action also carries with it an ironic twist. Unlike her ancient Mesopotamian sisters whose right to veil themselves came at the heavy price of subjugation to male authority, Demeter's veiling is, in effect, an act of defiance against male authority. She is insisting on her right to be treated with respect quite independently and in spite of male hegemony. As much as Zeus would like to force Demeter to submit to his demands and to dismiss her concerns in a cavalier manner, he is unable to do so. Demeter will not remove the veil at his behest; she will only remove it when she is ready.

In her examination of fairy tales in *Women Who Run with Wolves*, Clarissa Pinkola Estes also addresses the issue of veiling. Analyzing the role of veiling in a fairy tale, Pinkola Estes clearly demonstrates that veiling can be an act of defiance.[6] It can be a visible demonstration to the outside world that the person donning the veil is autonomous, free from man-made restraints, is one-unto-herself, and impervious to the demands placed on her by society. In other words, donning the veil can be seen as an act of tremendous courage and independence.

We can seek further assistance in our attempt to deconstruct the veil and its significance by turning to a religion that advocates the veiling of women: Islam. Much has been written about the religion of Islam and its ostensible discrimination against women. In fact, the veil has frequently been touted as a symbol of Islam's alleged propensity to oppress and control women. However, much of what has been promulgated as Islamic has little to do with the religion itself and everything to do with the Arab culture from which it originated. An understanding of the role that the veiling of women plays in Islam will help us to interpret the role it plays in Demeter's mourning. But we need to examine what the religion itself has to say about the subject and dispense with the misinformation that has frequently been presented as fact.

The Islamic religion encourages—but does not mandate—the veiling of women. The purpose of this veiling is to protect women from prying eyes when they enter the public sphere. The veil also acts as a visible manifestation of a woman's spiritual focus. It is a signal that even though she is in this world and of this world, her primary focus is not on this world but on the salvation of her soul after death. In other words, by veiling herself, a woman is attempting to direct her search for salvation inward and upward towards God.

According to Fatima Mernissi in *The Veil and the Male Elite: A Feminist Interpretation of Women's Rights in Islam*, the *hijab* (veil) literally means "curtain."[7] It is mentioned in the *Qur'an* as a barrier that is placed between two men, in this case between the Prophet Muhammad and one of his companions to preserve the privacy of the Prophet's bedroom. Mernissi argues, therefore, that the original intention of the *hijab* was to separate public space from private space, the profane from the sacred.[8] The veil has since been used as a method of segregating the sexes.

Mernissi deconstructs the concept of *hijab*. She claims that *hijab* is three-dimensional and that the three dimensions are interlinked.[9] The first dimension is visual: to hide something from sight. The second is spatial: to separate one space from another; to establish a threshold or border. The third is ethical: *hijab* designates forbidden space.

If we combine Mernissi's interpretation of the veil in Islam with the interpretations of Gerda Lerner and Clarissa Pinkola Estes, we are left with the understanding that the veil establishes a clearly delineated border between the person who is veiled and those who are left outside of the veil. It signifies to others that they may not proceed beyond this space, and that they may not see what the veiled person has hidden from sight or rendered invisible. And it places agency firmly in the hands of the individual who has donned the veil. As Pinkola Estes says, "When they [women] are in this veiled state, sensible persons know better than to invade their psychic space."[10] The veil, therefore, becomes a powerful symbol of strength, self-assertion, and autonomy.

The veil further demonstrates that the path to salvation and spiritual healing is inward—not outward towards the material world. The veil eliminates distractions and preoccupation with worldly matters. The veiled individual recognizes her need to direct her energy inward in search of peace and reconciliation. She is asserting her right to set her own agenda, in her own time and in her own space, for the purpose of embarking on the journey to heal herself.

Having deconstructed the veil, we can now begin to discern why Demeter dons the veil when in mourning.

The veil serves several purposes in this poem. At the opening of the poem, Demeter tears off her veil as she frantically searches for her daughter. Since what follows demonstrates Demeter's loss of perspective due to grief, the act of tearing off her veil symbolizes Demeter's temporary alienation from her true nature. She submerges her divinity and disguises herself as a mortal. She loses sight of who she is and engages in behaviors that are counterproductive and which serve only to delay the healing process. Her attempt to distance herself from the community of humans and to re-connect with her true nature is symbolized by her act of drawing the veil when she first enters the palace at Eleusis. However, this attempt is short-lived because Iambe is able to draw her back to the human fold through laughter. Shortly afterwards and as evidenced by the Demophoon episode, Demeter succumbs to the all-too-human tendency to desperately seek alternatives for the loss of a loved one.

Demeter dons the veil again when she enters the temple at Eleusis. Coming at the heels of the Demophoon episode, the veil represents Demeter's successful attempt to re-connect with her true nature—a re-connection that brings about a new awareness of the grieving process and a corresponding ability to strategize against the male-dominated power structure that deprived her of her daughter. Demeter realizes that in order to transcend the loss of her daughter, she must come to terms with her loss before she can begin to heal herself. She dons the veil of introspection. This is the veil of turning inward with the understanding that denial and displacement serve only to delay the healing process. It is the inner perspective that provides clarity. But it is also more than that.

Taking our cue from Fatima Mernissi's interpretation, this veil defines space and boundaries. It designates that which lies within its confines as sacred space. Intruders are unwelcome. The veil signals to outsiders that Demeter insists upon time and space to deal with her loss. And it demands respect. Through donning the veil, Demeter has made her space inviolable and protected in the same manner that her foremothers in ancient Mesopotamia were afforded protection when they entered the public sphere in a veiled state. Demeter also positions herself at the center of her own sacred space. She is a circle unto herself and has declared that all outside of the circle are peripheral to her concern.

Furthermore, the veil hides Demeter from prying eyes so that she can proceed with the serious business of coming to terms with her loss without distraction. She can begin on the path to authentic healing. Donning the veil is also an act of tremendous defiance and autonomy. Demeter signals to all in sight, including the messengers from Zeus, that she will no longer be distracted from or deterred in her goal: the release of her daughter. As Homer tells us:

> Never, she said, would she mount up to fragrant
> Olympus nor release the seed from the earth,
> until she saw with her eyes her own fair-faced child.
>
> (Lines 331–333)

The lessons to be learned from Demeter's actions are very evident. Part of being living, breathing human beings means we have to learn to deal with grief and loss. Many times, this task appears to be so overwhelming that we do all we can to avoid coming to terms with it. We seek substitutes—whether they are in the form of people, things, or activities. We engage in displacement. We experience denial. And by doing so, we delay the healing process.

In *The Change*, Germaine Greer's brilliant study on menopause, she argues that western culture shows little tolerance for grief.[11] Even after experiencing a serious loss, we are expected to don a stiff upper lip and carry on with the ostensibly more important business of life. We are not given permission to grieve, to weep, or to withdraw from human intercourse in order to understand what has happened to us. Greer argues that grief not only demands expression, but the expression of grief is a necessary precursor for feelings of relief.[12]

Demeter's lesson reinforces Greer's position: there is no substitute for dealing with grief and loss head on and for experiencing the pain and sorrow that accompany them. We have to go through the pain before we can move beyond it. Short-term solutions are just that—short term. There is no substitute for mourning. A failure to mourn trivializes our loss and renders it meaningless.[12] As Nancy Qualls-Corbett argues in *The Sacred Prostitute: Eternal Aspect of the Feminine*, mourning is a means of consciously integrating the fact that circumstances have changed and will never be the same again.[13] The ritual of mourning acts as a necessary transition to aid us as we move from one stage of our lives to the next. Just as Demeter learns she cannot deny or transcend her grief through her failed effort to find a substitute for her daughter by turning Demophoon into a god, we learn we have to confront our loss and come to terms with it. At the same time, we have to demand of others that they respect the psychological, emotional, and physical space that is necessary for us to accomplish this task.

Demeter's veiling does not constitute a morbid, self-destructive introspection—a wallowing in self-pity. It is an act that is undertaken of her own volition, with the courage and recognition that she needs space and time to deal with her grief. She can no longer deny her need to mourn. And it is only by consciously embracing loss that she is finally able to transcend her grief—a transcendence symbolized by the ultimate release of her daughter and the joy bestowed upon both of them as a consequence.

A Pomegranate

As a result of Demeter's intransigence, Zeus is forced to comply with her demand for the release of Persephone. Accordingly, he sends Hermes down to the underworld to inform Hades that he has to release the girl. Hades has no choice but to oblige. As Persephone is about to be whisked off to freedom, Hades reminds her of her new and powerful status: "You will have power over all that lives and moves / And you will possess the greatest honors among the gods" (lines 365–366). He then presents her with the pomegranate seed.

> ... But he gave her to eat
> a honey-sweet pomegranate seed, stealthily passing it
> around her, lest she once more stay forever
> by the side of revered Demeter of the dark robe.
>
> (Lines 371–374)

As we saw earlier, the fact that Hades gives her the seed after he has reminded her of her would-be powerful status as queen of the underworld suggests that Persephone knew what she was doing when she swallowed the seed. After all, had she not swallowed the seed, she would not be obliged to return to the underworld. Her claim to fame would be no different from that of the myriad young females in Greek mythology who had the dubious distinction of being raped by a god. But Hades was offering her more than the relative obscurity of being one among many. He was offering her power and status and autonomy and respect. He was offering her a unique position among the gods themselves. Ultimately, he was offering her the seed of death that was also the source of her power. In short, Persephone would have been a fool not to swallow the seed.

This is not to suggest that all women need men to gain access to power. For one thing, Hades is not a typical male according to patriarchal constructs because he exhibits many feminine qualities, as we shall see later. For another, Hades serves merely as the vehicle that brings Persephone to knowledge of her own internal power. That vehicle could be male or female. It could be circumstances or situations that occur in our lives. What we make of that vehicle and how we choose to use it is entirely up to us. Persephone chooses to pluck the narcissus that sends her plummeting to the underworld. She chooses to swallow the pomegranate seed that will guarantee her return to the underworld. She chooses to reap the benefits from her experience in the underworld. Ultimately, the power—and the choice—is within her.

Whether she was tricked or willingly swallowed the pomegranate seed, we know that she does, indeed, swallow the seed. As a result, she is compelled to spend four months of every year in the underworld since those who have eaten the food of death must return there periodically. Her return to the chthonic realm every year triggers Demeter's mourning and the corresponding seasonal death of the earth. Her emergence from the underworld signals the coming of spring. This cycle of events is precipitated by Persephone's swallowing of the pomegranate. What are we to make of this pomegranate?

First of all, the pomegranate contains a prodigious number of red seeds. The color red signifies blood. As such, red is associated with birth, death, and menstrual flow. Barbara Smith in "Greece" interprets the pomegranate as symbolizing Persephone's arrival at the menarche,[14] an indication that she has passed from one stage of her life to the next. Blood also issues forth at the breaking of the hymen. So we have associations of blood, birth, death, menstruation, and transformation.

The abundance of seeds in the pomegranate also makes it an obvious symbol of fertility. Medieval paintings frequently depict the Virgin Mary holding a pomegranate—perhaps suggesting that the prototype for Mary was Persephone. By swallowing the red pomegranate seed on her way out of the chthonic realm, Persephone carries with her the seeds of fertility to the surface of the earth. In the process, she has experienced a death of sorts (a transformation) in the underworld since she is no longer the same young virgin she was when she entered. And she has also experienced a re-birth since she is born anew when she emerges from the underworld. By literally

incorporating the seed into her own body, Persephone experiences a metamorphosis from which there is no return. And she carries within her seeds
from the realm of the dead which precipitate new life.

In addition, as Bruce Lincoln in *Emerging from the Chrysalis: Rituals of
Women's Initiation* has demonstrated, there are also male associations with
the word "seed." The term used in the Homeric *Hymn to Demeter* to desig-
nate seed is *kokkos*. *Kokkos* not only means seed; it can also signify "testicle."[15] Like the pomegranate, the testicle is round and contains a prodigious
number of seeds that are no less essential for fertility than the female egg.
Therefore, by swallowing the pomegranate seed, Persephone is also "swallowing" or internalizing the male experience. She has experienced a sexual
union with Hades not only through his forcible penetration of her body
but also through integrating the masculine seeds he offers her within her
own body. Through her voluntary internalization of this masculine seed,
Persephone is, in effect, fertilizing her egg and birthing herself anew.

Furthermore, the pomegranate, with its round, bulbous shape and its
red, flowing juices, is also suggestive of the womb. But the seeds it contains
are masculine. So the pomegranate encompasses both the male and female
experience. In "Politics and Pomegranates: An Interpretation of the Homeric *Hymn to Demeter*," Marylin Arthur reminds us that the pomegranate is
associated with both male and female fertility deities, and, as such, it ideally symbolizes the union of Persephone and Hades in this poem.[16] Persephone's swallowing of the pomegranate seed, therefore, suggests a union of
opposites: an assimilation of the masculine and the feminine, a fertiliza-
tion that leads to conception. Persephone/female/womb has internalized
Hades/male/seed, and it is through the synthesis of these opposites that
fertility, abundance, metamorphosis, and new life ensue.

How are we to understand this? To begin with, we know that Persephone has experienced a transformation in the underworld. She has been
initiated through rape. She is no longer Kore, the maiden, but Persephone,
queen of the underworld. However, her release from the underworld does
not immediately follow the abduction and rape. In fact, her release occurs
over one year after that traumatic event. Her release occurs only after she
has consciously assimilated (swallowed) the experience of the underworld.
It is as if the myth is telling us that self-absorption (the narcissus) will precipitate our descent into the underworld, but our release will occur only
after we have deliberately assimilated or internalized the meaning of our
experience and our tenure in the underworld (swallowed the pomegranate
seed). Persephone takes over one year to arrive at this understanding. In
our case, it may take a longer or shorter period of time since there are no
clocks in the underworld to regulate our release from the chthonic realm.
The only certainty the myth presents us with is that release and rebirth are

predicated upon a conscious assimilation of our experience in the underworld, upon our swallowing the seeds or fruit it has to offer.

What can we learn from Persephone's tenure in the underworld about the nature of the experience in the underworld? This will vary depending on what stage of our life we are in, what precipitates our "fall," and what we have to learn during our tenure in the underworld. But the fact that Persephone swallows *kokkos*, a masculine seed, can lead us to some conclusions about the qualities of what is being assimilated.

The meeting between a male and a female in myths and dreams carries with it a significance that is above and beyond a similar occurrence that takes place in the real world. As Marina Valcarenghi has argued in *Relationships: Transforming Archetypes*, the meeting between a male and a female is more than just a meeting between two characters if and when the meeting occurs in a myth or a dream. In such cases, the meeting also represents an integration of the masculine and feminine inside each of us, a union of our internal opposites.[17] The young Persephone, a female, swallows a male experience and is subsequently released from but simultaneously tied back to the chthonic realm. Apparently, the lesson we glean from our sojourn in the underworld has something to do with a marrying of opposites: the feminine and masculine, the yin and the yang. In other words, the myth promotes the importance of achieving internal balance, integration, assimilation, and union in order to arrive at transcendence.

This is not the only time we encounter an object in Homer that comes to symbolize a balance of opposites. We see it occurring in the *Odyssey*. In Book Ten, Odysseus and his men land on the island of the enchantress Kirke. Following his usual habit, Odysseus sends some of his men to explore the island. Drawn towards the sound of a woman's singing, the men find their way to Kirke's hall. There they encounter Kirke, singing and weaving on her loom. She graciously invites them in and offers them food and wine. No sooner do they drink the wine than Kirke waves her magic wand and transforms the men to swine. One of Odysseus' men, Eurylokhos, witnesses the event and runs back to the ship to tell Odysseus. Odysseus then proceeds to Kirke's hall to retrieve his men. On his way, he encounters none other than the messenger of the gods, Hermes, who gives him a *molu* flower that will protect him from Kirke's spell.

> He bent down glittering for the magic plant
> and pulled it up, black root and milky flower—
> a *molu* in the language of the gods—
> fatigue and pain for mortals to uproot;
> but gods do this, and everything, with ease.[18]

(Lines 331–335)

It is not insignificant that the flower that protects Odysseys from experiencing the same fate as his men, a fate that consists of a debasement of their humanity, is described in terms of a black root and a white flower. The color black represents the female; the color white represents the male. Once again, we see the importance of the integration of opposites and the achievement of balance in order to arrive at transcendence or higher knowledge. As Edward Edinger tells us in *The Eternal Drama: The Inner Meaning of Greek Mythology*, the molu represents a union of opposites and can best be understood as a symbol of an integrated self. Edinger argues that contact with the molu represents contact with wholeness, and it is this contact with wholeness that saves Odysseus from succumbing to Kirke's destructive snare.[19] The molu protects him, and, eventually, Odysseus succeeds in obtaining the release of his men as well as the assistance of Kirke as he continues his journey home.

It is also significant that Homer reminds us mere mortals cannot pluck the molu flower from the ground. It takes a god to do that. In other words, mortals cannot arrive at wholeness without the assistance of external forces. The task is too difficult for us to undertake alone. So we must be on the alert and ready to receive this gift from the gods or external forces when it is offered to us. In the same way that Odysseus' empowerment and ability to withstand a debasement of his humanity occurs as a result of accepting the gift offered to him by Hermes, Persephone's empowerment and ability to integrate and assimilate her experience in the underworld occurs as a result of accepting the gift offered to her by Hades. And in both cases, this gift from the gods represents a union of opposites, an integration of the masculine and feminine that is the necessary precursor to achieving wholeness.

In *The Creation of Patriarchy*, Gerda Lerner analyzes several of the surviving myths of ancient Mesopotamia. She concludes that in many of these myths, human beings acquire divine knowledge by eating and drinking substances which, in some cases, may be forbidden to them by the gods. Humans may also gain access to transcendence through sexual intercourse.[20] What is true of ancient myths is also true of Persephone: she gains access to higher knowledge through having sexual intercourse with a god and through ingesting the pomegranate seed offered to her by a god.

Through her person, Persephone serves as a vehicle for connecting the over-world with the underworld, life with death, the masculine with the feminine. And her marriage to Hades, as Kathie Carlson demonstrates in *Life's Daughter/Death's Bride*, is a marriage that serves the function of reconnecting the rest of humanity with our prepatriarchal feminine wholeness and placing the masculine in service to that wholeness and to life itself.[21] But Persephone can only serve as that vehicle when she has integrated her experience in the underworld, when she has married the masculine with the feminine within her own being, and when she is able to negotiate a unique space for herself between the two realms.

In *Woman's Mysteries, Ancient and Modern: A Psychological Interpretation of the Feminine Principle as Portrayed in Myth, Story, and Dreams*, Esther Harding argues that no human being is entirely male or entirely female. Each one of us is made up of a composite of both elements. In order to achieve wholeness, we need to recognize both aspects within ourselves and reconcile the two principles inherent in the very nature of being human.[22] This is not a new concept. In Kundalini yoga, for example, our ability to move up the ladder of spiritual enlightenment (the different stages represented by the chakras) is directly contingent upon our ability to achieve a balance between the masculine and feminine energies at every stage of the process. Without such a balance, we remain stuck in the quagmire of constant death and rebirth until we get it right and are able to move on.

Our release from the underworld must entail a comparable endeavor. In other words, if we want to be whole, we must face up to our unwholeness. In effect, what the pomegranate seed tells us is that time spent in the chthonic realm entails death, transformation, and re-birth. Release from the underworld is predicated upon an assimilation of the experience characterized by a union of opposites. And by assimilating the unity or synthesis of opposites, we have, in effect, transcended the limitations that are concomitant with a reliance on either the masculine or the feminine principle exclusively. Release and rebirth come as a result of integrating masculine and feminine in a transgendered dialectic that moves us beyond both. And when release and rebirth finally occur, like the prodigious number of seeds in each pomegranate, the rewards are abundant.

But birthing ourselves is no easy task. It may require nothing less than a complete dismantling of our old ways of thinking and our old ways of accepting socially constructed definitions, norms, and standards. It may require us to accept that an individual consists of qualities that have been socially designated as male, female, and all manner of variations in between; that even our definitions of maleness and femaleness are fluid and culturally defined; that we should not make the mistake of assuming a part of us represents or even speaks for the whole of us; and that the experiences, insights, perspectives, thoughts, and feelings of all aspects within ourselves must be heard, acknowledged, and accounted for before we can presume to speak for the whole person. And what is true for an individual is equally true for humanity as a whole. What is healthy for the microcosm is similarly healthy for the macrocosm. As a society, we must learn to acknowledge and value the diversity and multiplicity of voices that are out there. To negate, deny, repudiate, or stifle voices of the Other or to situate the Other on the peripheral banks of the rest of society performs not only a violence to those we have designated as Others, but also perpetrates a violence on the health of the organism as a whole. For as long as one part of the organism is marginalized and denied voice and access, the whole organism is going to suffer at one time or another and in one way or another.

We live in a culture that values and promotes the stereotypically masculine values of separation and individualism far more than it values and promotes the stereotypically feminine values of relationship and community. In fact, so much of what is wrong with society can be attributed to excessive separation and insufficient community. In order to rectify this situation, those values that have been designated as feminine—nurturance, community, relationships, mentoring, and networking—need to be given prominent positions in the public arena and should influence public discourse and public action because, ultimately, these values are far more human, humane, worthy, and conducive to health and wholeness for the individual, for society, and for the planet as a whole.

The journey towards wholeness is fraught with difficulties because we have to struggle against social institutions and a cultural climate that promote imbalance and unwholeness. So the journey to give birth to a new vision and a new self may require the assistance of experienced mentors, coaches, counselors, and therapists to guide us as we make our way through the birth canal. Fortunately, as we shall see in the next chapter, a significant feature of the Homeric *Hymn to Demeter* explicates this very role: the role of female mentoring.

CHAPTER 5

Female Mentoring

Female Mentoring

One of the most salient features of the Homeric *Hymn to Demeter* is female mentoring. Each of the females who appears in the poem plays a pivotal role in varying degrees to propel the story forward and bring it to suitable closure. These females are Demeter, Kore/Persephone, Hekate, the four daughters of Metaneira, Iambe (also known as Baubo), Metaneira, and Rheia. Persephone is the recipient of the action—not the performer. Since achieving her release is one of the goals, and since she appears only at the beginning and then at the end of the poem, Persephone does not participate in this fabric of female mentoring even though she is a beneficiary of its efforts.

Unlike their male counterparts who generally operate in isolation and are seen in isolation, Demeter, Hekate, the daughters of Metaneira, Iambe, Metaneira, and Rheia weave an intricate web in which each thread is essential for completing the whole. The females create a genuine sense of community. One of the contributing factors that makes the myth of Demeter and Persephone so unique is this very absence of the bitter, competitive rivalry that typically characterizes females in literature that privileges the male experience. With the exception of Demeter's initial antagonism towards Metaneira when the latter interrupted her during the ritualistic performance of purging Demophoon of his mortality, the modus operandi of these females is collaborative, supportive, and empathic. They are nurturing and compassionate. They guide each other and demonstrate by example. These women engage in female mentoring.

73

To mentor means to establish a system of connections and contacts with an individual, the purpose of which is to provide guidance and support for choices and behaviors for the individual one is mentoring. A mentor shares her knowledge, experience, and expertise. She has to bring certain skills to the project and must earn respect and trust if the relationship is to be productive. In addition to a shared, collaborative style of operation, a significant feature of mentoring is the willingness of those involved to learn from each other and, when the need arises, to defer to individuals who have recognized skills in other areas. Mentoring is predicated on the principles that no one individual has all the answers; that we need to guide each other and to fill in the gaps in our own areas of knowledge and expertise; that we must be willing to share our experiences and to learn from the experiences of others; and that our focus be on achieving the goal and not on self-aggrandizement. Mentoring functions much like the pieces in a puzzle: although each piece is different, each has a contribution to make, and each is essential for the completion of the whole.

This collaborative sharing of skills and resources in a non-competitive environment in which each part works for the betterment of the whole is increasingly being adopted by organizations in the public sector. This method of operation reflects a new style of leadership, one that is more conducive to the creation of a productive and healthy work environment within an organization. It is based on the assumption that each member of the team provides an informed and valuable perspective on her or his area of expertise, and, therefore, each has something worthwhile to contribute to the organization in terms of improving working conditions and increasing productivity. Power becomes a power shared *with* others instead of a power *over* others. As Stephanie Golden asserts in *Slaying the Mermaid*, power that is equally shared facilitates reciprocal relations which, in turn, enhance the power of all.[1]

This framework differs from the traditional leadership style that is hierarchical and characterized by the Western model of power *over* another. In this model, the person at the top seldom solicits or considers the opinions or advice of subordinates in the process of making decisions—even though those decisions will impact the quality of the work environment or the level of productivity of the employees. The assumption that underlies this approach is that the person in charge already knows all there is to know before making the decision and has no need to solicit input from others since they are subordinates. It is a very paternalistic approach and can be thoroughly counterproductive. Such a mode of operation makes employees feel useless and undervalued. Furthermore, it can have a debilitating impact on morale.

The contrast between the two styles of leadership is discussed in Sally

Helgesen's *The Female Advantage: Women's Ways of Leadership.* Helgesen focuses on four highly successful female executives and analyzes their style of leadership by comparing it to the leadership style of male executives. She concludes that female and male executives operate differently—with some differences being more significant than others. These differences stem from a difference in perspectives due to gender socialization. According to Helgesen, men in positions of authority perceive themselves as sitting on the top of the hierarchical pyramid. Because their position affords them a great deal of access to information, they perceive knowledge as power and are, therefore, reluctant to share it.[2] Female executives, on the other hand, view themselves as being in the center of things rather than at the top. Since it is more natural to reach out than it is to reach down, female executives deliberately structure their companies in the form of networks in order to facilitate the flow of information in all directions.[3] Knowledge is something to be shared, not hoarded. Helgesen concedes that the male-oriented, hierarchical style of organization is rapidly being replaced by a less formal corporate structure—one that attempts to maintain a level of fluidity and flexibility in order to keep pace with the changing economy and the transformations occurring within the workplace.[4] Helgesen continues to maintain, however, that this new style of organizational structure is more conducive to women who, because of the nature of their socialization, are already well-versed in flexibility, networking, collaboration, and the cultivation of relationships.[5]

The explicit goal in the Homeric *Hymn to Demeter* is the periodic release of Persephone from the underworld and her reunification with her mother. The veiled goal is to provide assistance to Demeter and Persephone as each journeys through her own underworld and emerges with new insight and knowledge. Demeter, Hekate, Iambe, Metaneira, and Rheia work together to achieve these two goals. At different times, each one has a unique mentoring role to play. They interact with each other, collaborate, share knowledge, and, overall, facilitate the process of movement towards individuation or self-awareness. In addition, they play contributing roles in the reunification of mother and daughter.

At the opening of the poem, Demeter is ignorant of the whereabouts of her daughter. She has heard her scream, but she doesn't know where she is or what has happened to her. We are told that Demeter roams the earth for nine days, depriving herself of food and drink in the frantic search for her daughter. The nine days represents the nine months of pregnancy, foreshadowing the rebirths that will take place at the conclusion of the poem. We know of at least three male gods who are well aware of Kore's whereabouts: Zeus, Hades, and Helios. But not one of them comes to her aid: "No one was willing to tell her the truth/not one of the gods or mortals" (lines 44-45). Until day ten, that is, when Hekate enters the picture. So let us begin our discussion with her.

Hekate

Hekate was known as the goddess of the threshold, that is to say, the goddess who guides us as we move from one stage of our lives to the next. She is the goddess of transitions, standing at the entrance to the under-world. She is thereby situated between the over-world and the underworld, between life and death. She was worshipped at intersections—particularly where three roads meet since it was believed she had the power to see the past, present, and future; the underworld, the earth, and the sky. At one point, she may have been identified with Cereberus, the three-faced dog who guards the entrance to Hades. She is associated with the darkness of nighttime and with the moon that lights the way at night. She is described as "tender of heart" and "of the delicate veil" (lines 24–25).

Hekate is in her cave when she hears Kore's cry. In many world mythologies, the cave is identified with the womb of Mother Earth. It is the symbolic place for death, birth, and regeneration because it is dark, hidden, and has an opening from which emergence takes place. Although these dark and damp locations inspire fear in some people, as Bettina Knapp argues in *Women, Myth, and the Feminine Principle*, in others they inspire anticipation for their association with fertility and their role as passageways to new worlds.[6] So it is fitting that Hekate should be in her cave at the moment of Kore's abduction since her presence there presages Kore's transformation and rebirth when she emerges from her own "cave," the underworld.

The poem tells us that Hekate seeks Demeter:

> But when the tenth Dawn came shining on her,
> Hekate met her [Demeter], holding a torch in her hands
> to give her a message.
>
> (Lines 51–53)

It is interesting that Hekate does not wait to see if Demeter comes to her. Instead, she is described as seeking Demeter out. There is no ego involved in her action—no self-centered self-absorption. As the goddess of the threshold and as the goddess associated with all transitions, she has every right to expect that Demeter should solicit her aid in determining Kore's whereabouts. After all, she is Demeter's equal. Demeter cannot claim to come from superior lineage since they are both goddesses. But after nine days, Demeter still hasn't sought Hekate's assistance. Demeter's behavior here parallels that of her daughter: she seeks help and guidance from male gods, but it is a female goddess who comes to her aid. Instead of feeling slighted and insulted at being overlooked, Hekate seeks Demeter out and offers her support. She recognizes that this is a grieving mother, frantically searching for her missing child. And her heart goes out to her. She shares with Demeter the little she knows:

> "Divine Demeter, giver of seasons and glorious gifts,
> who of the immortals or mortal men
> seized Persephone and grieved your heart?
> For I heard a voice but did not see with my eyes
> who he was. To you I tell at once the whole truth."
>
> (Lines 54–58)

Well, not exactly. She may not have seen with her own eyes the identity of Kore's abductor, but she knows enough of what has transpired so as not to refer to Kore in her maiden aspect. Instead, she refers to her as Persephone. In other words, Hekate knows that Kore is no longer kore, that her status has been changed irrevocably. But she chooses not to elaborate. We shall see why she makes that choice later.

Hekate does not abandon Demeter to fend for herself. Instead, she further demonstrates her solidarity and support by accompanying her as they solicit Helios, the sun god, for his knowledge of Persephone's whereabouts. She accompanies Demeter on her fact-finding mission to provide moral and emotional support.

> The daughter of fair-tressed Rheia [Demeter]
> said not a word, but rushed off at her side
> holding torches ablaze in her hands.
>
> (Lines 59–61)

In two of her works, *Goddesses in Every Woman* and *Goddesses in Older Women*, Jean Shinoda Bolen interprets a variety of goddesses as personifications of archetypes embedded within each woman. *Goddesses in Every Woman* focuses on the maiden and mother phases of a woman's life. *Goddesses in Older Women* focuses on the crone phase of a woman's life—her menopausal and postmenopausal phase. Bolen interprets these archetypes as energies that, when released, endow us with wisdom, spirituality, and a greater sense of Self.

Bolen sees Hekate as representing intuitive wisdom, a wisdom that is learned as a result of the experience that usually comes with growing older.[7] Hekate is constellated for women when they reach a threshold in their lives or a fork in the road that requires them to make a life-changing decision.[8] At such times, seeking the truth, speaking the truth, and confronting the truth are essential prerequisites for decision making.[9] Hence, Hekate's encouragement that Demeter seek the truth from Helios. Demeter cannot successfully progress on her journey of increasing self-awareness unless she is willing to forgo ignorance, denial, and self-delusion—all of which can delay genuine healing and growth.

In seeking the advice of someone more knowledgeable on the matter, Hekate is reflecting what has been typically designated as a female trait. Women socialized in a patriarchy are not embarrassed to ask for help. In fact, it has become almost a cliché in contemporary society to state that women will ask for directions when they get lost whereas men are quite prepared to drive around in circles for hours rather than stop and seek assistance. Once again, this difference in attitudes and behaviors has to do with differences in gender socialization.

Knowledge is power. An individual who has access to certain knowledge has power over individuals who don't. In some cultures, for example, American Indian cultures prior to European colonization, knowledge was to be shared with members of the community so that all could benefit. In such communities, an individual who hoarded knowledge was acting in violation of the ethical, moral, and social codes of conduct of the community. By way of contrast, in the Judeo-Christian tradition, originating with the claims of the male priestly class that it had exclusive access to Yahweh, knowledge was used as an instrument to control and dominate the "ignorant" masses. Knowledge, therefore, became equated with privilege, status, and hierarchy. From there emerged the concept that those who were not in the privileged position of knowing were obviously situated lower down in the hierarchy and were to be treated as inferior beings who were ignorant and powerless.

Since the onset of patriarchy, women have been marginalized and relegated to the bottom of the totem pole in terms of status and power. They were not expected to be knowers and were treated as ignorant and powerless. Consequently, knowledge for women does not have the same meaning as it does for men because, regardless of how much knowledge women possessed, they were still denied direct access to power. Women, therefore, have not been socialized to equate knowledge with power. Hence there is no incentive for them to hoard it. Furthermore, as members of an oppressed group, their very survival frequently depended on sharing knowledge, exchanging advice, and collaborating with others.

Men, on the other hand, because they could be rewarded in terms of status and power depending on how much knowledge they had, have learned to equate knowledge with power. Furthermore, they have been socialized to believe that an admission of incomplete knowledge or a lack of knowledge is equated with lower status. Hence, men are reluctant to admit if and when they do not know something they are expected to know because to do so suggests their status has been reduced to the weak, the powerless, and the "effeminate." In other words, their self-perceptions will fall short of socially constructed definitions of masculinity. For men socialized in patriarchy, knowledge equals privilege, equals power, equals high status, equals masculinity. Ignorance equals powerlessness, equals low status, equals femininity. That is why men are reluctant to ask for directions; that is why women are not.

The Homeric *Hymn to Demeter* provides us with a fitting example of women's willingness to share information and its corresponding power with one another. In this respect, the daughters of Metaneira once again demonstrate the impact on their behavior of their socialization as females. When they first encounter Demeter at the Maiden's Well, Kallidike responds to Demeter's inquiry about a place of employment by providing her with valuable knowledge about the male power structure in Eleusis.

> "To you I shall explain these things clearly and name
> the men to whom great power and honor belong here,
> who are the first of the people and protect with their counsels
> and straight judgments the high walls of the city.
> There is Triptolemos subtle in mind and Dioklos,
> Polyxenos and Eumolpos the blameless
> Dolichos and our own lordly father."
>
> (Lines 149–155)

By sharing this unsolicited information with Demeter, Kallidike identifies and situates the political forces in Eleusis. Furthermore, she establishes her father as a figure of authority. She is providing Demeter with valuable knowledge and advice. Such knowledge of the power structure of a city can prove to be of value to a stranger—if for no other reason than providing one with the knowledge of where one can turn for help. The fact that Kallidike spontaneously volunteers this information indicates her willingness to empower a total stranger. It also demonstrates that for her, sharing knowledge and power does not equate with a diminishment of her own power.

Hekate and Demeter are not averse to seeking knowledge from someone who is in a position to know more than they do. And Hekate shows no reluctance in going out of her way to help Demeter even though she is not directly involved in the situation. Throughout her interaction with Demeter, Hekate demonstrates her solidarity and support and performs the role of a mentor. In word and deed, she is telling Demeter, "You don't have to go through this alone. I am with you." She acknowledges Demeter's suffering and loss by demonstrating empathy and compassion for the frantic mother.

Hekate's example of one female coming to the aid of another who is experiencing trauma serves as a poignant reminder of how women frequently come to the aid of other women during their moments of crisis. For example, volunteers at rape crisis centers frequently attend rape-kit exams in hospitals to provide support to women who have experienced the trauma of rape. The rape-kit exam has to be conducted in a meticulous, precise, and often painful manner. Although the survivor of rape may understand the importance of submitting to this very arduous examination in order to increase the possibility of catching and convicting her rapist, the examination itself can, nevertheless, be very traumatic for a woman who has recently experienced rape. So the survivor needs generous amounts of support and compassion.

The primary function of volunteers who attend these rape-kit exams is to act as informed guides and designated "hand-holders" for these survivors in order to minimize the additional trauma that can be generated by the detailed and painful procedure of obtaining physical evidence of the rape. Like Hekate, they play the role of mentors and guides.

Such actions of female solidarity, support, and validation formed the foundation blocks for the feminist movement: women learning about the circumstances and commonality of their oppression through consciousness raising sessions; women coming to the aid of other women; women building solidarity with other women; women finding common cause with other women; and women bonding with other women to increase their power and strength and to make their voices heard. It is only by coming into consciousness of ourselves as women that we can begin to challenge male hegemony and move towards forging a new relationship within a transformed society.

After hearing from Helios about what has happened to her daughter, Demeter withdraws from the assembly of gods and goes to Eleusis. She goes alone because no mention is made of her companion, Hekate, until after the release of Persephone. The appearance of Hekate, her disappearance for most of the poem, and then her reappearance at the end of the poem with the emergence of Persephone is consistent with her role as the goddess of transitions and as an important contributor to this configuration of female mentoring.

As the goddess of the threshold, Hekate's role is to guide and assist us in our transitions—much like a counselor or therapist. Her role does not permit her to interfere with the process of death and renewal. Her role does not permit her to prevent it. Her role does not permit her to make decisions for us or to judge us. And her role does not permit her to act as our substitute. As we shall see later, no one can act as our substitute in the underworld. It is a journey we have to experience for ourselves, in our own way and in our own time. Otherwise, the excursion becomes meaningless.

Furthermore, much like a counselor or therapist, Hekate's role does not permit her to give us all the answers—even though she may be well aware of all the answers. As an objective outsider, one who is not intimately involved in the situation, she can have a clearer understanding than Demeter since the latter is carrying a great deal of emotional and psychological baggage with her that can cloud her vision. Hekate's role is to set Demeter—and us—on the right path, provide us with guidance, and ask us the questions that will spur us on to arrive at the answers for ourselves. Death and renewal involves process, and the process of working our way through the labyrinth to get to our destination is as important as the destination itself. In other words, how we arrive at the right answer is as essential a part of the journey as discovering what the right answer is.

In this capacity, Hekate assists Demeter as she makes her own journey to the underworld and experiences her own process of death and renewal. Without Hekate's assistance, Demeter may have been left floundering on earth indefinitely, searching fruitlessly for her daughter. As a result, she may not have learned anything about Persephone's situation. And, furthermore, she may not have experienced the growth and renewal that result from her own transformative journey into the depths.

Hekate appears, says just enough to propel Demeter on her own journey to inner transformation, and then she steps aside until both Demeter and Persephone emerge from their respective underworlds. She reappears again at exactly the right moment to usher them into a new phase in their lives.

True to the spirit of mentoring, Hekate provides her expertise and guidance when she is needed. But she has the sense not to interfere any further in the process. Like all good mentors, she doesn't meddle. She makes her contribution and steps aside so that the journey of death and renewal can proceed without impediment.

The last time Hekate is mentioned in the poem is after the release of Persephone and the ensuing reunification of mother and daughter:

> Hekate of the delicate veil drew near them
> and often caressed the daughter of holy Demeter,
> from that time this lady served her as chief attendant.

(Lines 438–440)

It is only fitting that since Persephone has to undertake the journey to the underworld on an annual basis, Hekate, the goddess of transitions, should be her constant guide, companion, and mentor.

The Daughters of Metaneira

After leaving the company of the gods and disguising herself as a "very old woman cut off from childbearing" (line 101), Demeter goes to Eleusis and sits by the Maiden's Well. There she meets the four daughters of Metaneira and Keleos, the queen and king of Eleusis. Although their inter-action and dialogue with Demeter is brief, the daughters of Metaneira serve to remind Demeter that she does not have to operate in isolation. Instead, she can rely on a network of support from other women in the community. Before Demeter has even attempted to solicit their sympathy by sharing with them a fictitious tale of kidnapping and escape, the daughters of Metaneira invite her to take advantage of this fabric of female support.

> "Who are you, old woman, of those born long ago?
> From where? Why have you left the city and do not
> draw near its homes? Women are there in the shadowy halls,
> of your age as well as others born younger,
> who would care for you both in words and in deed."
>
> (Lines 113–117)

The daughters of Metaneira are shocked to find an old woman alone on the outskirts of the community. They inform Demeter that, regardless of the nature of her problem, she does not have sever herself from the com-munity of women. They invite her to enter Eleusis and partake of the fab-ric of a female support structure in which women behave towards each other in accordance with the principles of sisterhood. They provide Demeter— and us—with a significant message: in times of distress, women can turn to other women for care, support, and nurturing. We do not have to experi-ence hardship alone but can rely on other women to assume the roles of mothers, daughters, and sisters to assist us in our struggles.

Women are particularly adept at empathizing and connecting with the suffering of others due to the nature of our socialization. This is a source of our strength. As Audre Lorde argues in *Sister Outsider*, a woman's need and willingness to nurture other women can be redemptive, not patholog-ical, and it is through arming ourselves with this knowledge that we can rediscover our power.[10] For unlike our male counterparts raised in a patri-archy, as women, we have been trained in the ethic of caring for others. Furthermore, our support does not have to come only from women of our generation. It can be cross generational, as the daughters of Metaneira inform us. It is important to keep reminding ourselves of this fact because a particularly insidious impact of patriarchy manifests itself in our willing-ness to sever our connection with other women and our complicity in sewing the seeds of distrust and suspicion between women of different generations, different races and ethnicities, different sexual orientations, and different economic classes.

Iambe

The next female to play a mentoring role in the story is the apparently minor figure of Iambe. We are introduced to Iambe in the house of Keleos. After receiving permission from their mother to do so, the daughters of Metaneira invite Demeter to their home. She follows them and, upon her arrival at the threshold, she fills the doorway with her radiance.

> Then to the house
> of their father they led her. She, grieved in her heart,
> walked behind them with veiled head. And her dark robe
> swirled round the slender feet of the goddess.
> They soon reached the house of god-cherished Keleos,
> and went through the portico to the place where
> their regal mother sat by the pillar of the close-fitted roof,
> holding on her lap the child, her young offshoot. To her
> they raced. But the goddess stepped on the threshold. Her head
> reached the roof and she filled the doorway with divine light.
>
> (Lines 180–189)

Metaneira immediately stands up and offers Demeter her seat. But Demeter declines the offer. Instead, she remains standing and aloof—that is, until "knowing" Iambe offers her a stool.

> She [Demeter] waited resistant, her lovely eyes cast down,
> until knowing Iambe set out a well-built stool
> for her and cast over it a silvery fleece.
> Seated there, the goddess drew the veil before her face,
> for a long time she sat voiceless with grief on the stool
> and responded to no one with word or gesture.
>
> (Lines 194–199)

Demeter declines offers of food and drink—that is, until "knowing" Iambe is able to make her laugh with bawdy jokes and antics.

> Unsmiling, tasting neither food nor drink,
> she sat wasting with desire for her deep-girt daughter,
> until knowing Iambe jested with her and
> mocking with many a joke moved the holy goddess
> to smile and laugh and keep a gracious heart—
> Iambe, who later pleased her moods as well.
>
> (Lines 200–205)

In some versions of the myth, Iambe's bawdy jokes and antics are revealed more explicitly. Carl Kerenyi in *Eleusis* suggests that Homer's poetic style forbids him from describing Iambe's behavior in greater detail.[11] Barry B. Powell's *Classical Myth* includes a translation of the poem that makes reference to the specific nature of Iambe's bawdy humor.[12] Demeter's laughter is apparently caused by the sight of Iambe pulling up her dress and exposing her vulva. Why would the sight of an old female with sagging breasts and wrinkled, flabby body performing this seemingly obscene gesture trigger Demeter's laughter?

Iambe's gyrating dance in which she reveals her female genitalia seems totally incongruous with Demeter's grief-stricken frame of mind. And yet it has the desired effect: Demeter is temporarily drawn out of her isolation and shares in the communion of laughter. A female beyond childbearing years, Iambe's shameless exposure of her vulva, her bawdy gestures and jokes, her obvious capacity to laugh at her aging body while, at the same time, her desire to celebrate her femaleness with such unmitigated audacity reveal that she is that all too rare a creature: a woman who is comfortable in her own body, with her own sexuality, and one who is proud to flaunt the vulnerabilities and frailties associated with aging. She wears her wrinkles like medals of glory. As Jean Shinoda Bolen in *Goddesses in Older Women* observes, Iambe's bawdy gesture serves as a potent reminder to Demeter that, in spite of her grief, she still retains the creative and sexual energy of a female.[13] By willing to expose herself in this manner, Iambe is able to connect with Demeter as a female and draw corresponding laughter from her.

Laughter constitutes an abandonment of restraint and inhibition and creates communion with those sharing in the laugh. Marylin Arthur in "Politics and Pomegranates: An Interpretation of the Homeric *Hymn to Demeter*" argues that Demeter's laughter, elicited as it has been by Iambe's display of sexuality, indicates an ambivalent acceptance on the part of Demeter of female sexuality. According to Arthur, through her laughter, Demeter temporarily abandons her sorrow and rejection of sexuality and makes initial, faltering steps towards reconnecting with her true self.[14]

Winifred Milius Lubell's definitive study on Iambe/Baubo, *The Metamorphosis of Baubo: Myths of Woman's Sexual Energy*, explores Baubo in all her manifestations and variations in world cultures. For Lubell, Iambe/Baubo represents the sexual and procreative energies of women that encompass the nurturing, transformative, and balancing agents necessary for the survival of civilization.[15] Lubell interprets Baubo's exposure of her vulva (an act called *ana-suromai*, a Greek verb that literally means lifting one's skirts) as a gesture of epiphany that reiterates the theme of feminine sacrality.[16] Lubell traces the ubiquitous presence of Iambe/Baubo like figures, postures, and gestures, as well as the many representations of the vulva, in the mythology and iconography of the ancient world. Her study leads to her assertion that through a process of re-visioning, we can remove the layers of tarnish that have distorted, demonized, and corrupted Iambe/Baubo throughout the centuries and recapture her original essence, an essence that celebrates and honors the fecundity and sexuality of the female. According to Lubell, the role of Iambe/Baubo in the Homeric *Hymn to Demeter* is to remind Demeter that, as females, they share in the mystery of the creative cycle of life, death, and regeneration in their bodies.[17]

Iambe's gyrations are a celebration of the physicality of the female body in all its stages of youth, maturity, and decay. In our youth-oriented culture, we have been taught to celebrate the female body only when it is young, svelte, and wrinkle-free. We panic at the first sight of muscles that sag, bulges that appear where no bulges should be, breasts that droop, thighs that reveal unsightly blemishes, and flabbiness that makes its ubiquitous presence visible here, there, and everywhere. We learn to think of our bodies in terms of fragmented bits and pieces instead of as totalities. And we support a billion-dollar industry to snip, tuck, vacuum, camouflage, add, and diminish these bits and pieces of our bodies in a futile, self-destructive attempt to conceal what is a perfectly natural and perfectly beautiful aging process. As Susan Brownmiller reminds us in *Femininity*, an intense preoccupation with preserving a youthful appearance is what society expects of us as women, while, at the same time, it holds us in utter contempt for being such a self-absorbed, narcissistic lot.[18]

Iambe is a beacon of light for all women who have been socialized to reject their bodies when those bodies do not conform to socially constructed standards of beauty. She reminds us that beauty is a relative term, that beauty can be found in bodies in a variety of shapes and sizes and in varying stages of decline, that we do not have to allow others to define beauty for us, and that postmenopausal women have a beauty and a sexuality and an autonomy that is all their own. She invites us to celebrate our aging bodies. And she invites us to join in her laughter.

In the face of the violence we have been socialized to perpetrate on our aging bodies, we have the image of a defiant Iambe, flamboyantly dancing and flaunting her sexuality. Iambe communicates the joy and pride she feels in a sexuality that is no longer restricted by a patriarchal insistence on female pre-marital chastity or one that reduces her sexuality to her reproductive capacities exclusively. She celebrates a sexuality that is all hers, one that has no other purpose but to give and receive unabashed pleasure.

Iambe serves to remind Demeter—and us—that there is joy and humor and liberation and sexual autonomy to be found in life after children. Many women justifiably derive great satisfaction and fulfillment from nurturing hearth and home and all those who dwell in it. They dedicate a big portion of their lives towards the service of others—whether it be spouse or children or both. But while in the process of dedicating their lives to serving others, many women neglect to serve themselves. They engage in what is frequently referred to as de-selfing: the process of continuously suppressing one's own needs and desires and aspirations for the sake of others.[19] De-selfing can lead to the loss of an independent identity by supplanting it with one that is totally reliant on others for its definition.

Consequently and more often than not, women who have engaged in de-selfing experience feelings of abandonment, futility, diminished self-worth, and depression when their adult children leave home. To exacerbate the situation further, this is a time that usually coincides with the onset of menopause, a time in which many women may already be experiencing an identity crisis due to the loss of their reproductive capacities. For the first time in their lives, many women may find themselves relieved of the responsibilities that had given meaning and definition to their lives: the caring and nurturing involved in meeting the physical, emotional, and psychological needs of others. This loss of purpose and meaning in life can be a terrifying time for some. But, as Iambe demonstrates, this third phase of a woman's life, the phase in which she is not constantly being interrupted by young children, no longer burdened by the needs and demands of others, and finally at a point in her life where her time, creativity, and energy can be channeled towards self-nurture and cultivation of self-interests can also be a joyous and exciting time for a woman.

In her comprehensive study of the historical and cultural significance of the post-menopausal female, *The Crone: Woman of Age, Wisdom, and Power*, Barbara Walker identifies the behavior that characterizes a woman's third stage in life in which she becomes increasingly self-directed as the nest-destroying behavior.[20] Walker correctly observes that although much attention has been devoted to a woman's nest-building instincts (since, after all, this instinct forms the economic foundation of a consumer society), little attention has been devoted to her attempts to simplify her life, to weed out her excess belongings, and to begin paying attention to her needs now that she is no longer consumed by meeting the needs of others.[21] Having arrived at this stage in her life, Iambe invites us to join her in collective celebration of our post-menopausal freedom, our autonomy, and our cronehood by embracing the potential they have to offer us. She invites us to join her in her raucous belly laugh.

Demeter's laughter in the midst of grief acts as a temporary relief from her sorrow and enables her to accept the hospitality, food, and nourishment offered by Metaneira. It is this laughter triggered by Iambe's earthy female-ness and unabashed celebration of cronehood that enables Demeter to move forward on her journey of growth and transformation. Through her example, Iambe inches Demeter closer towards her goal.

Metaneira

The next female to play a mentoring role in the story is Metaneira, the mother of Demophoon. Metaneira is ignorant of her role as an accomplice in the process of Demeter's individuation. But the fact that she is oblivious to her role does not make her any less significant. In fact, Metaneira probably has as much to contribute to Demeter's growth and transformation as any other female in the story.

As a mother, she has much in common with Demeter. She loves her child and is protective of him. She experiences alarm and fear when she assumes her child has been put in danger:

> But she shrieked and struck both thighs
> in fear for her child, much misled in her mind,
> and in her grief she spoke winged words.
> "Demophoon, my child, the stranger buries you
> deep in the fire, causing me woe and bitter cares."
> Thus she spoke lamenting.
>
> (Lines 245–250)

Demeter's initial reaction at being interrupted in her attempt to immortalize Demophoon is one of great anger. She lashes out at Metaneira and, by extension, at all humans:

> "Mortals are ignorant and foolish, unable to foresee
> destiny, the good and the bad coming on them.
> You are incurably misled by your folly.
> Let the god's oath, the implacable water of Styx, be witness,
> I would have made your child immortal and ageless
> forever; I would have given him unfailing honor."
>
> (Lines 256–261)

As we saw earlier, Demeter engages in displacement. She seeks a substitute for her own missing child. Unfortunately, she acts out of vengeance in the process. She snatches another woman's child to satisfy her aching need, and she does so without conferring with the mother. Perhaps Metaneira would have preferred to be consulted about the fate of her child. Perhaps then she would have given her blessing. But Demeter doesn't ask or inform. She appropriates. In this instance, Demeter replicates the behavior of none other than the bastion of patriarchy himself, Zeus. She flagrantly disregards the mother's feelings and operates under the assumption that the child is hers to do with as she pleases.

After lashing out harshly at Metaneira, Demeter reveals her identity. Then she softens her tone:

> "For I am honored Demeter, the greatest
> source of help and joy to mortals and immortals.
> But now let all the people build me a great temple
> with an altar beneath, under the sheer wall
> of the city on the rising hill above Kallichoron.
> I myself will lay down the rites so that hereafter
> you may propitiate my spirit."
>
> (Lines 268–274)

This appears to be an attempt at reconciliation. Demeter doesn't dwell on her anger or harbor resentment. Instead, she gives Metaneira and the people of Eleusis the opportunity to mollify her by building a temple in her honor. She gives them a way out of the quandary in which they find themselves. Eager to seize the opportunity, they rush to do her bidding. Metaneira's role in the story is now over.

Demeter's tone of reconciliation is perhaps an indication that, as Kathie Carlson observes in *Life's Daughter/Death's Bride*, Demeter recognizes that she has shared in Metaneira's erroneous—and very human—assumption about the finality of death.[22] Metaneira forcefully brings home the point to Demeter that what appears in human eyes to be a catastrophe of gargantuan proportions may not be a catastrophe at all. Instead, it may be the precursor to empowerment and new life. In other words, through Metaneira's very human reaction to the apparent death of her son, Demeter may have recognized that, like Metaneira, she may have misunderstood the apparent death of her daughter. As Nancy Felson-Rubin and Harriet M. Deal argue in "Some Functions of the Demophoon Episode in the Homeric *Hymn to Demeter*," Demeter recognizes that the foolishness of human beings is due to their shortsightedness and their bungling interference in divine plans.[23] This recognition forces her to confront and reevaluate her own daughter's apparent death. What seems like death when perceived through the lens of a very human Metaneira is, in fact, an attempt to bestow immortality on the young Demophoon. Similarly, what has the appearance of her daughter's death when perceived through the lens of a Demeter who has disconnected from her immortal identity and has assumed a human guise may, in fact, be the harbinger of new life.

Additionally, through her behavior, Metaneira acts as Demeter's mentor in another respect. She has the significant task of contributing to Demeter's metamorphosis as the latter undertakes her journey to self-knowledge by forcing Demeter to recognize that her attempt to immortalize Demophoon constitutes a violation of the mother/child bond. In other words, because of Metaneira's display of legitimate concern for the welfare of her child, Demeter seems to arrive at the recognition that her action of appropriating another woman's child for her own purposes is no different from what Zeus and Hades have done to her. Why else would she have been so willing to forgive or so quick to present Metaneira with the means by which to "propitiate" her spirit? It is by witnessing Metaneira's reaction that Demeter is able to connect with her, a connection that engenders empathy as well as self-awareness.

This recognition of the sanctity of the mother/child bond has the added effect of validating Demeter's feelings of outrage at the gods and at the flippant manner in which they summarily dismissed her concerns as a mother. When we experience pain or grief or outrage and all those around us make light of our emotions, we can begin to doubt ourselves and question the legitimacy of our reaction. We might even begin to question our own sanity. It isn't easy holding on to your sense of outrage at an injustice when the chorus around you is singing the triumphal hymn of "You're overreacting. Get over it!" But Metaneira validates Demeter's reaction. Her legitimate sense of outrage and fear at seeing her child snatched by another and put in harm's way has the effect of corroborating Demeter's own feelings. In effect, she reinforces Demeter's conviction that she has every right to feel outrage at the gods for daring to presume they can snatch her daughter away from her with impunity. And she has every right to insist upon respect for the mother/child bond.

Metaneira also provides an additional and much-needed jolt to Demeter. She forces her to begin to come to terms with her own loss by impressing upon her that there can be no substitutes for a lost loved one. Demophoon can never replace Persephone. Loss has to be confronted before it can be transcended. A helter-skelter pursuit for substitutes and quick fixes is no solution and serves only to delay the healing process.

Metaneira's role in this configuration of female mentoring is to help Demeter gain insight into herself, into the grieving process, and into having respect for the sanctity of all mother/child bonds—not just her own. As a mother, she is in a unique position to fulfill this role. Her experience parallels Demeter's, and it is only after Demeter recognizes this and empathizes with a concerned mother that she makes a genuine effort to come to terms with her own loss. Furthermore, Demeter's sense of outrage at the gods for their actions has been validated by Metaneira. And by the time this incident with Metaneira and Demophoon is concluded, Demeter has managed to move beyond guilt and begins to channel her anger where it belongs—at the gods on Mount Olympus. And as was the case with Hekate, now that her function is over, Metaneira disappears from the story.

Rheia

The next female to play a significant role in the story is Demeter's mother, Rheia. She has a small but important function in bringing the story to closure. After the release of Persephone, Zeus asks Rheia to intercede on his behalf with Demeter to assuage her anger towards him. Rheia delivers his message to Demeter.

> "Come, child, Zeus, heavy-thundering and mighty-voiced,
> summons you to rejoin the tribes of the gods;
> he has offered to give what honors you choose among them.
> He agreed that his daughter would spend one-third
> of the revolving year in the misty dark, and two-thirds
> with her mother and the other immortals.
> He guaranteed it would be so with a nod of his head.
> So come, my child, obey me; do not rage overmuch
> and forever at the dark-clouded son of Kronos.
> Now make the grain grow fertile for humankind."
>
> (Lines 460–469)

Demeter agrees to her mother's entreaties. The earth grows fertile again, and Demeter reconciles with the gods. Rheia performs her function in this configuration of female mentoring by successfully resolving the situation and bringing the story to closure. Who better than a mother to plea for reconciliation between feuding siblings?

Rheia is a fitting illustration for Carol Gilligan's claim in her influential work *In a Different Voice* that, because she is a female, she values relationships over abstract honor.[24] Rheia is not concerned with who is right and who is wrong in this situation. Instead, she focuses on salvaging the torn relationship between her offspring and restoring harmony. As an agent of reconciliation, she works by advocating a compromise—one in which neither side emerges as the total victor or the absolute loser. And like her female counterparts in this tapestry of collaboration and support, Rheia is ideally suited for the role she has to play.

In addition to performing the role of mentors, Hekate, Iambe, Metaneira, and Rheia also perform the role of mediators. In order to be successful at mediation, a person has to have the ability to see both sides of an issue and to advocate for a middle ground that will help opposite sides arrive at a compromise and reach an agreement. The qualities of a good mediator are usually perceived to lie within the sphere of the feminine since successful mediation entails a willingness to hear both sides of an issue, an ability to see things from another's perspective, good listening skills, and a large dose of empathy—qualities that are usually associated with the female because of the manner in which her identity has been constructed by social forces.

Hekate mediates between Demeter and Helios. She also mediates Persephone's transition to and from the underworld. Iambe recognizes Demeter's grief and is able to mediate her movement towards growth and transformation through the redeeming quality of uproarious laughter. Metaneira mediates with the Demeter who has yet to gain self-knowledge and with the Demeter after she has gained self-knowledge. She further mediates her understanding that loss is loss—whether it is experienced by a mortal mother or an immortal one. And Rheia mediates between her feuding offspring. As Tanya Wilkinson has observed in *Persephone Returns: Victims, Heroes, and the Journey from the Underworld*, Rheia is the mediating mother who bridges the conflict between the domineering Zeus and the angry Demeter.[25] Finally, Demeter and Persephone also act as mediators. Demeter mediates between the mortal and immortal worlds while she is in Eleusis, disguising herself as a human and traversing both worlds at the same time. Furthermore, through the initiation of her mysteries, she mediates an increased awareness for humanity on the meaning of life and death and the lessons to be learned from both. And Persephone performs the role of mediator between the two realms of the over-world and underworld. As Hades reminds her, she will have honor among the gods (the skies), honor among mortals (the earth), and honor among the dead (the underworld).

Hekate, the daughters of Metaneira, Iambe, Metaneira, and Rheia appear in the poem as mentors and perform the necessary two-fold functions: to propel Demeter and Persephone as they undertake their respective journeys to the chthonic realm and experience transformation and rebirth and to assist in the reunification of mother and daughter. Hekate leads Demeter to the brink of the chthonic realm. She is there to greet her and Persephone when the two emerge from their respective odysseys. The daughters of Metaneira remind Demeter that she can seek support and assistance from other females in times of crises. Iambe's laughter propels her forward on her journey and reminds her that there is much to celebrate in life after children. Metaneira impresses upon Demeter the legitimacy of her feelings of outrage and the necessity of grieving in order to transcend loss. And Rheia addresses the issue of reconciliation. These women act as guides and mentors and, collectively, they take us through the stages of death and regeneration. In many ways, they also perform the role of psychological midwives.

Until comparatively recent times, women have been the only ones at the side of pregnant women during the difficult process of childbirth. Such women were known as midwives. Hekate, the daughters of Metaneira, Iambe, Metaneira, and Rheia perform a function similar to that of midwives. Through mentoring, they assist Demeter and Persephone—and, by extension, all individuals—to experience the complex process of successfully birthing themselves.

In many respects, this illustration of females working together to help other females is needed more today than it was over one thousand years ago when the ancient Greeks gathered at Eleusis to commemorate the mysteries. To this day, it is still relatively rare for women to find authorities and guides of their own sex to serve as their mentors and role models. For centuries, patriarchal institutions have mercilessly indoctrinated women into complying with and contributing to their own subordination in society. Patriarchy has actively sought to prevent them from working collectively to change the conditions of their subordination and oppression. As women, many of us have internalized our oppression to such a profound degree that we have come to view all women, including ourselves, negatively. We have consumed the prevailing attitudes, myths, and stereotypes about women that bombard our sensibilities on a daily basis. Through the media, through popular culture, through education, through socialization, and through religion, we are told that women are unintelligent, powerless, shallow, and inconsequential. Above all, we are told that women are not to be trusted.

Fairy tales are particularly effective in packaging these pernicious messages. They implant the self-destructive notion that women are useless, passive, dependent, and ineffectual. They articulate the proposition that we are totally inept at redeeming ourselves and need the muscular arm of a handsome Prince Charming to rescue us from our miserable, humdrum lives, and, not coincidentally, from the cruelties inflicted on us by nasty, jealous women—women who are typically depicted as postmenopausal females. They tell us that Prince Charming will come to our rescue only if we are passive, supine, asleep, or virtually dead. And, of course, we have to be unnaturally thin, virginal, and very, very beautiful as part of the bargain.

Furthermore, fairy tales encourage us to believe that women are not to be trusted—especially women across the generations. An older woman, in the form of a stepmother or an old "witch" who lives alone, subjects the beautiful, innocent, adolescent female to cruelties beyond belief. Younger women are taught that older women envy them for their youth and vitality. This message can have a devastating impact on young girls who can become alienated from their own future since that future holds only the promise of being ridiculed and treated with contempt and derision by a society that worships all things young, firm, and perky.

Time and time again, heroines in fairy tales are shown as incapable of rescuing themselves or each other. Portrayed as helpless, pathetic little victims, they are totally inept at taking even the most innocuous course of action to defend or protect themselves from harm. Instead, they are victimized by a magic sleep that renders them supine and helpless; they tolerate all manner of abuse with a cheery, can-do attitude; or they encounter the big, bad wolf who is eager to gobble them up as soon as they transgress their circumscribed boundaries. In all these cases, the helpless and hapless victim has to rely on the handsome prince or the virile hunter to come to her rescue from all manner of evil. She never rescues herself; she is never rescued by other women. These insidious messages contribute to the creation and reproduction of a culture in which women are socialized to depend on men—and only men—for their protection and security.

To add to this cornucopia of misogynism, women are taught that all other women are on the prowl, in constant competition for the attention and affections of the all-powerful male in their lives. Never mind that the man in our lives may be far removed from Prince Charming. Every woman is surely desperate to have him. Never mind that the man in our lives may be one notch above a Neanderthal and anything but God's gift to the universe that he perceives himself to be. We still have to be on our guard for potential rivals. And if, for whatever reason, our man abandons us for a younger, more beautiful female, we only have ourselves to blame. We obviously didn't try hard enough to fight off the marauding women who are out to capture him in their seductive snares.

Centuries of a constant barrage of such misogynistic constructs have convinced women that men are more honest, sincere, important, and interesting than their female counterparts. Western culture does not encourage women to develop strong and meaningful bonds with other women. In fact, relationships between women that exclude men are often perceived as peripheral and devoid of significant meaning. As a consequence of internalizing these perceptions, women are cut off psychologically and emotionally from members of their own sex. We are left floundering for a support structure.

In her perceptive discussion and analysis of fairy tales in *Kiss Sleeping Beauty Good-bye: Breaking the Spell of Feminine Myths and Models*, Madonna Kolbenschlag argues that the estrangement at the root of women's psyches is not caused by alienation from the world of men but by alienation from the friendship and support of women.[26] If a woman cannot love and respect other women, how can she be expected to love and respect herself? If she cannot love and respect herself, how can she be expected to love and respect other women? And if she harbors low self-esteem and ill will towards herself, how can she be expected to believe in her ability to help others?

If we are serious in our pursuit of self-empowerment and wholeness for all of humankind, we need to remedy this situation. And we need to do so quickly. We need to challenge negative stereotypes about women and expose them for what they are: attempts to weaken and separate women from each other; attempts to devalue women and all things womanish; attempts to perpetuate the subordination of women. We need to dissect, discuss, deconstruct, and subject the far-reaching tentacles of patriarchy to the scrutiny of a gendered analysis. We need to grasp the fundamental truth that patriarchal institutions, systems, and ideologies cannot survive without our cooperation and complicity. We need to demand the right to self-definition, self-determination, and self-expression. We need to recognize that our sex is irrelevant to our ability to think or to do. We need to affirm that our destiny is not determined by our biology. We need to promote the female perspective and argue for a paradigm that includes the female experience. We need to defend ourselves and to come to the defense of our sisters when they are under attack. We need to cultivate self-reliance and nurture collaborative working relationships with women and men who share our goals. We need to learn to trust other women. And, perhaps more importantly, we need to become women who are worthy of trust.

That is why the illustration of female mentoring and collaboration in the Homeric *Hymn to Demeter* is invaluable and essential. As Mary Daly reminds us in *Beyond God the Father*, healing cannot take place in isolation since our sense of reality is contingent upon communal validation.[27] According to Daly, a woman needs the support of other women in her struggle for psychic wholeness because she is setting herself in opposition to a system with enormous resources at its disposal whose purpose is to persuade her that she is wrong, evil, or mad to think, feel, and behave the way she does.[27]

Demeter's attitude towards Metaneira was initially competitive, aggressive, and hostile—an attitude that replicated patriarchal power relations. But with the help of Metaneira, Demeter transcends that and learns one of many valuable lessons in the process: the importance of empathizing with another woman in distress. We need to feast our eyes on the image of Hekate, coming to the assistance of Demeter and Persephone in the true spirit of sisterhood. We need to revel in the glory of a mother's successful challenge to patriarchy and of her stubborn refusal to abandon her daughter to the clutches of a patriarchal power structure that uses and abuses them both. We need to remind ourselves of the message of the daughters of Metaneira, namely, that there are women across the generations who are able and willing to help us in times of distress or trauma. We need to cultivate Iambe's ability to laugh at our aging bodies and celebrate the female power and sexuality they embody in all their wrinkled and sagging glory.

And we need to honor the negotiating skills of Rheia who reconciles feuding siblings and the clashing, gendered perspectives they represent.

These are positive female role models who hold out the possibility of nurturing, constructive, healthy, empowering, and rewarding relationships between women. We need to celebrate their accomplishments and follow their example. We need to remind each other and ourselves that such non-hierarchical, woman-centered, collaborative, and transformational relationships between women and women and between women and men are possible—in spite of what the constructs of a misogynist culture would have us believe.

Before concluding this chapter, let us turn to a scene that offers us a moving demonstration of the compassion and support that women can provide for each other, and let us feast our eyes, once again, on the delightful, young daughters of Metaneira. We are told that when Metaneira interrupts Demeter's ritual with Demophoon, she cries out in horror. Demeter immediately snatches the child from the flames and "cast[s] him away from herself to the ground" (line 254). She then reveals her identity to Metaneira and lashes out at her and at all mortals for their ignorance. Metaneira is bewildered, speechless, and motionless. Her knees buckle, and Homer tells us, "For a long time she remained voiceless, forgetting / to pick up her dear only son from the floor" (lines 282–283). Meanwhile, the infant has been abandoned on the floor and is crying hysterically. His sisters hear his cries, and at once, there is a flurry of frenzied female activity:

> But his sisters heard his pitiful voice and
> leapt from their well-spread beds. Then one took
> the child in her arms and laid him to her breast.
> Another lit the fire; a third rushed on delicate feet
> to rouse her mother from her fragrant chamber.
> Gathering about the gasping child, they bathed
> and embraced him lovingly.
>
> (Lines 284–290)

This delightful image of young girls rushing to the aid of a distraught mother and her weeping child serves as a potent reminder of the ability of females to soothe and comfort those suffering from the blows of pain and injury. Without prompting or guidance, the daughters of Metaneira jump right into action like the cavalry charging to the rescue. But unlike the cavalry, their mission is not to destroy, invade, conquer, or subjugate. Their mission has a nobler purpose: to alleviate human suffering. They know what has to be done, and they do it. Their flurry of female activity, designed to mitigate the hurt inflicted on others, reminds us how strong and capable and nurturing and loving females can be towards each other and towards those in pain. We should not forget that image or the message it sends. We should not allow the pernicious agenda of patriarchy to bury that image beneath layers and layers of mistrust, suspicion, and woman-hating.

In contrast to these collaborative, nurturing, power sharing, and horizontal-style relationships, patriarchy posits individualism, power over relationships, and hierarchy as its ideal, a subject we shall explore next in our discussion of Zeus and Helios.

CHAPTER 6

Zeus and Helios: Male Power and Masculinities

Three of the male deities in the poem are Zeus, Helios, and Hades. They subscribe to the same patriarchal ideology that posits women as the property of men. As males, they also share a common goal in much the same way that their female counterparts share a common goal. The males conspire to bring about the abduction and rape of Kore and then to cement her stay in the underworld as Persephone, the bride of Hades. The females, on the other hand, seek to mitigate the harsh repercussion on the mother and daughter of the forced separation, abduction, and rape; to reunite mother and daughter; and to facilitate the growth and rebirth of mother and daughter. But the difference between the two groups is more than just a difference in their goals. It can also be evidenced in their mode of operation.

Although they share a common goal, unlike their female counterparts, the males in the poem do not work together as team players, striving to achieve this common goal. They do not interact with each other; they do not dialogue with each other; and they are not in physical proximity to each other. Zeus, Helios, and Hades operate independently of each other, and, with one exception, they operate in relative isolation. There is no evidence of the networking or mentoring that were such prominent qualities in the behaviors of their female counterparts. Mentoring, as we saw in the previous chapter, is predicated on the assumption that we can all learn from each other; that we can benefit from each other's expertise; and that we have the potential for growth. Apparently, the male gods in the Homeric *Hymn to Demeter* are so secure in themselves that they do not feel the slightest need to seek each other out or to learn from one another. They obviously think they know it all already.

The opening of the poem presents us with the one exception. We are told that Hades had sought and was granted permission from Zeus to abduct Kore:

> Against her will Hades took her by the design of Zeus
> with his immortal horses—her father's brother,
> Commander- and Host-to-Many, the many-named son of Kronos.
>
> (Lines 31–33)

But this conversation between Zeus and Hades had already transpired and the agreement cemented before the poem begins. So we are not made privy to their dialogue or to the nature of their interaction. In fact, throughout the whole poem, and quite unlike their female counterparts, these three male gods never interact directly with each other. Each is situated in his own sphere of influence; each stays within that sphere and does not encroach upon the other's territory. As we shall see below, the nature of the interaction between these three gods illuminates the nature of patriarchal power relations and masculine structured hierarchies. Furthermore, their mode of operation provides us with some insight into the nature of masculinities.

Since Hades exhibits a greater complexity than either Zeus or Helios, his role in the poem will be discussed at length in the following chapter. For now, let us turn our attention to the grand, old patriarch himself, Zeus.

Zeus

As the father of the patriarchs, Zeus represents the ruling class. He is the king of the gods on Mount Olympus. We learn of his role in the abduction and rape of Kore in the opening lines of the poem:

> Zeus, heavy-thundering and mighty-voiced, gave her [Kore]
> without the consent of Demeter of the bright fruit and golden sword
> as she played with the deep-breasted daughters of Ocean.
>
> (Lines 3–5)

Furthermore, we are told that Gaia (Earth) grew the fatal narcissus in order to satisfy Zeus:

> And the narcissus,
> which Earth grew as a snare for the flower-faced maiden
> in order to gratify by Zeus's design the Host-to-Many,
> a flower wondrous and bright, awesome for all to see,
> for the immortals above and for mortals below.
>
> (Lines 7–11)

Later, we are told that as Kore was being abducted by the lord of death, she calls out to her father:

> The lord Host-to-Many rose up on her
> with his immortal horses, the celebrated son of Kronos;
> he snatched the unwilling maid into his golden chariot
> and led her off lamenting. She screamed with a shrill voice,
> calling on her father, the son of Kronos highest and best.
>
> (Lines 17–21)

However, as we noted in an earlier chapter, Zeus was too busy or too indifferent to pay any attention to her call:

> But he [Zeus] sat apart
> from the gods, aloof in a temple ringing with prayers,
> and received choice offerings from humankind.
>
> (Lines 27–29)

Apparently, now that Zeus has agreed to deliver his daughter to his brother, Hades, he considers the matter closed. He shows no concern for Kore or for her plight in the underworld. This flippant disregard for the welfare of his daughter reflects the prevailing marriage customs practiced by the ancient Greeks. As Nanci DeBloois has argued in "Rape, Marriage, or Death? Gender Perspectives in the Homeric *Hymn to Demeter*," the consent of the father is required before the marriage can proceed; however, neither the consent of the mother nor the young bride was required or even sought.[1]

Unfortunately, this attitude still prevails in many parts of the world where young girls continue to be forced into marriages against their own wishes. Zeus is acting well within the parameters of patriarchal ideology that posits all women as no more than fertile wombs for producing offspring and as the property of men to be dispensed with as they see fit—especially in matters of marriage. Having given his consent and having provided for the abduction, Zeus now turns his back on the situation. He would like to consider the matter closed and return to business as usual. Unfortunately for him, Demeter has other ideas in mind.

Through this casual dismissal of his daughter, Zeus also reflects a flagrant disrespect for the sanctity of the mother/child bond. The ancient Greeks perceived the female as merely fertile soil for male insemination. She was viewed as a vessel, a baby-maker. There was no accommodation made for the fact that a mother might form a bond with the infant in her womb or the baby at her breast. There was no consideration given to the fact that because she gave birth to that child, because she nurtured and loved that child, that she has a right to insist upon having a say in the welfare of that child. Women were a means to an end. In the words of the god Apollo in Aeschylus' trilogy, *The Oresteia*:

> The woman you call the mother of the child
> is not the parent, just a nurse to the seed,
> the new-sown seed that grows and swells inside her.
> The man is the source of life—the one who mounts.
> She, like a stranger for a stranger, keeps
> the shoot alive unless god hurts the roots.[2]
> (Lines 666–671)

This attitude towards women is reflected in the manner with which Zeus summarily ignores Demeter. He fails to consult with her about their daughter's marriage, and he seems genuinely baffled by her fierce insistence on getting her daughter back.

The misogynism evident in the behavior of Zeus does not reflect the way communities operated at all times and in all places. In *When God Was a Woman*, Merlin Stone cites evidence of the historical existence of matrilineal societies, societies in which the line of descent was traced through the female. Inheritance rights were transmitted through the female. Husbands, sons, and brothers gained access to property and power only through their relationship to a particular woman.[3] In such societies—for obvious reasons—women held a high status and were treated with respect. However, it bears mentioning that even though there is documented evidence of the existence of matrilineal and matrilocal societies (where the family unit is located in the community of the female instead of the male), there is no evidence to support the existence of matriarchies—communities in which women subordinate, subjugate, and enslave males, and in which women exert total power and control over males in the same manner and to the same degree that patriarchy continues to exert over females.

Again, in *When God Was a Woman*, Merlin Stone postulates that the shift from matrilineal societies to patriarchy occurred as a result of the concern among the Indo-European invaders, and later by the Hebrews, with imposing male inheritance rights and with institutionalizing the male's ability to acquire and accumulate power and property independent of the female. A female kinship system based on matrilineal descent patterns pays only tertiary consideration for the paternity of the children. Therefore, it became crucial for the Indo-Europeans to supplant the matrilineal system of the older religion of the indigenous peoples (based on goddess worship) with a patrilineal system that firmly established the child's paternity.[4]

In order to accomplish this onerous task, the Indo-Europeans and their Hebrew descendents had to suppress any hint of goddess worship and its corresponding advocacy of female sexual autonomy. It was only by doing so could the male guarantee that his sons were, indeed, his sons and not the fruit of some other man's loins. The female, therefore, had to be placed firmly under the control of the male—first her father, then her spouse. Strict prohibitions were placed on her sexual activity before marriage or outside of marriage. There was no corresponding stricture placed on a male's virginity before marriage or his sexual fidelity within the marriage.[5]

The ubiquitous presence of biblical assaults on women; the many references to them as harlots and whores; the brutality by which "deviant" females are punished; the constant comparisons between an Israel that has deviated from Yahweh and a female who has committed lewd, sexual crimes—all of these are interpreted by Stone as evidence of the political maneuvering on the part of the Hebrews and then the Christians to squash worship of the female deity wherever it existed for the purpose of wresting political power and property from the hands of the female and delivering it to the hands of the male.[5]

It is important for us to know how and why things changed. It is also important for us to know that things have not always been the way they are now. As Gerda Lerner has documented in *The Creation of Patriarchy*, patriarchy entered into human history at specific times and in specific places and as a result of specific circumstances.[6] It coalesced to become the overpowering force we know it to be today. But knowledge of a time when human communities operated differently, when the sexes related to each other in an equitable and just manner, and when difference did not mean hierarchy holds out the possibility for change. We can transform our current society just as our ancestors transformed theirs in the past. We can work towards building a new society, one that conforms more closely to the ideals of equality and inclusivity and one which is modeled on an egalitarian relationship between men and women. And we can transform existing institutions so that they reinforce the fundamental principle of the equality and worth of all of humanity and not just its male half. Patriarchy had a historical beginning. Patriarchy can, therefore, have a historical ending.

Riane Eisler's *The Chalice and the Blade: Our History, Our Future* explores this subject further. Eisler articulates her cultural transformation theory in which she proposes that we view history in terms of a series of movements beginning with an initial partnership model (goddess-centered and life-generating), followed by a transitional period of chaos and disruption, followed by the establishment of a dominator model (patriarchal and life-threatening).[7] She argues that the root problem of our society is that we worship the technologies that are symbolized by the power of the blade and whose purpose is the domination and destruction of life.[8]

Eisler's exploration of Neolithic art leads her to conclude that the predominant theme of the Neolithic period was a celebration of life in all its forms, of the regenerative powers of the goddess, of spiritual and material nurturance, and of the unity of all life. The central image was a female giving birth, not a male dying on the cross.[9]

According to Eisler, the ideology that holds the most promise for challenging the dominator model of society in which human beings are ranked based on their ability to perpetrate violence is none other than feminism.[10] Only feminism makes explicit the connections between the systemic violence against women, against people of color, and against the planet. Only feminism holds the promise of a better future.[11]

Embedded within Eisler's concept of a dominator society is a gendered understanding of power and the role of power. Stephanie Golden in *Slaying The Mermaid* takes this one step further by incorporating race in her analysis of power. According to Golden, the concept of power as it is conceived in Western culture differs from power as it is conceived among women in the African-American community.[12] Basing her analysis on the work of sociologist Patricia Hill Collins, Golden claims that African-American females conceive of power as something to be shared with others for the common goal of the betterment of the community. Their approach grew out of African models of community derived from extended female networks that included all female care-givers, whether they were blood mothers or "othermothers."[13] Golden concludes her discussion by asserting that women, since they have a greater level of comfort with connecting with others and are less prone to perceive power as domination, are better equipped to generate a balance between maintaining the integrity of one's personal selfhood with the selfhood of the other.[14] Her discussion reinforces the contrast between the power *with* nature of female mentoring, as we saw earlier, with the masculinist concept of power *over*, control, and domination that we see illustrated in the conduct of the male gods.

In *The Creation of Feminist Consciousness*, Gerda Lerner articulates the position that men's power over women—specifically their power to define reality—has had an insidious effect on women's development. It has forced women to expend their energies on defensive arguments in which they try to counteract prevailing patriarchal assumptions of their inferiority and incompleteness as human beings; it has channeled their thinking into circumscribed arenas of knowledge; it has impeded their ability to cultivate an awareness of themselves as a collective entity; and it has aborted and thwarted their intellectual capacities for thousands of years.[15] Lerner's analysis elucidates why women's struggle for emancipation and equality has gone on for so long. And why we still have such a long way to go.

We encounter Zeus again after Demeter has caused the earth to experience drought and famine for one year. Zeus becomes aware of the problem because of the paucity of sacrifices and offerings to the gods:

> She [Demeter] would have destroyed the whole mortal race
> by cruel famine and stolen the glorious honor of gifts
> and sacrifices from those having homes on Olympus,
> if Zeus had not seen and pondered their plight in his heart.
> (Lines 310–313)

So Zeus proceeds to send an entourage of immortals to try to cajole Demeter into relinquishing her mourning and restoring the earth to its fertility. Demeter is intransigent. Once Zeus realizes that she refuses to submit to his will, he is forced to submit to hers: he sends Hermes down to the underworld with instructions for Hades to release the girl.

The last time we encounter Zeus is after the release of Persephone. He sends his mother, Rheia, to mediate between Demeter and himself. Through Rheia, Zeus invites Demeter back to join the company of the gods in Mount Olympus and to resume her function as the goddess of the grain. In return, he agrees to allow Persephone to spend two-thirds of the year with her mother in the over-world, and one-third of the year with Hades in the underworld. Rheia is able to broker a reconciliation between the feuding siblings. And Zeus has been forced to acknowledge the significance of the mother/child bond.

Zeus' behavior conforms to male norms as posited by patriarchal ideology. History provides us with a plethora of examples of males using power and privilege to oppress and subordinate females. Zeus is no exception. He acts from a position of male privilege and male hegemony. He behaves aggressively, takes what he wants when he wants it, and disposes of women as he sees fit. And he thinks he is entitled to do all of this without question. So Demeter's audacious challenge to the male hegemony that he embodies comes as somewhat of an unexpected setback. However, as we noted earlier, Zeus does not comply with Demeter's demands out of a sense of regret or possible transgression on his part. At no point in the poem does he express remorse for his actions or admit to any wrongdoing. Neither does he act out of sympathy and compassion for either his sister or his daughter. He seems as indifferent to them at the end of the poem as he was at the beginning. He agrees to Demeter's demands for one reason and one reason alone: it serves his self-interest.

Zeus does not show any signs of internal conflict or suffering. If he suffers at all, it is because Demeter's strangulation of the earth has caused him to experience deprivation: human kind is no longer able to provide "choice offerings" at his altar. But one never gets the sense that he understands the extent of his responsibility in starting the chain of events that precipitated the current dilemma. He does not see himself as being even partially accountable. From his perspective, the source of his suffering is external and is due exclusively to the unreasonable demands of a willful female. And because he does not fault himself, because he fails to accept some measure of responsibility, Zeus fails to experience the internal growth that comes from learning from one's mistakes.

Zeus, however, does learn to modify his behavior. He learns not to underestimate Demeter or to trivialize the role of the mother. But these lessons are forced on him through external circumstances. They are not internally arrived at since he fails to acknowledge his level of culpability in the course of events. From beginning to end, he has shown no compassion for either Demeter or their daughter. One gets the distinct impression that he is completely baffled by Demeter's intransigence and is taken unawares by her actions. He just doesn't seem to get it. But perhaps that is of little significance in the grand scheme of things.

As many of us know, it is extremely difficult—if not impossible—to change a person's attitude. We all have the liberty to harbor whatever offensive attitude we want and to think as we please. However, if our thoughts were such that we would risk dire repercussions were we ever to articulate those thoughts into words or into actions, we may eventually arrive at the conclusion that it is more prudent to keep our thoughts to ourselves and not articulate them in their full grandeur for the whole world to hear and see. For as far as the rest of the world is concerned, what we actually think is a matter of little significance. It is what we say and what we do that will elicit a response and have an impact.

An individual cannot be forced into changing attitudes or thoughts; however, an individual can always be cajoled or coerced into changing behaviors. We cannot prevent individuals from harboring racist or sexist attitudes towards other human beings. But we can—and should—censure them if and when they articulate those thoughts to us. And we should do so even if those offensive thoughts are articulated in the guise of "harmless" jokes. There is nothing harmless about words designed to demean or strip any group of its humanity even if those words have the ostensible purpose of eliciting laughter. Furthermore, we can and do punish individuals if they act upon offensive thoughts and engage in discriminatory and abusive behav-

iors towards others. In fact, one of the hallmarks of living in a civilized society is the enactment and enforcement of laws that punish those who engage
in discrimination and abuse.

In the case of Zeus, since we are not made privy to his thoughts but
only to his words and actions, we are on somewhat secure ground in spec-
ulating that he probably maintains the same misogynistic attitude towards
females that he has always had. However, that is of little consequence. What
matters to Demeter, to Persephone, and to the rest of the world is that he
has been forced to modify his behavior in compliance with the rules of living in a civilized society, a society that affords respect and protection to
human beings in all their diversity. Ultimately, in mythology as well as in
life, that is all that counts.

It is interesting to note that in his interaction with others, Zeus makes
demands, bellows orders, and acts from a position of strength. He consents
to the abduction and rape of his daughter; he arranges for the creation of
the narcissus in order to snare the young girl; he orders his entourage of
immortals to cajole Demeter; he instructs Hermes to inform Hades that he
has to release the girl; and, finally, he launches his mother on a mission of
reconciliation. In all of these instances, Zeus conducts himself as the head
of the hierarchy—which he is. His status is firmly established. This brings
us to the interesting issue of the role dialogue plays in establishing and
reflecting status.

In *You Just Don't Understand: Women and Men in Conversation*, Deborah
Tannen observes that status is asymmetrical in that individuals are posi-
tioned differently in a hierarchy. One of the primary means of establishing
status is by giving orders and having others obey them.[16] Zeus' interaction
with others is marked by an absence of give and take, an absence of compromise or willingness to accommodate to the needs of his subordinates since
he perceives them to be his inferiors. Zeus makes no attempt to mentor
or mediate—behaviors that are evident in his female counterparts. His
approach is top down and reflects the hierarchical, masculinist perspective
of people in positions of power in patriarchal institutions.

The only exception to this behavior is reflected in his final acquies-
cence to Demeter's demands. Here, he is forced to compromise. He has to
accommodate to his sister's demands while at the same time satisfying his
brother's desire to retain Persephone as his wife in the underworld. This is
the only instance in the poem Zeus acts from a position of weakness. He
needs something only Demeter can give him. And it is the only instance in
which we see him treating someone as an equal—no doubt, much to his
chagrin.

According to Deborah Tannen, unlike the masculine emphasis on status, the feminine emphasis is on connection, which, by definition, is based

on symmetry.[17] In symmetrical relationships, individuals are perceived as equals. By forcing Zeus to compromise and treat her as an equal, Demeter is also forcing Zeus to behave in accordance with the feminist principles of connection and symmetry—something he is not in the habit of doing. However, even here, he tries to maintain a distance between himself and everyone else. Yes, he has had to succumb to Demeter's demands and acknowledge her right as a mother. Yes, all the other gods witnessed that Demeter, a female, was able to bring him to his knees. But he will not allow her to rub his face in her victory and his defeat. He doesn't address her directly but sends his mother, another female, to mediate and broker a peace between them—as if by maintaining his distance from the victor, he is also preserving some measure of dignity for himself. In effect, Rheia's intervention enables Zeus to maintain the appearance of power, authority, strength, and autonomy. She enables him to save face—something that women are particularly adept at doing because of the nature of their socialization.

The Homeric *Hymn to Demeter* illustrates the principle that even from their positions of subordination, females can still exact a fierce revenge if they feel their rights have been violated. Even Zeus learns a valuable lesson as a result of the events: regardless of whatever personal views you may hold on the subject of motherhood, do not trample on the rights of mothers because you may end up paying a heavy price. And Zeus also learns he can no longer treat the sacred bond between the mother and child in such a cavalier manner. He must afford it the respect it deserves.

Helios

Like Zeus, Helios, the sun god, endorses the patriarchal perspective on marriage and reinforces the fact that this is a gendered perspective. When Demeter asks if he knows the whereabouts of her daughter, he reveals the truth:

> No other
> of the gods was to blame but cloud-gathering Zeus,
> who gave her to Hades, his brother to be called
> his fertile wife.
>
> (Lines 77–80)

It is obvious that Helios views Kore's abduction and rape as a marriage. His use of the word "wife" reflects that. He advises Demeter to refrain from mourning. He even implies that she should celebrate her good fortune at having such a worthy son-in-law:

"But, Goddess, give up for good your great lamentation.
You must not nurse in vain insatiable anger.
Among the gods, Aidoneus is not an unsuitable bridegroom,
Commander-to-Many and Zeus's own brother of the same stock.
As for honor, he got his third at the world's first division
and dwells with those whose rule has fallen to his lot."

(Lines 82–87)

From Helios' point of view, this is a desirable marriage. As was the case with Zeus, Helios considers it to be inconsequential that Persephone was unwilling, that the young girl has been violated, that she is traumatized, and that she is, in many respects, dead since she is forced to inhabit the underworld as the spouse of the lord of the dead. And as was the case with Zeus, Helios does not seriously consider the trauma inflicted on her mother. His attitude epitomizes the gender bias that permeates patriarchal ideology. In effect, Helios suggests that Demeter overlook the fact that her daughter has been kidnapped and violated and that she continue to support and feed the very system that is responsible for her daughter's abduction and violation. It is no wonder that Demeter responds with outrage.

It is interesting to contrast Helios' matter-of-fact response to Demeter's question with Persephone's response to her mother's related question after her emergence from the underworld. The differences in narrative structure and content highlight the differences in gender socialization. Helios is very factual. He summarizes succinctly the sequence of events in a straightforward, unemotional manner: Zeus agreed to Kore's abduction; Helios snatched her to the underworld; she is now his bride. His narrative is devoid of detail and provides little context. He sticks to the facts, pure and simple. And then he moves on to urge Demeter to reconcile herself to the situation.

Persephone, by way of contrast, provides her mother with nearly 30 lines of details when responding to Demeter's question, "By what guile did the mighty Host-to-Many deceive you?" (line 404). Persephone tells her story by reversing the chronology of events. She begins with Hermes' announcement to Hades that Zeus has declared she should be released from captivity. Then she moves backwards in time and tells her mother how she was playing in the meadow, picking flowers with her friends, when she plucked the narcissus and was abducted to the underworld. But that is not all she tells Demeter. She lists the names of her friends—all 23 of them! She even lists the flowers, using descriptive adjectives and a simile to boot. Persephone's narrative, unlike the narrative of Helios, provides context and colorful detail. She rearranges the sequence of events to suit her narrative purpose. And she doesn't omit even the most apparently inconsequential bits and pieces of information.

According to Bettina Aptheker in *Tapestries of Life: Women's Work, Women's Consciousness, and the Meaning of Daily Experience*, the structure, sequence, and details of a woman's narrative have been influenced by the daily routines she performs in the domestic sphere.[18] Housework, childcare, and other repetitive tasks that constitute home-making socialize a woman to pay attention to details, to situate her activity in a context, and to increase her sensitivity to the cyclical nature of life—the awareness that life doesn't progress in a neat, linear fashion. The repetitive tasks performed in the domestic sphere are, by definition, cyclical in nature, for housework is process: it never ends.

That Persephone's response to her mother's question omits no detail that she can remember and situates the event within a context reflects the nature of her socialization. For her, and for women in general, it is in the telling of the details that one provides a complete picture of the event. You ask a woman, "What happened?" and she will provide you with details galore, ranging from who said what to the intricacies of what each one was wearing, eating, or drinking. The event itself is only a part of the fabric. For women, socialized as we are to focus on the dailiness of life, context is everything. By contextualizing our daily activities and situating them in a larger framework, we are able to derive meaning and significance to our work as women.

In his capacity as the lord of the sun, Helios further accentuates the differences between genders. As Esther Harding demonstrates in *Woman's Mysteries, Ancient and Modern: A Psychological Interpretation of the Feminine Principle as Portrayed in Myth, Story, and Dreams*, the sun as masculine principle rules the day, consciousness, work, achievement, understanding, and discernment.[19] The sun is constant in shape and size. Unlike the moon, it does not wax and wane. It appears in the daytime and brings with it light and clarity to the surface of the earth. It is also associated with the light of reason (logos), the light that operates on our conscious level through analysis, dissection, and logical procedure. In the overwhelming majority of cultures throughout the world, the sun was perceived as a masculine deity and is associated with the masculine principle.

The moon, on the other hand, experiences metamorphosis. It waxes and wanes. It disappears for a period of time. It is visible at night and is associated with darkness, dreams, and shadows. It represents the level of our psyche that operates beneath the conscious level. Because it experiences the same type of ebb and flow changes of a female during pregnancy and menstruation, and because it is associated—and, at one time, was held directly responsible for—her menstrual cycle, the moon was viewed as the visible representation of the feminine principle (Eros) in most ancient cultures and was perceived as a female deity. Esther Harding reminds us that, as the feminine principle, the moon controls those mysterious forces beyond human understanding.[19] In the Homeric *Hymn to Demeter*, Hekate is associated with the moon and with darkness and shadows, and as such, she is the polar opposite of Helios.

When Helios argues in favor of reason and logic, he is promoting the masculinist point of view. In effect, he tells Demeter to accept what she cannot undo. He presents sound arguments in favor of Hades. He is being perfectly logical, perfectly rational, and perfectly realistic. However, he is virtually devoid of empathy and totally disregards emotions—qualities that are usually designated as belonging within the sphere of the feminine. It matters not to him that Persephone may have been traumatized by the experience. It matters not the slightest that her mother is grief-stricken over the loss of her daughter. These factors are inconsequential as far as he is concerned. Helios is the voice of reason that commands us to snap out of it, to get a grip on reality, to stop mooning about over circumstances we are powerless to change. In a sense, he is right and is giving us sensible advice. However, Helios and the voice of reason he represents fails to take into consideration that in order to arrive at this rational understanding of a situation that has traumatized us, in order to accept what cannot be undone, we need to undergo a process of coming to terms with it emotionally and psychologically. We need to grieve and to mourn. We need time. We need to journey to the depths and reap the seeds of acceptance, understanding, and assimilation. Failure to go through that sequence serves only to delay healing process.

Demeter reminds us that we need time and space to mourn and grieve. Eventually, she arrives at the conclusion that Helios recommends by accepting that her daughter is no longer Kore and that she is now Persephone, the bride of death. However, she can only do so after she has experienced her own journey to the chthonic realm and has dealt with her grief on an emotional and psychological level before being able to transcend it and adopt a rational approach to the situation. Helios' disregard for this all-important step is tantamount to negating the essential role that emotions have to play in the healing process. And since emotions continue to be culturally designated as belonging to the province of the female, Helios is also showing his utter contempt for all things deemed feminine.

Males who exhibit Helios' tendency of denying the importance of emotions deprive themselves of the opportunity of experiencing wholeness. Audre Lorde in *Sister Outsider* argues that men who are afraid to experience feelings for themselves keep women around for the purpose of experiencing feelings for them vicariously. At the same time, these men will dismiss women for their ostensible weakness to feel deeply. Lorde concludes that men who are afraid to feel or who expect women to feel for them deny their own humanity and become entrapped in dependency and fear.[20]

In *Goddesses in Older Women*, Jean Shinoda Bolen contrasts logos with gnosis. Logos is that which can be known and demonstrated objectively whereas gnosis is that which can only be known and experienced subjectively.[21] Bolen associates gnosis with the Sophia archetype. She argues that gnosis is a type of knowledge that is revealed or intuited as being true. It is an insight that resonates with our spiritual core. Referred to as "soul knowledge" and then later as "women's intuition," gnosis is, according to Bolen, a source of inner wisdom in women.[22]

Using Bolen's definition, we can see that gnosis provides us with a type of knowledge and a means of intuiting that knowledge in ways that are inaccessible through logos. Similarly, logos can provide us with a type of knowledge and a means of arriving at that knowledge in ways that are inaccessible through gnosis. However, that does not make one better than the other. What is required is not an either-or oppositional stance or the establishment of a hierarchy of values. Neither logos nor gnosis is sufficient in and of itself. Both types of knowledge are necessary. Both will come into play with alternating prominence depending on the circumstances and situation at any given time. Their relationship to each other is complementary, not antagonistic.

Helios projects the masculinist perspective by valuing reason over intuition, thinking over feeling, mind over body, logos over gnosis—with the former quality in each case being culturally associated with the masculine and the latter being culturally associated with the feminine. It is unfortunate that all binaries have been gendered in this way. As Andrea Dworkin observes in *Woman Hating*, one consequence of this dualistic stance is that masculine and feminine are constantly pitted against each other. They are seen as polar opposites whose mode of interaction is plagued with conflict.[23]

In *Slaying the Mermaid: Women and the Culture of Sacrifice*, Stephanie Golden argues that the orientation of Western philosophy since the time of the ancient Greeks has been to divide, separate, and distinguish.[24] It sets up as polar opposites spirit and nature, mind and matter, male and female. According to Golden, the contribution of the seventeenth-century philosopher René Descartes was to claim a position for reason as the best tool to control those elements considered as being the inferior half of the dichotomy: nature, matter, female, and all things feminine. But in the process of rejecting feelings, intuition, and sensory experience, Golden argues that the Cartesian method engenders feelings of alienation, separation, and a disconnection from others as well as from the material world.[24] Obviously, this is not a desired state.

Patriarchy attributes a higher value to the qualities associated with the masculine than it does to those qualities associated with the feminine. But the reality, as both Demeter and Persephone demonstrate, is that the two modes of operation are not hierarchical. They are not even oppositional. They are complementary. Both are equally important; both are essential to bringing about wholeness. As Susan Griffin argues in *Pornography and Silence: Culture's Revenge Against Nature*, our notions of what it means to be a male or a female have nothing to do with reality. They are simply cultural expressions of the choice we make to sacrifice and divide ourselves.[25] This decision can have a deleterious impact on our development as human beings.

In *The Moon and the Virgin: Reflections on the Archetypal Feminine*, Nor Hall stresses the importance of balance in achieving wholeness. She argues that to be whole, we must know the sun consciousness, the phenomenal world as it is revealed to us in the bright light of reason, while, at the same time, maintaining our connection with lunar consciousness, the unconscious night realm of the moon that reveals the spirit world with its shadows, dreams, and visions.[26] We are reminded of Persephone's transformation in the underworld—a transformation that encompasses the same message of balance between the feminine and masculine realms, between the yin and the yang, between underworld and over-world, between darkness and light. Persephone assimilated the masculine experience before she gained her release from the underworld. Similarly, we must strive towards maintaining a balance between solar consciousness and lunar consciousness before we can be released from our own journeys to the chthonic realm and move ourselves one notch closer to achieving wholeness.

Throughout his interaction with Demeter, Helios adopts what Bettina Aptheker in *Tapestries of Life: Women's Work, Women's Consciousness, and the Meaning of Daily Experience* identifies as a masculinist process which accentuates the oppositional, the either/or dichotomies.[27] From Helios' perspective, there is no compromise. You either accept the situation as it is, or you fight a losing battle and suffer in hopeless misery—preferably in some dark corner where you don't disturb the rest of the universe with the sound of your whimpering.

Demeter is able to challenge such rigid dichotomies. By tapping into her inner strength and acting from a position of power, she forces a compromise: she and Hades will share Persephone throughout the year on a rotating basis. In this manner, there are no outright winners; there are no outright losers. The masculinist perspective as promulgated by Helios has been exposed for what it is: unnecessarily rigid, uncompromising, skewed, and detrimental to the health and well-being of individual development.

Zeus and Helios present the rigidly dichotomized perspective of humanity and human development. Theirs is not only a distorted view of humanity. Theirs is also a very damaging perspective in its insistence upon fragmenting, severing, and, ultimately, rejecting an essential part of what constitutes our humanity. If adopted and promoted, this perspective—a perspective that constitutes a violent injury to our sense of well-being and completeness—can only portend disaster: an annihilation of wholeness, a self divided and alienated from itself. Furthermore, because of this masculinist tendency to strip each act of its context and to treat it as an isolated event, both Zeus and Helios suffer from an inability to empathize with another—an ability that can only be engendered through connection with another.

What is true on an individual scale is also true on a societal scale. Just as an individual has to integrate both the masculine and feminine principles within her/his own being in order to achieve wholeness, so society has to give equal validity and treat with equal respect the contribution of what falls under the feminine as well as the masculine sphere of influence. In reality, human civilization could not have developed had it not been for the different tasks performed by women and men. But to say that women and men have made different contributions to society is not to say that one gender's contribution is significantly more important than another's. Difference is not synonymous with inequality. In fact, as Gerda Lerner has argued in *The Creation of Patriarchy*, societies have existed in which sexual asymmetry carried with it no connotation of superiority and inferiority.[28] A gender-specific difference in roles does not necessarily equate with a difference in value or worth.

The private work that takes place inside the domestic sphere—the cooking; the cleaning; the washing; the clothing, feeding, and caring for children; the nurturing; the healing—in short, all those tasks that keep a household running are essential for the maintenance and reproduction of the foundation block of any society, the family. Without these tasks—tasks that society has designated as coming under the jurisdiction of the female—we could not have survived or developed as a species.

The work of the male, on the other hand, occurs in the public sphere where there is always an audience to witness his heroic performances. Hence, validation for him comes from outside the home. History is replete with examples of his heroism. Songs have been sung and stories have been written celebrating his magnificent accomplishments. But who is at home, witnessing the heroic accomplishments of his female counterpart? Who is singing songs and writing stories about the heroism involved in performing the same arduous tasks day in and day out, tasks that are no less essential for the sustenance of a household? When was the last time we acknowledged her vital contributions?

The reality is obvious for those who want to analyze it: if it weren't for the "little" woman who stayed at home keeping the home fires burning, the male could not have ventured forth, seeking the fame and glory of the hunt, the battle, or the paycheck—all of which are, without a doubt, equally essential for the survival of the species, but all of which seem to get a disproportionate amount of the credit. After all, when was the last time we had adoring fans to cheer us on and applaud while we were changing dirty diapers or scrubbing the grunge from bathroom tiles? Maybe these jobs aren't quite as "heroic," romantic, or exciting as arming oneself with a suit, tie, and briefcase, and galloping off to the public sphere to perform heroic deeds of immense proportions. But are they any less essential?

Society has designated the work performed inside the home as "women's work" and, as such, has proceeded to undervalue, underrate, and demean it. A woman's work is invisible in that no one notices it if and when it gets done. But we begin to notice when it doesn't get done: when the laundry starts to pile up and we run out of clean clothes to wear; when the house is a mess; when there is no home-cooked meal waiting to greet us after a hard day at the hunt, the battle, or the office. On the one hand, we insist and rely on women's unpaid labor to sustain us; on the other hand, we refuse to acknowledge the value of her labor or the essential role it has played in our sustenance.

This skewed, imbalanced, warped, and hypocritical value system needs to change if ever we are to achieve wholeness and health as a society. Instinctively, we know the importance of "women's work." But we must do more than just know it and remain silent about it. We must do more than assuage our guilt by remembering to buy her a gift on Mother's Day. We must openly recognize, acknowledge, reward, and honor the vital contributions that she has made and continues to make.

What is true for the health and well-being of the individual is also true for the health and well-being of society: we must restructure gender relations based on reciprocity and not on social and cultural stratification; we must maintain a balance between the feminine and the masculine, internally and externally; we must acknowledge their complementarity; we must honor and respect their different contributions; and we must openly recognize the essential roles they play in achieving health and well-being on an individual as well as on a societal scale.

In his exploration and analysis of the subject of masculinities, R. W. Connell in *Masculinities* traces the history of masculinities and defines its many permutations and varieties. He argues that as a social construct subject to the vicissitudes of time and culture, masculinities has a historicity which is defined and manifested in a diversity of forms depending on a variety of categories, including race, class, and sexual orientation. Historically and currently, the different types of masculinities interact with each other to establish systems of domination and subordination.[29] In other words, there is a gender politics that operates within masculinities.

Connell further demonstrates that hegemonic masculinity is not fixed for all times and all places. It is a fluid construct continuously challenged by other forms of masculinity as well as by femininities.[30] According to Connell, masculinity has to contrast itself with femininity in order for it to exist.[31] Hence Connell concludes that any attempt to dismantle hegemonic masculinity has to encompass a degendering strategy which he defines as "a degendered rights-based politics of social justice," applicable at the level of culture, institutions, as well as at the level of the body.[32] Abolishing hegemonic masculinity involves abolishing violence, hatred, and the cultural climate that produced it.[33]

The Homeric *Hymn to Demeter* presents us with a successful (albeit short-lived) challenge to male hegemony and the masculinity of the ruling class that it embodies. Demeter's insistence that her wishes and perspective be accommodated is the equivalent of forcing the patriarchal power structure—whether it be in the form of Zeus or Helios—to recognize that the continuation of life itself depends upon an accommodation of the female as well as the male perspective. These two perspectives are not polar opposites but complement each other. By insisting on her rights as a female and as a mother; by reminding us of the sanctity of the mother/child bond; by rendering visible the virtues of nurturance and care; by insisting that the voice of the female be recognized, valued, and validated Demeter has forced an acknowledgement of the essential role that the female and the feminine principle play in the attainment of health, balance, and healing for all of us—female and male alike.

Unlike either Zeus or Helios, the third male in the poem, Hades, does not subscribe to such inhuman, unnatural, and schizophrenic dichotomies. He shows greater complexity both as a character and as god of the underworld—a subject we shall explore in our next chapter.

CHAPTER 7

The Underworld
and Hades: Death,
Transformation,
and Rebirth

For the ancient Greeks, Erebos, otherwise known as the underworld or chthonic realm, was a dark, mysterious place, the exact location of which was unspecified. It was in a nebulous region under the earth or across a large expanse of water. In Greek mythology, the underworld is the afterlife inhabited by the shades of the dead. Although recognizable in shape and form, shades were transparent figures that couldn't be held or touched—as Odysseus learned when he visited the underworld in Book XI of Homer's *Odyssey*.

But the underworld is also psychic space, and, as such, its location transcends time and space. Esther Harding in *Woman's Mysteries, Ancient and Modern: A Psychological Interpretation of the Feminine Principle as Portrayed in Myth, Story, and Dreams* explains that whereas the ancients projected the underworld as an unknown region outside of themselves and thought of it as an actual geographical place, we tend to recognize it as the hidden and unknown depths of our unconscious.[1] Jean Shinoda Bolen in *Goddesses in Older Women* concurs. She understands the underworld to be a metaphor for the personal and collective unconscious.[2]

115

One of the many attractions of the Homeric *Hymn to Demeter* for a contemporary audience lies in our ability to interpret the underworld as psychic space. As can be evidenced by the tremendous appeal of the Eleusinian
Mysteries for the ancient Greeks, perhaps they, too, came to understand
the underworld as more than just a geographical location. Participation in
the rites suggests a belief, however inchoate and embryonic, that the underworld consists of more than just a physical locale. It came to signify a psychic space that contains within it the potential for health and healing—a
potential that transcends a geographical location.

In the Homeric *Hymn to Demeter*, after Persephone has been whisked
off to the underworld, we do not encounter her—or the underworld again—
until Hermes is sent down to retrieve her. We are provided with scant detail
of what transpires during her tenure in the underworld. The little we do
know is this: she is taken against her will by Hades who then rapes her and
claims her as his bride. And while she is in the underworld, Persephone
spends her time longing for her mother and hoping for release:

> So long as the goddess gazed on earth and starry heaven,
> on the sea flowing strong and full of fish,
> and on the beams of the sun, she still hoped
> to see her dear mother and the race of immortals.
> For so long hope charmed her strong mind despite her distress.
>
> (Lines 33–37)

We next encounter her through the filtered lens of Hermes. After
receiving the command from Zeus to inform Hades that he has to release
the girl, Hermes sets off on his mission:

> Hermes did not disobey. At once he left Olympus's height
> and plunged swiftly into the depths of the earth.
> He met lord Hades inside his dwelling,
> reclining on a bed with his shy spouse, strongly reluctant
> through desire for her mother.
>
> (Lines 340–344)

Persephone has apparently spent the whole year in the underworld by pining away for her mother. Even though she has been raped and gained sexual experience, she is still described as a "shy" spouse. However, as we saw
in our discussion earlier, there is a suggestion that Persephone is not quite
as gullible or as naïve as she used to be and that she has, in effect, gained
knowledge and insight during her tenure in the realm of death. The apparent causal relationship between Hades' enticement of the power and respect
that will be bestowed on her as his bride concomitant with her apparent
willingness to swallow the pomegranate seed and ensure her annual return

to the underworld suggests that Persephone knew exactly what she was doing. She may have been "shy" but she certainly can no longer be considered naïve.

Even though Persephone's year in the underworld is shrouded in secrecy, we know that her time there has had a positive impact on her: from the innocent, virginal Kore, she has metamorphosed into an autonomous, compelling figure, relishing in her newly found power and status. As mysterious and dark as it is—or, perhaps, because of its mystery and darkness—the underworld can therefore be interpreted as the psychological space where death and the potential for transformation and rebirth can occur for all human beings.

In her exploration of goddesses as archetypes, *Goddess in Older Women*, Jean Shinoda Bolen argues that the underworld or chthonic realm can symbolize deep layers of the psyche: it is the place which harbors our personal memories and feelings in the personal unconscious, and it is also the place which harbors the images, patterns, instincts, and feelings that we share in common with all of humanity in the collective unconscious.[2] Seen in this light, the underworld becomes not just a physical location, that is to say, a place located under the earth or across the sea, as the ancient Greeks understood it to be; it can also become a psychological location, a place that transcends both time and space. Sylvia Brinton Perera articulates a similar perception of the underworld. In "The Descent of Inanna: Myth and Therapy," Brinton Perera claims that we make descents into the underworld in the service of life "to scoop up" what has been held captive in our unconscious by the Self.[3] The underworld becomes the realm of the human psyche. And herein lies its meaning and relevance for us.

As the realm of death, the underworld is also, paradoxically, the realm of rebirth. Rebirth in this context should be understood as a place of metamorphosis, of transformed consciousness. Pregnant with the potential for new life, the underworld manifests an amorphous chaos with a fructifying force. Unfortunately, the western world has cultivated a fear of the underworld, that psychic space in which we experience death, transformation, and rebirth. We have invented drugs that numb our senses and deaden our pain in order to avoid experiencing the underworld in its full force. In so doing, we fail to recognize that the underworld can also be our source of life: for without death, there can be no life; without pain and suffering, there can be no growth. By indulging ourselves in drugs that induce a mindless stupor and blunt the impact of confronting the harsh reality of the underworld—a reality that, in the words of Hamlet, our flesh is heir to—we are, in effect, condemning ourselves to living in the domain of death indefinitely. Until we embrace pain and suffering and are prepared to stare into our own psychological abyss with unflinching honesty, we can never hope to assimilate the life-altering experience and actualize the potential for health and wholeness the underworld has to offer.

In *Reinventing Eve: Modern Woman in Search of Herself,* Kim Chernin refers to the underworld as "a uterine shrine," "a sacred cave of rebirth."[4] Chernin images the underworld as a dark and mysterious primal womb, the center of our psychological and spiritual being, a place that nourishes and protects us until we are ready for emergence.[4] And when we are ripe for reemergence, when we are ready to experience rebirth and transformation, we cannot do so without shedding our old "skin" and giving birth to ourselves anew. And just as with all birth and death, pain is central to the process.

This dark and foreboding psychic space of the underworld can be terrifying. Experienced in isolation, the underworld is a place where an individual can feel utterly desolate, abandoned, and bereft of community. It is associated with times of depression and feelings of separation. Surely no one in his or her right mind would want to venture into those depths voluntarily. Hence, like Persephone who has paved the way before us, we have to be periodically abducted—abducted from our preoccupation with the material world into a realm that offers us the opportunity to explore our hidden depths. But like Persephone who fervently retains the hope to return to Mother, while we are there, we have to sustain the hope of returning to our psychological surface. Furthermore, we have to use our time there wisely, reaping the benefits that are offered to us in terms of insight and knowledge and ingesting the fruits of the underworld when we are finally released from captivity.

The successful journey into the depths is not for the faint-hearted. We are reminded that Persephone has a "strong mind." Those who are unequipped for negotiating the journey into the depths and those who are faint-hearted will seek a myriad of ways to numb the pain and deaden their senses in order to avoid confronting the stark, unadulterated reality the underworld represents. But by so doing, they may be condemning themselves to reside in the underworld indefinitely. As we saw in our discussion with Persephone, although we may have little or no control over our abduction into the underworld, we continue to be responsible for our successful emergence.

Even those who are strong of mind and will and who may have already experienced the underworld approach subsequent journeys with trepidation. We know that once there, we will experience a psychological death. As Christine Downing has argued in "Persephone in Hades," in a sense, all psychological deaths consist of an abduction since no one really expects to die or wants to die. Hence, we have to be kidnapped.[5] Psychological death also consists of a violation since there is nothing we can do to deny death access to our minds and our bodies.

This process of experiencing a psychological death is frightening, lonely, and can be plagued with perils. Unflinching honesty with one's self is required in order to experience the process fully. We have to be prepared to do some deep excavating in our unconscious and bring to the conscious level even the most ugly and cruel truths about ourselves and to ourselves if we are to experience genuine rebirth. We have to poke around in all the nooks and crannies that the underworld makes available to us. We have to stare with brutal candor at our strengths, weaknesses, frailties, and vulnerabilities. We have to assimilate the negative experiences and energies that sent us plummeting to the underworld and recycle them into positive energies that produce new life. Having done that, we must be prepared to go a step further: we must incarnate the insights we have gained through implementing the necessary changes in our selves, in our perspectives, and in our lives. Otherwise, our time in the underworld is time not well spent.

Descent into the underworld can happen at different times in our lives, and the time spent in each descent can vary in duration. The process is cyclical: death, transformation, and rebirth inevitably followed by another death, transformation, rebirth, and so on. When, how, why, and for how long our abduction will last is a mystery. As humans, we act with partial knowledge. We experience the descent whenever we make a decision or pursue a course of action that backfires on us in a traumatic way. Sometimes our descent may be caused by unexpected circumstances or unforeseen turmoil such as the death of a loved one, the end of a relationship, or the loss of something we value. Descents serve to remind us of our own limitations and frailties.

When the descent takes place early in our lives, it can act as the catapult to propel us to greater maturity. When the descent takes place later in our lives, it can push us toward a deeper awareness of our very being. As Marion Woodman and Elinor Dickson have argued in *Dancing in the Flames: The Dark Goddess in the Transformation of Consciousness*, the mid-life descent frequently necessitates a reorientation of our identity, a new direction in our lives.[6] It is a time of changing focus: from the material world and its outer journeys to the internal world and its inner journeys. Jean Shinoda Bolen concurs. In *Goddesses in Older Women: Archetypes in Women Over Fifty, Becoming a Juicy Crone*, Bolen argues that middle age consists of a time pregnant with the potential for self-expression, inner and outer freedom, and autonomy. According to Bolen, middle age coincides with the third phase in a woman's life, the phase she terms the "green and juicy crone" phase.[7]

Persephone and Demeter experience parallel journeys in the underworld. Both are abducted into the underworld by circumstances beyond their conscious control: Persephone by her uncle and Demeter by the abduction and rape of her daughter. Persephone's descent into the underworld causes her to experience the death of her virginal phase and to enter upon the second phase of a woman's life—the one associated with being a wife and mother. Similarly, Demeter's descent into the underworld causes her to experience the death of the mother phase in her life and enter upon the third phase of life, the postmenopausal or crone phase.

We are not provided with the detailed stages of Persephone's transformation in the underworld. We first meet her as Kore. And we meet her again just before she swallows the pomegranate and exits the underworld. By now, she has become the empowered queen of the underworld, one who has assimilated the lessons made available to her in the underworld by transforming her loss of innocence (her symbolic death) to an opportunity for growth and development.

By way of contrast, Demeter's stages while she is in the underworld are clearly delineated for us. Demeter is plummeted to the underworld as a consequence of the abduction and rape of Persephone. As soon as she learns the whereabouts of her daughter, Demeter disguises herself as a crone and wanders from one city and field to the next until she arrives at Eleusis.

> There she sat near the road, grief in her heart,
> where citizens drew water from the Maiden's Well
> in the shade—an olive bush had grown overhead—
> like a very old woman cut off from childbearing
> and the gifts of garland-loving Aphrodite.
> (Lines 98–102)

Demeter's decision to disguise herself as a crone is heavily significant. Having learned that her daughter is now the bride of Hades, Demeter recognizes the immutability of Persephone's altered status. By assuming the guise of a crone, Demeter foreshadows a corresponding shift she will now have to experience in her own life in terms of her self-definition as well as in terms of the changing dynamics in her relationship with her daughter. Persephone has flown the nest. This transformational event concludes Demeter's role of mothering as she once knew it. The death of the old Demeter presages the birth of the new: her movement from mother to crone. But acknowledgement that she has passed from one phase to the next does not necessarily mean that Demeter has internalized or reconciled herself with the changes that have been forced upon her. In fact, she has taken only the first, fledgling step in what is to be a clearly articulated but non-linear progression towards embracing her new role in life. Demeter's progression, as Kathie Carlson in *Life's Daughter/Death's Bride* accurately characterizes it, consists of a shifting back and forth between her human ignorance and goddess understanding.[8]

Kim Chernin in *Reinventing Eve: Modern Woman in Search of Herself* argues that initiation shares the qualities of all change: it is an unpredictable, non-linear process in which we get glimpses of insight and intuition interspersed with times of confusion and reflection.[9] According to Chernin, like all change, initiation circles around itself, pursues seemingly meaningless detours, deludes us into believing that we are back where we started without having made any progress whatsoever, and then, when we least expect it, we find ourselves shoved across a threshold where we discover we have moved on to a new plateau.[9] This is the meandering pattern that Demeter follows as she navigates her path through the transformative process of the underworld.

Demeter's stages of transformation while she is in the underworld are prompted by the events and the people she encounters—each of whom helps her to arrive at a new understanding of herself and of a new awareness of death and life as transformative experiences. Her fabricated story of abduction and rape by pirates indicates that she feels she has experienced a rape of sorts—a psychological trauma that has penetrated her psyche and changed her irrevocably. Her encounter with Iambe serves to remind her that her entrance into the crone phase of life does not necessarily entail depression and grief. Instead, it can be perceived as a new beginning—one in which she can celebrate her autonomy and sexuality free from the restraints that patriarchy can impose on women during the first two stages of life. Her attempt to immortalize Demophoon followed by Metaneira's understandable grief at the possibility of loosing her child propel Demeter on her journey forward in the underworld by impressing upon her the value of reconciling oneself with loss; the importance of grieving; the sanctity of the mother/child bond; the strength that can emerge when one reconnects with one's internal source of power; and a new understanding of the meaning of life, death, transformation, and rebirth.

Demeter's progression in the underworld is gradual and oscillates between ignorance and knowledge. Like Persephone, her experience in the underworld teaches her to transform loss into potential for growth and renewal. And like Persephone, her transformation is complete before her release from the underworld. Persephone eats the pomegranate and internalizes her transformation before she emerges from the underworld. Similarly, Demeter internalizes her transformation, displays her impenetrable and determined new self at the temple in Eleusis, and forces the male hegemonic structure to acquiesce to her demands. She does not emerge from the underworld until the release of her daughter. The joyous reunification of mother and daughter signifies their simultaneous release from their respective underworlds. Having internalized the lessons the underworld offered them, both mother and daughter experience release, rebirth, and transformed consciousness.

As the land of plenty, the underworld has much to offer us. In the Homeric *Hymn to Demeter*, Hades, the lord of death, is frequently referred to as the Host-to-Many. His is the richest realm because all that lives will eventually come under his jurisdiction: all living things must eventually die. In *Descent to the Goddess: A Way of Initiation for Women*, Sylvia Perera deconstructs the story of Inanna, the Sumerian goddess who undertook a journey to the underworld. According to Perera, all descents to the underworld can serve as initiations that provide us access to the different levels of consciousness, thereby expanding our understanding and enhancing our lives creatively.[10] We emerge from the darkness with a new perception of the internal and external forces that govern our lives and with a greater understanding of our roles within our own lives and in relation to the lives around us.

Like Kore, we enter the underworld in a virginal state; and, like Persephone, we have the potential to emerge utterly transformed, and utterly empowered. Hence, the underworld becomes a place where we can learn about who we are, what we can become, and how we fit into the grand scheme of things. We can use the experience, in the words of Christine Downing in *The Long Journey Home*, as "occasions for deep seeing."[11] Marina Valcarenghi in *Relationships: Transforming Archetypes* declares that descent into the underworld, far from contributing to the construction of a "neurotic nucleus," can perhaps be the most radically transformative experience in the psychic development of a female.[12] Or a male, for that matter.

How we choose to understand our experience in the underworld will, in great measure, determine the nature of the underworld we experience. Once we understand the role the underworld can play in our psychological and spiritual development, we can begin to recognize that these excursions have the capacity to become fertile periods in our lives, ones in which we can glean insight and experience genuine transformation and rebirth, although we do not necessarily welcome the trips. As Tanya Wilkinson argues in *Persephone Returns: Victims, Heroes, and the Journey from the Underworld*, descents to the underworld are inevitable but returns are possible.[13] Perhaps, after racking up frequent flyer miles with our many visits, some of us may even begin to embrace these abductions into the depths as opportunities for experiencing genuine growth spurts. Some may even welcome Hades as our initiatory guide to these depths. And some of us may even leave the realm of death secure in our knowledge that, like Persephone, we'll be back for more growth, more transformation, and, unfortunately, more of the pain that growth and transformation inevitably engender.

One trip to the underworld does not guarantee that we have learned all there is to know. Persephone conveys the message that if we are abducted to the inner depths of the underworld, we are able not only to survive the experience, but we can also transform the ordeal into something life-enriching. For if we have used our time in the underworld wisely, we will emerge with greater understanding. We will know what sent us plummeting down there in the first place, and we will know enough to avoid making that same mistake again. However, this is no guarantee that we will be able to avoid making mistakes altogether. No human being can avoid doing that. So sooner or later, we will make another mistake—one that will send us tumbling down again. The mistake may take a different guise, a different form, occur under different circumstances, but it will happen. And it will happen for one reason and one reason alone: because we are human and, by definition, we are fallible. Our fallibility is the source of our downfall as well as the source of our glory.

Persephone's emergence from the underworld and her obvious joy at reuniting with her mother sheds light on our own emergence from the underworld. Yes, the time spent there can be beneficial and transformative. Yes, it can be a period of psychological and spiritual growth. However, it is also a relief to have emerged from the experience on the other side, thankful for having undergone the experience, but relieved at putting it behind us and getting back to the business of living on the surface. In that sense, like Persephone, we are overjoyed to return to Mother, to return to the source of our origin—only now, we are wiser, more experienced human beings better equipped to handle life's hurdles. Now we can use the knowledge we have garnered in the underworld to guide us as we journey through life.

What does the Homeric *Hymn to Demeter* tell us about the catalyst for our own journeys into the underworld, the nature of our stay there, and the catalyst that propels us out? The hymn is very short on specifics and long on generalities. We know the catalyst that sets Persephone off on her journey is the plucking of the narcissus, which, as we saw earlier, represents her abandonment of community and indulgence in self-absorption. We know little about the nature of her stay in the chthonic realm since the only time we see her in the underworld is when Hermes finds her, lolling about in bed with Hades. This hardly serves to provide us with clues as to how we are to spend our time in the underworld. Her exit from the underworld is precipitated by Demeter's defiance of male hegemony through assertion of her rights as a mother. Her annual return to the underworld is precipitated by her swallowing of the pomegranate seed. The significance of the narcissus and the pomegranate seed was explored in an earlier chapter. So let us focus our attention on Persephone's tenure in the underworld and what it can tell us about our own experiences in the chthonic realm.

Persephone is apparently passive in the underworld. She is victimized by Hades. She can do nothing to help herself out of her predicament. She just seems to lie around in bed, waiting and hoping to be reunited with mother. She can hardly serve as a role model for those of us who encourage women to seize control of their lives and exercise their own agency. But perhaps by expecting Persephone to act, to do something—anything—to save herself, we are completely misconstruing the point of time spent in the underworld.

Time spent in the underworld should not be confused with time spent in the over-world. While we are on the surface, we are expected to act, perform, and achieve in a multitude of ways that are tangible and measurable. We are encouraged to keep moving and to strive for bigger and better things. But time spent in the underworld is precisely a time to transfer our energy from worldly pursuits and direct it towards internal growth. It is a time for taking advantage of the stillness and the nurturing quality that saturates the psychic fabric of the underworld. It is a time for going back to the womb and bathing in its protective waters. We have to be psychologically still if we want to recognize and benefit from moments of transformation and illumination. Time in the underworld is a time for introspection, for gestation. It is a time for plummeting into our own depths. It is a time for "donning the veil" while appearing to be doing nothing. Quite simply, it is a time for learning what it means to *be* without the distraction of having to *do* anything.

For women, the experience can be paralleled to undergoing a full-term pregnancy. Pregnant women continue to perform their daily chores and duties to the best of their abilities. They try to function on the surface level as if nothing were happening inside them. But the reality, as any woman who has undergone a pregnancy will confirm, is that pregnant woman are fully conscious of the fact that the activity in the womb is, in many ways, far more significant and meaningful than anything they can be doing on the surface. With each butterfly movement experienced from within, with each belly-punch and kick that jerks her consciousness, a pregnant women is reminded that nothing in life has greater value than the activity of creating new life within her womb, an activity that occurs hidden from prying eyes on the surface.

As with any pregnancy, the journey in the underworld is experienced internally. So for those of us on the outside and looking in, little seems to be taking place. In reality, a great deal may be taking place on the subconscious level that is not evident to the naked eye. This is a productive and fertile time for spiritual and psychological gestation. Persephone's apparent passivity in the underworld can be seen as the symbolic equivalent of Demeter's entrance into the temple at Eleusis: they both engage in an external passivity that belies an internal fermentation.

The process of rebirth and transformation is shrouded in secrecy, mystery, and darkness. It has to be—not just for Persephone but for all of us. In *Relationships: Transforming Archetypes*, Marina Valcarenghi demonstrates that one of the conditions for conquering the labyrinth (a synonym for the underworld) is solitude because any truly creative activity requires introversion and is experienced differently by each person.[14] Just as the fetus grows and develops in the mother's womb shrouded in solitude and, until recent times, in mystery and darkness before it emerges, we, too, experience the process of giving birth to ourselves as a fertile period in our lives equally shrouded in solitude, mystery, and darkness.

Encounters with the underworld frequently entail a loss of appetite. Persephone goes for one year without eating anything in the underworld until she swallows the pomegranate seed just prior to her release. Demeter initially refuses food and drink when she first enters the palace at Eleusis. But we are creatures of flesh and blood that, unlike Persephone, cannot survive for a year without food. Interestingly enough, however, many of us do lose weight when we are in the underworld. We may find difficulty eating and drinking during the initial stages of our encounter with loss and grief. But like Demeter when she assumes the guise of a mortal at Eleusis, we, too, will eventually accept offers of food and drink. Our survival depends on it.

As mortals, we live and operate in the over-world, going through the motions of functioning in the material world while the life of our psyche, our process of birth and renewal, is occurring in the underworld, hidden from prying eyes. This process is likely to be apparent only to us. To everyone else, we may appear to be lolling about in bed, doing nothing, twiddling our thumbs, munching on bonbons, watching Oprah, and waiting for Prince Charming to come a-galloping to our rescue.

Audre Lorde's distinction between pain and suffering in her collection *Sister Outsider* provides us with further insight on our journeys to the underworld. Lorde argues that pain is an event or experience that must be acknowledged, named, and eventually transformed into a source of strength and knowledge, and a course of action.[15] In other words, one experiences the pain, assimilates it, and moves on. Pain becomes a steppingstone to higher knowledge. This is to be distinguished from suffering, which, according to Lorde, is the nightmare of reliving the same pain on a continuous basis due to a lack of understanding and assimilation. One condemns oneself to the inescapable cycle of suffering if one does not use pain constructively, grow from it, and move beyond it.[16] Suffering is undigested pain.

Although the journey into the underworld, the time spent there, and the journey out of the underworld is unique for each individual, we can gain insight from the experiences of others who have journeyed there before us. We can also learn from our own experiences during previous visits. With each successive visit, we learn something new and gain new insight. And if we utilize our time in the underworld constructively, each trip can make us a little tougher, a little stronger, and a little more confident in our ability to survive the experience and to emerge from the depths with greater wisdom. As Esther Harding argues in *Woman's Mysteries: Ancient and Modern*, to engage in a periodic psychological withdrawal from the demands of external life and nurture our inner life produces a healing effect in which our inner and outer lives find at least a temporary reconciliation.[17]

The fundamental concept that determines the outcome of our journeys to the underworld is agency. Life is constantly throwing hurdles in our direction over which we may have little or no control. The circumstances that sent us plummeting to the underworld may have been unavoidable and traumatic. However, what we do once we get there is a question of agency. In the words of Jean Shinoda Bolen in *Goddesses in Older Women*, we can become "choicemakers" and assume the role of protagonists in our own life story.[18] Or not. We can choose to allow others to continue to make decisions for us; we can choose to allow the circumstances to overwhelm us; or we can choose to exercise agency and take control of our lives. Either way, we are making a choice. However, the first two choices trap us in a quagmire of victimization and powerlessness; the third choice in which we exercise agency and become "choicemakers" in our own lives opens up the doors for empowerment, health, growth, transformation, and new life.

At the end of the Homeric *Hymn to Demeter*, we are told that Demeter returns to Eleusis and teaches the people her mysteries. Homer describes the mysteries with the following words:

> ...holy rites that are not to be transgressed, nor pried into,
> nor divulged. For a great awe of the gods stops the voice.
> Blessed is the mortal on earth who has seen these rites,
> but the initiate who has no share in them never
> has the same lot once dead in the dreary darkness.
> (Lines 478–482)

Blessed, indeed, was the mortal who witnessed these rites. And blessed is the mortal who experiences the depths in all its pain, suffering, and loneliness, and who emerges as a result of the experience stronger, wiser, and more powerful—in short, as one who has experienced the privilege of successfully undergoing the death, transformation, and rebirth that constitute the seductive lure of the underworld.

Having deconstructed the underworld, let us now turn our attention to the god of that realm—and, not coincidentally—our abductor, Hades. As Christine Downing in *The Long Journey Home: Re-Visioning the Myth of Demeter and Persephone for Our Time* tells us, Hades represents both the male as rapist and the male as agent of self-discovery.[19] He forcibly separates Perse-phone from her old self and her mother. At the same time, he provides Persephone with the opportunity to gain a new understanding of herself and exercise her own agency by encouraging her to take the first step that will propel her in the direction of realizing her potential. Furthermore, he makes it possible for her to forge a new relationship with her mother, one that is not based on need and dependency but on cooperation, equality, and autonomy.

It is important to note that the Hades we encounter at the end of the Homeric *Hymn to Demeter* differs significantly from the Hades we encoun-tered at the beginning. As we shall see below, Hades experiences change and growth. This change and growth can only be attributed to his interac-tion with Persephone during her tenure in the underworld since nothing else new has happened to him. Initially, Hades sees what he wants in the young Kore, snatches her without seeking her consent, rapes her, and declares her his bride. Throughout this initial stage, Kore's permission has not been sought or given. Hades engages in typical patriarchal behavior that reflects typical patriarchal attitudes. He conforms to sadistic behavior as Susan Griffin defines it in *Pornography and Silence*: he doesn't seek permis-sion from but takes possession of the other, and his goal is domination and control—not closeness or union.[20]

But after having spent a year with Persephone in the underworld, Hades' treatment of her and his attitude towards her reflects a major change. By the end of the poem, he appears to be taking into consideration her feel-ings, validating her sense of being wrongfully treated, deeming her worthy of persuasion, and communicating with her respectfully. In short, before he releases her, Hades seems to be treating Persephone as his equal. This is a far cry from the Hades we encountered at the beginning of the poem who appropriates what he wants when he wants it with the cavalier attitude of patriarchal entitlement. Hades has apparently changed during Perse-phone's tenure with him in the underworld. His dialogue and actions illus-trate that his encounter with the feminine force she embodies has had a positive impact on him. It has enabled him to connect with the feminine in his life and render him a more complete individual.

Hades is unique among Greek male deities in that by the time we encounter him in his deathly realm at the end of the poem, he has assumed many "feminine" traits. He exhibits a degree of androgyny that is not evi-dent in either Zeus or Helios. First of all, before releasing her, he feeds Persephone. By doing so, he performs a role traditionally associated with women. As Christine Downing has observed in *The Goddess: Mythological Images of the Feminine*, food is associated with women because not only were they responsible for cultivating it and preparing it, but also because their bodies were a source of food and of life.[21] Through her breasts, the female is able to provide both physical and psychological nourishment and comfort to new life. And in life as in death, nothing can change or grow without being fed or without serving as a source of food for others.

Additionally, the female has been affiliated with the power of transformation. Until our ancestors made the connection between male insemination and female fertility, it was believed that women alone had the mysterious ability to transform their own blood into new life. In fact, as Kathryn Rabuzzi observes in *Motherself: A Mythic Analysis of Motherhood*, out of the half million to million years of humanoid existence, humans understood the concept of paternity only within the last 12,000 years.[22] This means that the role of the male in the creation of new life is a relatively new discovery. The female, perceived as the sole creator of life, was a powerful entity in her own right. The goddess was parthenogenetic. Pre-patriarchal cultures, therefore, worshipped the female because of her reproductive capacities, because of her inexplicable ability to give birth to a being that was like her (a female child) and different from her (a male child), and because, through her breasts, she had the ability to transform her internal fluids into nourishment for her newborn infant.

Through their bodies, women transform raw material into new life. Through their bodily fluids, they transform raw material into sustenance. Through their cultivation of crops and cooking, they transform raw material into food. Through their weaving and sewing, they transform raw material into clothing. Through their shaping and baking, they transform raw material into containers and utensils for transporting and serving food. It was perfectly logical, therefore, for our ancestors to assume that women, since they were responsible for transformations that took place within the physical realm, were also responsible for transformations that took place within the spiritual realm. Just as a woman gives birth to new life in the form of an infant, so, too, she is the gateway for our own spiritual rebirth. Since women traditionally were—and still are—associated with transformation, in his role as the agent that precipitates Persephone's transformation, Hades further illustrates his androgynous qualities.

Hades' uniqueness among male deities is reinforced by his adoption of the feminine role of the transformational agent. He becomes the instrument that guides us to our own underworld to explore our own depths. And as the god of the underworld, the fertile womb where transformation takes place, Hades becomes our "caretaker," our surrogate mother. In this respect, his role parallels the role of his female counterparts: Hekate, Iambe, Metaneira, and Rheia. By assisting Persephone as she undergoes the difficult experience of giving birth to herself, Hades assumes the role of a midwife.

Hades further deviates from his male counterparts, Zeus and Helios, in that he apparently takes into consideration Persephone's emotions. He recognizes she has been hurt and is experiencing feelings of pain and betrayal. At the same time, however, he tries to comfort her by suggesting that she curb her anger. In the process of doing so, he validates the legitimacy of her feelings. He tells her:

> "Go, Persephone, to the side of your dark-robed mother,
> keeping the spirit and temper in your breast benign.
> Do not be so sad and angry beyond the rest."
>
> (Lines 360–362)

By acknowledging Persephone's sadness and anger at her abduction and violation, Hades performs the same role that Metaneira had performed earlier for Demeter: he validates her right to experience sadness and anger at what has been done to her. But unlike Helios when he counsels Demeter, Hades does not negate or trivialize Persephone's feelings of loss and violation. He does not approach her with the cavalier attitude of, "You can't do anything about it now, so get over it and move on." Instead, he acknowledges the existence of her emotions as legitimate, inevitable, and necessary for the healing process.

The masculinist tendency to negate or repress emotions begins very early on in the socialization process of males within patriarchy. In their landmark study on the American educational system, *Failing at Fairness: How America's Schools Cheat Girls*, Myra and David Sadker expose the gender inequities in America's schools through analyzing data accumulated during a decade of classroom observation and research. They conclude that although they are sitting in the same classroom, reading the same assignments, and listening to the same teachers, boys and girls are receiving very different educations. According to the Sadkers, this inequity begins in grade school and continues through graduate school.[23]

Although the primary focus of their work is on gender inequity in education where it has its most pervasive impact on the development of girls, the Sadkers also observe that gender inequity in education can have an adverse impact on the development of boys. Their research demonstrates that boys submit to social and cultural pressures to purge themselves of any hint of femininity for fear of being ostracized or exposed to cruel epithets by their male peers. Unfortunately, parents, teachers, and other adults frequently reinforce these social stigmas by discouraging boys from engaging in behavior associated with girls. According to the Sadkers, this can have a devastating impact on the development of boys. Since everyone, male and female alike, can benefit from the healthy expression of emotions as well as the experience of caring for and nurturing others, when these opportunities are denied to boys, it causes them to disengage from their own emotions.[24] The Sadkers

argue that when socially constructed masculinities valorize risk-taking, violence, and sexual aggression while simultaneously belittling care-taking activities and the nurturing of oneself and others, the distorted profile that
emerges can be detrimental to the healthy development of males and to the
development of a good society.[25]

The uncanny thing about emotions is that they don't go away. But they
can be buried temporarily. However, if emotions are not addressed appropriately, they may eventually surface in ways that can be violent, destructive, and horrifying—as the recent spate of male-perpetrated school killings
serve to remind us. In many ways, the work of Myra and David Sadker has,
unfortunately, proved to be prophetic.

Emotions must be acknowledged and addressed appropriately. But that
does not mean that they should not be given free reign to dictate our behavior. Hence, while acknowledging the legitimacy of Persephone's feelings,
Hades also cautions her not to allow those feelings to overwhelm her by
abdicating control over her own spirit and temper: "Do not be so sad and
angry beyond the rest." In other words, Hades is promoting balance: legitimate emotions tempered with rational control. Once again, this sets Hades
apart from Zeus and Helios who advocate reason to the total exclusion of
emotions. Hades guides Persephone to an understanding of the importance
of balance, a lesson her mother does not learn until after the episode with
Demophoon.

Furthermore, the fact that Hades tries to convince Persephone to
view him as a suitable spouse indicates a recognition on his part that she
is not only someone who is worthy of convincing but that she is someone who needs to be mollified—which means he understands that he is
guilty of inflicting pain on her and is now trying to make amends. His words
further indicate his recognition that Persephone now has the freedom to
choose to accept him or reject him—a choice that he initially denied her.
Agency is in her hands. Hades understands that it is not the abduction
or the rape that guarantees Persephone's return to the underworld. It is
her tacit agreement to swallow the food that he offers her from the land of
the dead. She can reject the pomegranate seed, in which case he will be
deprived of her company forever. Or she can swallow the pomegranate seed,
in which case he will be assured of her company for at least a few months
of the year.

Just as in the case of his brother Zeus, Hades wants something that
only the female can give him. Zeus wants Demeter to abandon her strangulation of the earth. Hades wants Persephone to join him in the land of
the dead—even if it is only for a few months of the whole year. Both male
gods want something from a female goddess. But unlike Zeus who, as we
saw earlier, shows no remorse, no recognition of his wrongdoing, nor any

acknowledgement of his role in causing the catastrophic events, Hades approaches the female with humility that comes from acknowledging the pain and hurt he has caused her while, at the same time, asking her not to allow these feelings—justified though they are—to overwhelm her. His behavior here reflects a sensitivity and compassion that is entirely absent in the words and behavior of Helios or Zeus. Furthermore, his attitude and approach differ markedly from Zeus' handling of Demeter. Zeus doesn't seem to get it; Hades eventually does.

In many respects, when we encounter Hades and Persephone in the underworld, we see him treating her as an equal. If he viewed her as his subordinate, as an object to be dispensed with as he sees fit, why would he even bother to comfort her or to try to convince her of his suitability as her spouse? He would just bark his orders in the manner of Zeus. He would treat her the way he treated her while she was in her Kore aspect: as an object to be appropriated without consideration for her feelings or her pain. But Hades knows that the Persephone who has spent a year with him in the underworld has been impacted by her tenure there. She is no longer the weak, naïve, and innocent victim she once was before she entered the under-world. She is now Persephone, an empowered female with the potential to exercise her own agency and capable of inflicting pain on him by leaving him. And there is not a thing he can do any more to force her to abide by his wishes.

So he addresses her in a conciliatory tone—speaking to her as his equal, trying to cajole her to his side:

> "Do not be so sad and angry beyond the rest;
> in no way among immortals will I be an unsuitable spouse,
> myself a brother of father Zeus."
>
> (Lines 362–364)

Hades sounds almost like a suitor, approaching his would-be bride with words affirming his suitability and credentials to be her spouse.

Hades further distinguishes himself from his male counterparts in that he deems Persephone to be worthy of direct communication and as an individual who is capable of being educated. So he tells her of her strength and power.

> "And when you are there,
> you will have the power over all that lives and moves,
> and you will possess the greatest honors among the gods.
> There will be punishment forevermore for those wrongdoers
> who fail to appease your power with sacrifices,
> performing proper rites and making due offerings."
>
> (Lines 364–369)

Perceiving her as someone capable of learning and growing, Hades takes on the role of her teacher. He educates her on the extent of her power. By doing this, he assumes another role that is traditionally ascribed to females since, for the most part, women are the ones who continue to perform the overwhelming majority of tasks associated with the education and rearing of children.

In *Life's Daughter/Death's Bride*, Kathie Carlson provides a similar reading of Hades as experiencing transformation. In the process of deconstructing Hades and the Hades-identified man, Carlson argues that at some deep level, Hades is aware that he needs the feminine to complete him and to connect him with life.[26] So he behaves in a way that conforms to patriarchal definitions of masculinity: he snatches Kore with violence and aggression because that is the only way he knows how to gain her as his bride. But after spending a year with Persephone in the underworld, Hades has apparently been initiated into the ways of the feminine. He has disengaged from the patriarchal perspective of power *over* the female and has replaced it with a balanced perspective of power *with* the female. Just as he has acted as the guide who facilitates Persephone's transformation from the naïve Kore to the empowered queen of the underworld, Persephone has acted as the guide who assists him in making the transition from an unequivocal adherence to the patriarchal image of masculinity to a newly constructed image of masculinity, one that integrates the feminine within its boundaries and experiences wholeness as a consequence.

In *Pornography and Silence*, Susan Griffin deconstructs pornography and the pornographic. She argues that pornography is an expression of human fear of bodily knowledge and desire and constitutes an attempt to silence the erotic—a love of life and body.[27] When a man sexually objectifies a woman for the purpose of destroying her spirit and humiliating her, he is acting pornographically.[28] In the process, according to Griffin, the pornographer also seeks to humiliate, punish, and possibly destroy that part of himself that experiences feelings, the body, and knowledge of the body from which those feelings emanate.[29] Ultimately, Griffin argues, the pornographer seeks to reject a part of himself and to exclude from his self-image that which is feminine since the pornographic culture fuels a rejection of nature, flesh, feelings, body, and sexuality—all of which are associated with the female and the feminine.[30]

Using Griffin's distinctions, one can argue that Hades moves from the pornographic mode of behavior, which seeks to control, dominate, and degrade the female and the feminine within, to the erotic, which seeks to embrace the female and the feminine within in order to arrive at wholeness. Hades' recognition of a void in his life leads to his abduction of Kore as a means of filling that void. Initially, he operates according to the pornographic mode because no alternative mode of behavior is available to him. But as a result of his year-long interaction with Persephone, he relinquishes his desire for domination of the female and the feminine and replaces it with the erotic mode of conduct—one which fosters the life-giving force that propels us to experience feelings, wholeness, love, and community and that engenders in others the ability to experience the same.

We know that the Eleusinian Mysteries appealed to both men and women. The appeal it held for women is obvious since the myth privileges the female position and deals with perennial female concerns centered on the bond between mother and child and the nature of community. But the appeal it held for men is not so readily apparent. We know that all the initiates, male and female alike, adopted feminine names and assumed the role of Demeter. And we know that as a result of their participation in the rites, initiates arrived at a new understanding of themselves and of the meaning of life and of death.

In *Gender War, Gender Peace*, Aaron Kipnis and Elizabeth Herron argue that men and women receive different behavioral training beginning with their infancy. Our cultural conditioning leads to feelings of dependency and disenfranchisement for many women; it leads to disengagement from feelings, inability to engage in self-care, and disenfranchisement from family and community in many men.[31] According to Kipnis and Herron, our conditioning has empowered men and women in dissimilar ways: women develop greater capacity for experiencing emotions, cultivating relationships, and engaging in care-giving and nurturing of others; men develop greater capacity for behaving independently, for thinking logically, for negating pain, and for engaging in goal-directed activity.[31]

Again, the issue becomes one of balance. The qualities enumerated by Kipnis and Herron are desirable and should be cultivated in every human being, regardless of gender, to be called upon as the need arises. Participation in the Eleusinian Mysteries helped to develop these qualities since the rituals exposed initiates to gender-coded qualities and behaviors in order to liberate those qualities and behaviors from their gendered associations. The mysteries encouraged the integration and internalization of desirable and empowering qualities and behaviors in all participants. Furthermore, they facilitated the transcendence of socially constructed gender norms in order to diminish alienation and cultivate wholeness.

Pertinent to this discussion is Barbara McManus' description of a transgendered moment or behavior as she articulates it in *Classics and Feminism: Gendering the Classics*. McManus defines transgendered moments or behaviors as those that are still governed by gender expectations and gender power differentials but that have now been adopted by both men and women and considered to be appropriate for both. However, McManus cautions us that such moments or behaviors are not interpreted and evaluated according to the same set of standards when performed by the different sexes.[32] Women who seek to negotiate or appropriate a transgendered space for themselves are perceived to be striving for that which is powerful and which has been socially defined as having greater value and superiority.[33] The issue is far more complex and conflicted for men who seek to appropriate transgendered space because they run the risk of provoking accusations of weakness, inferiority, and effeminacy.[33] McManus' discussion sheds light on the difficulties some men may encounter in their attempts to embrace a masculinity that accommodates and assimilates those qualities conducive to wholeness but violate socially constructed norms of masculinities since they have been stereotypically ascribed to the province of the female.

The male initiate in the Eleusinian Mysteries required to assume the guise of a mother grieving for her lost child and then experience reunification with that child is being made to experience life through a feminine lens. In similar fashion to Hades who is initiated into the ways of the feminine as a result of his interaction with Persephone, the male initiate experiences a corresponding initiation into the feminine perspective through his participation in the rites. In this respect, Hades becomes the role model for all male initiates who are steeped in patriarchal tradition but who recognize it to be limited, narrow, and unremittingly destructive of individual and collective life. He holds out the possibility that transformation and wholeness is possible for those who are willing to relinquish rigid patriarchal constructs of masculinity in favor of masculinities that embrace and acknowledge the feminine as equal partners in life. The death of old perceptions and the birth of new ones remains a possibility for everyone in the underworld—male and female alike.

Hades is unique among the male gods in that he adopts feminine qualities and assumes a feminine role. As such, he plays a constructive role in Persephone's process of individuation. But as much as one may wish to applaud Hades for his role in facilitating Persephone's transformation, for his apparent burgeoning sense of compassion for Persephone, for acknowledging his role in inflicting pain and suffering on her, and for his ultimate embrace of the feminine, one must not lose sight of the fact that Hades has initiated Persephone by kidnapping her and violating her bodily integrity through brutal rape. This is a subject we will explore in our next chapter.

CHAPTER 8

Rape

And now we come to the difficult subject of rape. In order to explore the role and significance of Persephone's rape in this story, we must address the not unrelated issues of the function, meaning, and impact of rape; the role of rape in mythology; and rape as a possible metaphor for psychological transformation.

It should be stated at the outset that the physical act of rape—the forcible bodily penetration of one human being by another—has little to do with sex and everything to do with power over another individual. Rape is the sexual expression of a violent act perpetrated by an individual or individuals for the purpose of exerting power over, dominating, subjugating, and humiliating the victim. It is an abominable act that has nothing to do with an uncontrollable drive to satisfy sexual urges. If a woman chooses not to engage in sexual intercourse with a man and he chooses to force himself on her, then he is committing the act of rape. It bears repeating that this holds true regardless of what the victim may or may not have been wearing at the time, regardless of the nature of any of her previous sexual encounters with that man or with any other man, and regardless of the nature of the relationship between the victim and the perpetrator of the rape. Rape constitutes a violation of the bodily integrity of a human being. Simply put, rape is sexualized violence.

The proclivity to commit rape signifies a distinguishing feature of the human species. Elaine Morgan reminds us in *The Descent of Woman* that every piece of evidence concerning animal behavior confirms that the sexual drive in animals is a mutual affair that both partners feel the need to satisfy and that both experience as a consummatory act. However, *Homo sapiens* are the only mammals where the female experiences the dubious distinction of being mated against her will. For the rest of the animal kingdom, the female must be a willing partner before copulation can proceed. As Morgan succinctly tells us, monkeys don't commit rape.[1] In some species the female's willingness seems even more apparent than the male's. So in this instance, at least, our evolution to the position of the most advanced species on the planet seems to be less of a case of progression and more of a case of regression: we have the unique distinction of engaging in anomalous, abhorrent behavior that is not evidenced anywhere else in the animal kingdom.

In *Against Our Will: Men, Women, and Rape*, Susan Brownmiller's comprehensive and influential study on the subject of rape, Brownmiller speculates that the first rape ever committed probably consisted of an unexpected battle caused by the first woman's refusal to submit to the male's sexual advances.[2] However, if the first rape was stumbled upon, the second and all subsequent rapes were, in the words of Brownmiller, "indubitably planned."[2] Brownmiller postulates that gang rape of a woman was probably one of the earliest forms of male bonding.[2] Rape became a male prerogative; male genitalia became a universal weapon of force against woman, generating fear.[2] Brownmiller argues that rape is a conscious and deliberate attempt on the part of all men to intimidate all women and to keep them in a state of fear.[2] She draws a parallel between rape and lynching: rape as the ultimate physical threat by which all men are able to keep all women in a state of psychological intimidation in much the same way that lynching kept all blacks in a state of psychological intimidation.[3]

As we saw earlier, patriarchy designates women as the property of males. Because of this, when rape eventually came to be considered a crime, it was initially conceived of as a crime perpetrated by one man against another man's property—a violation of his rights.[4] The fact that rape violated the bodily integrity of the female and constituted a violent crime against her was not even open to consideration until many centuries later. According to Brownmiller, the female was, in fact, the male's first piece of tangible property. Once this male ownership of the female had been firmly established, it was followed by other forms of ownership in which the male expanded his territory to include possession of their offspring, of slaves, and of property. The subjugation and ownership of the female, therefore, constituted the foundation block of what was later to become the patriarchy.[5]

Rape serves several functions: it is a means by which a male can physically and brutally exert his power over another human being; it is a means of subordinating a female and of forcing her to submit to male hegemony;

it is a sexual means of manifesting aggression; it is a means of violating the psychic and bodily integrity of the victim for the purpose of inflicting pain, humiliation, degradation, and trauma; and it is a means of keeping all women in a state of fear and apprehension. Regardless of whether a woman has ever experienced rape, she will modify her behavior based on the knowledge that she is susceptible to this violation because of her gender.

Historically and currently, rape serves the additional function of humiliating and degrading the opposing side in times of war. The nature of the war—whether it is fought for religious, political, or economic gain—is irrelevant. War has always been accompanied by rape. War provides men with the perfect excuse to release their anger, pent-up frustration, and contempt for women in general and for the enemy in particular. As Ruth Seifert has argued in "War and Rape: A Preliminary Analysis," in the context of war, rape represents the ultimate means by which to humiliate the male opponent.[6] It is designed to expose and reinforce the vulnerabilities of adversaries since they are unable to serve as protectors for their women. Since patriarchy has assigned the role of protector to the male, any male who is unable to fulfill that function is automatically emasculated. In other words, during times of war, the sexual violation of women is used as a means to an end—the end being the forcible subjugation of the female and the corresponding erosion of the opponent's masculinity. In the words of Brownmiller, "The body of a raped woman becomes a ceremonial battlefield, a parade ground for the victor's trooping of the colors."[7]

In *The Creation of Patriarchy*, Gerda Lerner demonstrates that the practice of raping the women of a defeated army has been an intricate part of warfare and conquest from the second millennium B.C.E.[8] Then, as now, its purpose was twofold: it served to humiliate and degrade women and, by extension, it served as a means of symbolically castrating men since they were unable to preserve the sexual purity of their women folk.[8] Lerner argues that the sexual enslavement of captive women was an essential step in what was later to become the patriarchal system. According to Lerner, the sequence was as follows: men learned to exert sexual control over women within their own group; then they learned to exert it over captive women of other groups; and then they exerted it over captive men of other groups.[9] In other words, the enslavement of a people, the system of hierarchies in which a privileged group exerts total domination and control over all aspects of the lives of members designated as subordinate, began with the enslavement of women. In the words of Lerner, "Sexual dominance underlies class and race dominance."[10]

The literature and mythology of classical Greece is littered with examples of women being carted off as spoils for the victor to serve in the roles of concubines or sex slaves. Women were perceived as part of the loot to be plundered, apportioned out, and distributed to the leaders and to the rank and file of a victorious army. In Homer's *Iliad*, for example, the opening quarrel between Agamemnon and Achilles was over just such a situation. Agamemnon is asked to return his female prize, the Trojan Chryseis, to her father in order to appease the god Apollo. He agrees to do so, but only after he has been suitably compensated with a substitute female. Since all the booty had already been apportioned out, and since Agamemnon felt it was unfair that he alone should be without a concubine, he decides to appropriate for himself Achilles' concubine, Briseis, and to make her his own sexual slave. Agamemnon's conduct is interpreted by the Greek army exactly as he means it to be: as an affront to Achilles and as a challenge to his masculinity. It is this wrangling over the distribution of the female as booty, the appropriation of one man's "property" by another, that ultimately causes Achilles to withdraw temporarily from the war against the Trojans, a decision that has disastrous consequences for the Greek army.

For many centuries and throughout different parts of the world, this forcible sexual subjugation of women was treated as a natural by-product of war and was a means of rewarding loyal soldiers. A victorious army tramples through defeated enemy territory, raping and pillaging the land and every thing and every one on it. According to Brownmiller, during medieval times when the common foot soldier was paid with irregularity, one means of rewarding him was to allow him free access to rape and loot as he pleased.[11] Eventually, however, talk of rape in war became increasingly distasteful in polite society. It became a dirty little secret, the existence of which no one wanted to acknowledge. But incidents of rape did not disappear. Rape simply went underground, and the occurrence of the mass rapes that continued in wars either went unreported, underreported, or treated as isolated phenomena.

It is only in recent times—particularly after the occurrence of mass rapes in Bosnia—that rape has been exposed as an instrument of war, punishable with the full force of international law. Through the United Nations war crimes tribunal at The Hague, the international community has finally come to recognize rape as a weapon of war and as a crime against humanity. In the year 2001, through its conviction of some Bosnian Serb soldiers for the systematic rape and torture of Muslim women and girls during the 1992–1995 war in Bosnia, the war crimes tribunal took a giant leap forward in recognizing rape in war for what it is: a crime against humanity and one that should be punished by the full force of international law. Rapes have always occurred in wars and will probably continue to do so for many years to come. But at least now there is a glimmering of hope that perpetrators will not be allowed to engage in this barbaric practice with such impunity.

Rape can also serve as a means of attacking or undermining a culture or an ideology. In *When God Was a Woman*, Merlin Stone affirms that goddess-centered religions were ubiquitous in the ancient world. Eventually, these were overcome by the competing ideology of patriarchy, an ideology that was transported and transplanted by Indo-Europeans, a northern people who worshipped male deities.[12] In their incursions into goddess-worshipping communities, Indo-Europeans had to combat an ideology that was antithetical to the hierarchical, blade-oriented, male-god worshipping, dominator ideology that they espoused.

One means at the disposal of the patriarchy to weaken an ancient and well-established ideology was through appropriating the powers and the sacred shrines of this older, goddess-worshipping culture for its own male sky gods. And patriarchy did just that. Another means was through rape. Elinor Gadon observes in *The Once and Future Goddess* that rape metaphorically depicts the patriarchal suppression and appropriation of the goddess and her culture in addition to demonstrating the change in attitudes towards women.[13]

The transition from a goddess-worshipping ideology to a god-worshipping ideology was characterized by violent incursions, brutal massacres, and territorial conquests. In *Living in the Lap of the Goddess*, in which she articulates the principles of the feminist spirituality movement in America, Cynthia Eller claims that many spiritual feminists express frank puzzlement as to why and how the patriarchal revolution took place.[14] Although a variety of hypotheses have been proposed, most spiritual feminists agree that the first steps towards the establishment of patriarchy occurred as a series of violent invasions in which the indigenous peoples were murdered, raped, or forced into slavery.[15] But, as Eller indicates, such tactics can succeed only in the short run. In the long run, patriarchy could only succeed in gaining control of a people by gaining control of their thinking. Patriarchal indoctrination, therefore, took the form of rewriting goddess mythology to portray the goddess in a diminished and weakened state; transferring her power to male deities; demonizing her; minimizing her role in procreation; and killing her off.[15]

The battle that led to the demise of goddess-worshipping communities was consequently waged on many fronts and frequently evidenced in the culture's mythology. In fact, as Merlin Stone proposes in *When God Was a Woman*, the mythology of a culture records the "intricate interlacing of two theological concepts." One was espoused by the indigenous people, and the other was transported by the Indo-Europeans.[16] In *Life's Daughter/Death's Bride*, Kathie Carlson argues that the myth of Demeter and Persephone can be seen as a transitional myth in that it depicts the tensions and oppositions of two competing ideologies with both sides having to compromise and with neither side having yet emerged as the clear victor.[17] Eventually, though, mythology was to record the attitudes and perceptions that led to the suppression of goddess worship and to the victory of patriarchal ideology.

The plethora of rapes committed by the gods in the Greek pantheon served the additional function of undermining the culture and ideology of goddess-worshipping communities. In this case, stories of the rape of female deities or heroines by male gods constitute a mythological rendition of the demotion and subjugation of the powers of the goddess—a necessary component of the war waged against women by patriarchy since it depicts the goddess as powerless to overcome her own violation. And if the goddess cannot protect herself, how can she be called upon to protect other females?

The issue is one of control of the female by a male hegemonic power structure. The message delivered by patriarchy is loud and clear: women are to be stripped of agency. They are powerless to protect themselves or each other and need the assistance of males to ward off attacks from other marauding males. And the price patriarchy exacts from females for this protection is steep: their total subjugation and subordination to the males in their lives and to a system that, by its very nature, is designed to oppress them and reproduce the means for their subordination.

Regardless of the specific circumstances, in all cases of rape, the female body is used as a vehicle, a means to an end, a bridge the perpetrator crosses to arrive at his destination. The destination may vary: the desire to feel assertive, in control, and powerful; the desire to humiliate one's enemy in times of war; the desire to weaken and transplant one ideology with another; the desire to suppress opposition and dissent through fear and the threat of violence; the desire to weaken and humiliate; the desire to inflict pain; the desire to vent one's anger and frustration; the desire to claim ownership; or a combination of some or all of these. Regardless of the goal, however, the vehicle is the same: the oppression and brutal violation of the bodily and psychic integrity of another human being, usually a female, to achieve the desired end.

As the bastion of patriarchy on Mount Olympus, Zeus spends much of his time raping at will. By doing so, he demonstrates his feelings of absolute entitlement to the female body. The only concession he occasionally makes is to disguise himself as an animal in order to prevent his wife, Hera, from knowing of his shenanigans. But even here he shows his abject contempt for the female: his attempts at disguise are frequently half-hearted, cavalier, and not entirely successful. And once he has satiated his appetite with the helpless victim who has had the dubious distinction of being the object of his desire, Zeus frequently stalks off without even giving her so much as a perfunctory, "Thank you, ma'am."

Patriarchy will squash any attempt at female empowerment or female resistance to male oppression. But the problem goes even deeper than that. The hand of patriarchy deals with any effort on the part of a female to connect with her inner source of power, her Eros, and to experience that power in all its manifestations, including her sexuality, with swiftness and brutality. Eros, as defined by Audre Lorde in *Sister Outsider*, is a woman's assertion of her life force, all aspects of her creative energy (including sexual energy) that propel her to actualize her potential.[18] According to Lorde, experiencing the erotic in our lives brings us internal satisfaction and empowerment.[19] In other words, the erotic functions in a manner that is diametrically opposed to the pornographic since the latter serves to demean and debilitate and fragment.[20] Feminine Eros threatens patriarchy. In *Archetypal Patterns in Women's Fiction*, Annis Pratt, Barbara White, Andrea Lowenstein, and Mary Wyer argue that within patriarchal constructs, women heroes who seek erotic freedom—the freedom to exercise choice in their lives—have to contend with the full force of patriarchal opposition. Accordingly, patriarchy not only discourages feminine Eros, but it posits rape as a substitute.[21]

As we have seen, the Homeric *Hymn to Demeter* is a story about transformation. A transformation can usually take place in one of two ways: either the heroine or hero experiences a sudden, cataclysmic event that precipitates immediate metamorphosis; or metamorphosis occurs after a long, arduous struggle in which self-knowledge and insight gradually seep into the consciousness of the individual. Occasionally, the two types of transformation occur in the same story. More often than not, however, the cataclysmic event acts as the catalyst for precipitating a journey to the underworld in which self-knowledge and insight slowly ooze their way into our pores, into the very fiber of our being. The motion can be so slow that we are hardly conscious of our own transformation even while it is occurring.

Demeter's metamorphosis, as we saw in a previous chapter, occurs gradually and is precipitated by the abduction of her daughter. Persephone's metamorphosis is precipitated by the cataclysmic event of her abduction and rape. However, unlike what occurs in the case of Demeter, we are not given access to Persephone's process of transformation. We see her before the abduction, and we see her just prior to her release from the underworld. But by the time we encounter her in the underworld, she has already experienced a metamorphosis of sorts: she has transformed from the young, naïve, virginal girl to a mature and empowered female who is eager and ready to seize the opportunity to become her own person, an autonomous entity in her own right. Persephone has become connected with her own erotic power and is able to manifest this power through her decisions and actions.

As a result of her abduction and rape in the underworld, Kore experiences an irrevocable transformation. She crosses the threshold from the young, innocent, and virginal maiden who is tied to her mother's apron strings to Persephone who is queen of the underworld, powerful, autonomous, and feared. Somehow, this transformation has to be thoroughly cemented in her being. It also has to be irrevocable so that she is denied the option of regressing to her infantile state of dependency on mother, regardless of how much she may wish to do so. The transformation is manifested in her rape.

According to Bruce Lincoln in *Emerging from the Chrysalis: Rituals of Women's Initiation*, initiation through rape is a typical pattern of many male-centered, misogynist cultures. [22] Kore has been initiated through rape and there is no going back. No matter how hard Persephone or her mother tries, neither can undo the rape/transformation. As Tanya Wilkinson has argued in *Persephone Returns: Victims, Heroes, and the Journey from the Underworld*, Persephone's rape demonstrates that some tears in the fabric of life can never be mended; some directions taken in life—even those that were not chosen or that occurred as a result of circumstances beyond our control— can never be reversed because the self is irrevocably transformed by them. [23] Persephone can never go back to being un-raped; Persephone can never undo her transformation.

In order to understand fully the role of rape in the story of Persephone, rape has to be placed within the context of its time and culture. According to Brownmiller in *Against Our Will*, the earliest form of establishing a permanent bond between a male and a female, a bond that later culminated in the institution of marriage, appears to have come about through the male's forcible abduction and rape of the female chosen for the dubious distinction of being his bride. [24] This practice was known as bride capture. Through a violent penetration of her body, the male was able to stake his claim for her person in much the same way that a man penetrates the earth with his nation's flag, thereby claiming territory for himself or for the glory of king and country. Again, according to Brownmiller, men viewed this forcible seizure as a perfectly acceptable way of acquiring women. The practice existed in England into the fifteenth century. [24]

It bears repeating that Persephone's abduction and rape by Hades is a heinous act. It constitutes a violation of the bodily and psychic integrity of the young girl. In its initial stages, patriarchy may have viewed this as an acceptable method of selecting a bride, but it wouldn't be unreasonable to assume that even in those times, women espoused a different opinion of this abominable practice—as evidenced by Kore's shriek for help and her mother's reaction. However, the patriarchal context is what we have to work with, and the Homeric *Hymn to Demeter* is steeped in patriarchal tradition. If placed within its cultural context, Hades' abduction and rape of the young girl lies well within the acceptable patriarchal norms of his society. Viewed through the historical and cultural lens of the time, it was a logical means for obtaining a bride. It is only when we view this practice through a modern lens that we recoil with horror.

It is a scathing indictment of our society that all too many people have experienced rape and know it to be a traumatic event that can devastate a human being for life. The cultural and historical contextualization of Kore's rape in the preceding paragraph is not intended to trivialize the experience of rape or to justify abduction and rape. It is merely an attempt to place Hades' action in a cultural and historical framework and to demonstrate that the prevailing ideology of the time did not view this abominable act in the way that it is currently viewed in many parts of the world today.

As abhorrent as this practice is when viewed through a modern lens, it behooves us to acknowledge, however, that to this day, communities throughout the world continue to deny women the right to exercise control over their own bodies; continue to promote the male's right to appropriate the female body in whatever way he deems suitable; endorse rape as a legitimate means to marriage; and not only allow the rapist to go unpunished but seek to punish or mutilate the victimized female.

Rape is the only crime in which the victims are required to prove that they resisted the attack. As Susan Brownmiller argues in *Against Our Will*, victims of robbery and assault are not asked to provide evidence of their resistance, or evidence that their consent was withheld, or evidence that the criminal exerted sufficient force or threat of sufficient force that they had no choice but to acquiesce to the criminal's demand.[25] In fact, in cases of robbery, the police encourage the victim to submit to the criminal's demands, report the crime, and then turn the matter over to the justice system. The prevailing view is that if one can emerge from a robbery or an attempted assault relatively unscathed, one should consider oneself lucky.

But rape is handled differently. The victim is asked to provide evidence that she resisted. Her sexual history is put on trial. Her lifestyle is put on trial. Her clothing is put on trial. The nature of her relationship with the rapist is examined and cross-examined. In short, in cases of rape, the burden of proof that a crime has been committed is firmly placed on the shoulders of the victim. The fact that most rapes go unreported can be partially—if not wholly—attributed to a legal system that in many ways continues to be a hostile environment for victims of rape. However, in spite of the difficulties that a woman can encounter in reporting a rape, she should try to pursue justice since, as Audre Lorde reminds us in *Sister Outsider*, her silence will not protect her.[26]

Rape and the threat of rape as an instrument of patriarchy can flourish only if we continue to keep silent about its occurrence. It bears repeating that a pernicious impact of patriarchy is the disruption or severing of female bonding. Females are socialized to internalize blame and to experience shame and guilt in cases of domestic violence, sexual harassment, or sexual assault. Feelings of shame and self-blame hamper their ability to connect with other females and to discover the commonality of their experiences. The situation is further exacerbated by the fact that females in patriarchy frequently are haunted by the specter of seeking male validation to the exclusion of all else.

An example of this is illustrated in Athena Devlin's "The Shame of Silence" in which Devlin narrates her experience of being sexually assaulted by a football player in her high school.[27] Devlin observes that the experience generated a series of consequences: it served to solidify male bonding because other members of the football team were permitted to view the assault—which meant that it had obviously been pre-planned; it also caused her intense feelings of shame and guilt to the degree that she did not share her experience with others. But, according to Devlin, the most devastating impact of the whole experience was her subsequent ostracization by the females in her class who not only distanced themselves from her as much as possible but also contributed to her humiliation by maligning her reputation and generating a slew of rumors and whispers about the incident. Their sole purpose was to ingratiate themselves with the power structure—the popular males in the school, some of whom were the same males who had witnessed the assault.[27]

The absence of female solidarity, the unwillingness to confront and challenge male violence, the silence and passivity of victims, the propensity to engage in self-blame and guilt, the reluctance to share stories of humiliation and abuse with other victims, the inability to defend oneself against the onslaught—these are all contributing factors to female oppression. And these are all factors that enable the abuse, the harassment, the rape, the assault, and other forms of violence against women to take place undeterred.

The reality is that as long as one woman remains vulnerable to misogynistic assaults, all women are vulnerable. As long as we allow patriarchy to classify women as being either chaste and virginal or whores and sluts, we are participating in our own subordination. As long as we align ourselves with the forces that arbitrarily and hypocritically determine which one of us is deemed respectable and which one is deemed disreputable, we are separating ourselves from our sisters. And as long as we continue to uphold a system that pits one woman against another, we are not only impeding the formation of our own feminist consciousness, but we are obstructing its formation in others.

The rape of Persephone fulfills all the functions of rape as outlined above. First and foremost, Hades rapes her in order to lay claim to her as his bride. Although this does not minimize the trauma on the young girl, when placed in its cultural and historical context, Hades' actions were well within the acceptable patriarchal constructs of the time.

Second, the rape serves the function of attempting to inculcate in Persephone—and by extension, all women—the notion that their proper role consists of submission to male hegemony. Rape unequivocally endeavors to reinforce Persephone's subordinate status in patriarchy. In a sense, the entire patriarchy colludes to rape her, and she is powerless against the onslaught.

Third, the rape serves as a metaphor for the demotion of the goddess and the usurpation of her powers by the male sky gods of patriarchy. Persephone is, after all, the daughter of a goddess. By subjecting her to rape, patriarchy is also snubbing its nose at her mother, the goddess Demeter. As in times of war—in this case, the war against women and all things female waged by patriarchy—the rape of the young girl serves to "emasculate" Demeter because she is unable to protect her daughter from the violation. However, as we saw earlier, Demeter is not entirely without resources to retaliate.

Fourth, the rape serves to indicate that Persephone has been "marked," that is to say, irrevocably transformed. She can no longer regress to the state of the young Kore, innocently picking flowers. But having once crossed the threshold from maiden to powerful queen, Persephone seizes the opportunity to capitalize on her new status: she embraces Hades as her bridegroom, and, not coincidentally, as the guide who facilitates her initiation into womanhood. She moves from victim to survivor. Her rape, therefore, functions as the instrument that severs her connection to mother and propels her on the path of independence, maturity, and autonomy. Through rape, her old self is penetrated, and her new self is born.

What does the role of rape in the Homeric *Hymn to Demeter* say to a modern audience? We certainly should not arrive at the conclusion that all women need to be physically raped in order to become autonomous individuals in their own right. That would be an abomination. Furthermore, we should not conclude that just because Persephone chose to return to her abductor and rapist that all women secretly love their rapists and harbor a clandestine desire to be raped. That would be an equal abomination.

What the rape does say to us is this: when we undergo an experience that is traumatizing, we cross a psychological threshold and are plummeted into our own underworld. Just as the underworld designates psychic space, so rape designates a psychological intrusion. The nature of the rape experience is such that it should not necessarily entail a violent, physical penetration of our bodily integrity. However, it must constitute a violent intrusion into our psyche—an intrusion that transforms us irrevocably and one from which we cannot return. In other words, rape should not be understood in solely physical terms. Instead, it must be read as a metaphor for a violent penetration of the psyche, a breaking of the psychological hymen that precipitates a transformation in consciousness. For the reasons outlined above, within the cultural and social milieu of ancient Greece, the violent penetration was described as a physical rape. But for a modern audience, operating in a different cultural and social milieu, the rape symbolizes a violent psychological penetration—a penetration that pierces the threshold, the psychological hymen, and one that presages the death of the old self and the birth of the new.

Persephone's journey of abduction and rape bears parallels with the journey of the infant son of Metaneira, Demophoon. Like Persephone, Demophoon is abducted by a god (in his case, the goddess Demeter) who attempts to sever his connection with his mother by altering his status (in his case, from a mortal to an immortal). As was the case with Persephone, this attempt meets with partial success: Persephone alternates between the realm of her mother and the realm of her spouse, never fully belonging to either realm; Demophoon alternates between the mortal realm and the immortal one through Demeter's attempt to grant him immortality. And like Persephone, Demophoon undergoes an irrevocable transformation as a consequence of his encounter with the abductor: he experiences a psychological rape. The poem reveals that after he has been discarded by Demeter, in spite of his sisters' efforts to comfort him, Demophoon's "...heart was not comforted / for lesser nurses and handmaids held him now" (lines 290–291).

It is interesting to note that although this may be a thoroughly modern reading of the rape, Demeter herself seems to suggest this reading by demonstrating her cognizance of the psychological rendering of rape. When she meets the daughters of Metaneira by the Maiden's Well at Eleusis, she fabricates a story about being abducted and raped by pirates and taken on a journey across the sea.

> "I will tell you my tale. For it is not wrong
> to tell you the truth now you ask.
> Doso's my name, which my honored mother gave me.
> On the broad back of the sea I have come now from Crete,
> by no wish of my own. By force and necessity pirate men
> led me off against my desire."
>
> (Lines 120–126)

As Kathie Carlson observes in *Life's Daughter/Death's Bride*, Demeter's fabricated tale remarkably parallels the fate of her daughter.[28] Like Persephone, she was kidnapped from her mother, forced to enter unfamiliar territory bereft of a familial support structure, and raped. However, Demeter's story, unlike Persephone's, is pure fiction, but like all lies, as Patricia Berry argues in "The Rape of Demeter/Persephone and Neurosis," this one contains a kernel of psychological truth.[29] The fact that Demeter chooses to parallel her fabrication with what has actually happened to her daughter indicates she recognizes that, like Persephone, she has experienced a trauma that will have a profound impact on her life and change her irrevocably. In other words, because of what has transpired with her daughter, Demeter experiences a psychological rape from which there can be no turning back. Why else would she choose to fabricate a story about abduction, rape, trauma, and dislocation from all that is familiar? At some level, she must recognize that she, too, has crossed a psychological threshold.

A threshold is a passageway that connects different realms of existence, different ways of being. But a threshold can also be a barrier: it can prevent people from entering; it can also prevent people from leaving once they have entered. Our ability to cross the threshold out of the underworld successfully is contingent upon how we cope with the trauma that yanked us down there in the first place. Did we learn from the experience and thereby transcend it? Or did we allow it to consume and destroy us? Some of us cross the threshold and plunge into the underworld, never to reemerge. Some of us avoid the pain, and, consequently, the potential for growth that the underworld offers. We may do so by indulging in drugs—legal or illegal—that numb our capacity to feel or to think. We may refuse to confront the truth and live in denial. We go down that precipitous path away from community and towards greater isolation. Some of us are able to emerge from the underworld but only with the assistance of experienced guides, counselors, and therapists. Some call upon friends and family to help us out. And some seek guidance and assistance through books.

Our journeys to the underworld are always painful. But if we use the experience wisely, we can move beyond the pain and escape the underworld with new knowledge and insight. However, if we do not understand and assimilate the painful event or experience appropriately, we condemn ourselves to lifelong misery in which much of what we experience in life will be perceived through the murky lens of perpetual, tortured suffering. This self-destructive perspective will impact our future decisions and attitudes, will reinforce our suffering and concomitant feelings of powerlessness and victimization, and will extend our stay in the underworld indefinitely.

Persephone comes to terms with her traumatic experience and embraces the lessons the underworld has provided. By doing so, she is able to cross the threshold successfully and emerge on the other side. She transcends her trauma. Demeter experiences a parallel fate. Similarly, we have to come to terms with our trauma—be it physical, psychological, or both—in order to transcend it and gain our release from the underworld. This can be a very difficult and painful process, but it is one that is essential for healing. We can allow the trauma to paralyze us and remain psychological captives in the underworld for the rest of our lives. Or we can squeeze every ounce of insight from the experience and use it to increase our understanding of who we are, where we went wrong, and where we went right.

Ultimately, to view one's life as consisting of a series of journeys to the underworld is to believe that each painful experience in our lives provides the ongoing potential for growth, insight, and transformation. In that respect, the underworld can come to represent the fructifying force of the womb from which all life emerges. We have a choice: we can allow the trauma or psychological rape that sent us plummeting down to the underworld to immobilize us, or we can use the experience as a steppingstone that catapults us to a greater wisdom—a wisdom that can be called upon when needed to provide us with guidance and direction in our own lives and in the lives of others who may find themselves in similar circumstances.

The choice is ours to make.

CHAPTER 9

Unraveling the Mysteries: Guidelines for Healing and Knowledge

The Homeric *Hymn to Demeter* has taken us down a meandering path of insight, knowledge, and healing. Along the way, it has shown us how to steer a course through the bumps and hurdles of life and emerge from each experience with greater wisdom, strength, and empowerment. We have learned about and about coping with loss and with trauma. We have learned about the social construction of gender and how social and cultural forces define, limit, and influence our perspectives, words, and actions. We have learned about the dynamics that operate in relationships. We have learned about accepting responsibility for our mistakes while, at the same time, moving beyond them. We have learned about the mother and child bond. We have learned about the stages of a woman's life and the importance of embracing each stage for the unique pleasure and opportunity it brings us. We have learned about gendered communications, gendered behaviors, gendered attitudes, and gendered lives. We have learned about the necessity of establishing a network of support to assist us in our struggles. We have learned about respecting diversity in others as well as respecting it in ourselves. And we have learned about the importance of agency and self-definition.

But if there is one thread that weaves its way prominently throughout all the permutations of this wonderful tale, it is the importance of negotiating balance in our inner and outer lives. At almost every turn of the story, we are provided with yet another illustration of the importance of maintaining balance and of the disastrous consequences to ourselves and to our communities that can ensue if we favor one side of our consciousness to the exclusion of the other or favor one half of humanity over the other.

Balance in Grieving

Demeter learns the importance of balance in the grieving process. Her initial grief at the loss of her daughter led her to pursue a helter-skelter path of denial and displacement. Drowning in grief, she sought the quick fix in Demophoon to dull the pain. Her unbridled emotions almost led to dire consequences for innocent bystanders in her war against Zeus. It is only after Metaneira forces her into a recognition of the parallels between her action and the action of her brothers that Demeter is shocked into tempering her grief with a balanced course of action. She dons the veil of introspection, consciously embraces her grief, and devises a plan to gain the release of her daughter. After successfully negotiating this balance between accepting her loss or immersing herself in denial, Demeter transcends the grief and moves forward.

In contrast to Demeter, we have the reactions of Zeus and Helios. They approach grief with a cavalier attitude and a flippant disregard for the pain of loss. Through their reliance on logic and reason to the exclusion of emotions, they represent the opposite but equally unbalanced perspective illustrated in Demeter's initial reaction. Logic and reason may dictate that we accept that what is done is done and cannot be undone. But logic and reason are insufficient for healing to take place. We need to work through our loss emotionally before we can accept it logically. We need to allow ourselves to experience the pain involved in coping with loss. We need time and space to mourn and grieve. And we need to have our emotions validated and respected by our community. As a result of Demeter's actions, Zeus and Helios are forced into an accommodation of a balanced perspective on grieving. They learn that in spite of all their wishes to the contrary, the loss of a loved one cannot be summarily dismissed in such a cavalier manner. Healing is a process. It requires time. And it requires balance.

Balance in Coping with Trauma

Demeter and Persephone demonstrate the importance of balance in coping with trauma. Demeter experiences the trauma of the loss of her daughter; Persephone experiences the trauma of betrayal, abduction, and loss of innocence. Whether we brought it on ourselves or just happened to be in the wrong place at the wrong time, trauma can immobilize us and strip us of agency. But it all depends on how we handle it.

Demeter and Persephone illustrate the principle that we can move beyond trauma. They come to terms with their experience, internalize the lessons each experience offers, and then use the experience as a stepping-stone for greater knowledge, wisdom, and empowerment. This entails a recognition that dwelling on the details of who, what, where, when, how, or why it happened, continuously reliving the experience in all its tortured gyrations, may trap us in the underworld forever. At some point, like Demeter and Persephone, we have to come to terms with the fact that what is done cannot be undone. And like Demeter who says no more on the subject when she hears that Persephone has cemented her return to the underworld by swallowing the pomegranate seed, we need to embrace the new reality and move on.

This involves a precarious balancing act. While we do not welcome our trips to the underworld, once we are there we need to maintain a balance between reaping the benefits the underworld experience offers us while simultaneously being ever on the alert for our way out. On the one hand, if we dwell too long on reliving the experience itself and berate ourselves for making the choices we made, we may never be able to get the psychological distance we need to approach the experience analytically and learn from the insights it can provide. On the other hand, if we distance ourselves too far from the experience and deny it ever happened, like the early Demeter, we risk engaging in a mad scramble for substitutes and alternatives to dull the pain. By indulging in such behaviors, we also delay the healing process. Balance is essential for coping with trauma: the balance between understanding the experience and cultivating the ability to move beyond it.

The ultimate goal is always to facilitate healing, to move beyond the trauma and emerge from the underworld a stronger and wiser human being. Some of us, like both Demeter and Persephone, require assistance in the journey. If so, we should not be embarrassed or ashamed to seek help from experienced guides, trained professionals, or those who have gone there before us. But once again, we need to understand that in order to be successful, our guides need to negotiate a delicate balancing act. Like Hekate, Iambe, Metaneira, her daughters, and Rheia our aids should step in and provide us with just enough assistance to propel us forward and upward. But then they need to step back and allow us to proceed on our own, step by faltering step. Too little help could keep us wallowing in the quagmire indefinitely. Too much help could have the same effect by fostering an unhealthy dependency on others. We need support, encouragement, and guidance. But we also need to acknowledge that the journey through the trauma and out of the underworld is one we each have to undertake alone. Mentors and midwives can cheer us on and propel us forward, but the process of birthing ourselves is one we have to experience for ourselves. There can be no substitutes.

Transgendering

Finally, we come to what may be the most important balancing act of all: transgendering or moving beyond the socially constructed limitations of gender. The myth of Demeter and Persephone dramatically illustrates the masculinist forces of patriarchy pitted against feminist forces whose goal is to undermine and ultimately dismantle patriarchy. The myth promulgates the necessity of maintaining an internal as well as an external balance between masculinities and femininities and by doing so transcending the limitations of both.

The qualities associated with masculinities, as demonstrated by Zeus and Helios, consist of a flagrant disregard and disrespect for all things feminine and all things that fall under the feminine sphere. Hierarchical relationships are valued over horizontal relationships. Communication is one way and top down. Reason is promoted over emotion and intuition; logos is promoted over eros. The father/child relationship usurps the position once held by the mother/child relationship. Individualism and separation replaces community and intimacy. In short, there is a hierarchy of values in which the activities and perspectives of one half of humanity garner greater respect than the activities and perspectives of the other half of humanity.

The qualities associated with femininities, as demonstrated by Demeter, Kore/Persephone, Hekate, Iambe, Metaneira, her four daughters, and Rheia are care-giving, nurturing, collaboration, and a concern for community. These are positive qualities that should be cultivated by all of us. But, again, they need to be balanced with qualities associated with masculinities. The Homeric *Hymn to Demeter* demonstrates over and over again that the promotion of one side of our consciousness to the exclusion of the other will lead to disaster for the individual and the community. For example, while the ability to nurture is a positive attribute, if we nurture others and neglect to nurture ourselves, we risk causing damage to ourselves and to those we nurture. An equilibrium must be maintained between a love of self and a love of others. Masculinities that promote individualism must be balanced with femininities that promote care for the community in order to achieve a healthy sense of well-being. If a love of self totally overpowers concern for others, we become self-absorbed and walk down the precipitous path of isolation and alienation. If love of others totally overpowers love of self, our identity assumes parasitical tendencies: we begin to view any step towards another's burgeoning independence as a threat to our own identity and we attempt to stifle it. There is a time to nurture and support others. But, as Demeter shows us, there is also a time for letting go.

Similarly, emotions and intuition must be balanced with reason and logical thinking. Lunar consciousness must be integrated with solar consciousness. As we saw with Demeter, giving free license to our emotions to guide our behavior leads to muddle-headed activities. And as Zeus and Helios demonstrate, denying the legitimacy of emotions and advocating a response based on reason exclusively leads to negating a big part of our psychological make-up as well as to possible disastrous consequences for the community. Repressed emotions will eventually surface—and sometimes they do so in very damaging ways. Emotions must be respected and validated. But they also need to be tempered with clear, logical thinking. Again, there is no hierarchy of values. These qualities should be cultivated in all human beings to be called upon as circumstances dictate. Like Persephone who swallows the pomegranate seed and assimilates the masculine experience it symbolizes, as females we need to internalize and assimilate the masculine experience. And like Hades who undergoes a feminist transformation as a result of his interaction with Persephone, as males we need to internalize and assimilate the feminine experience and all that it embodies.

Transgendering also entails moving beyond the limitations of socially constructed gender norms in our communities. We need to explode ridiculous and antiquated notions that the performance of certain tasks and behaviors and the cultivation of certain values and perspectives should be considered norms for one gender but not the other. We need to build communities that afford the same respect to the role of caregiver and nurturer as they do to the breadwinner. We need to applaud women who balance their femininities with the masculine qualities of individualism and autonomy. And we need to applaud men who balance their masculinities with the feminine qualities of the nurturance and care of others. For as the myth demonstrates, the repetitive activities involved in nurturing and caregiving generate a perspective that is more conducive towards cultivating empathy and connection with others. The *Hymn* illustrates the principle that what operates well in one sphere can be applicable to the other sphere with equally positive results. We should not allow the gendering of productive attributes to be limited in their application to one side of humanity but not the other.

The Homeric *Hymn to Demeter* also advocates the position that we need to move beyond perceiving the female as merely an ornamental digression in the lives of men and, instead, foster a respect for the female, her activities, her values, and her contributions. Difference does not have to be oppositional. Difference can—and should—be complementary. The *Hymn* demonstrates that we need to reconstruct gender relations on the basis of reciprocity not hierarchy. And this change must occur at the individual as well as at the institutional and societal level.

Patriarchy distinguishes between the public sphere and the private sphere and designates the former as a masculine province—one that is endowed with greater value than the private sphere, which has been designated as a feminine province. The Homeric *Hymn to Demeter* obliterates this hierarchy of values, and while it continues with the assignation of public as male and private as female, it blurs the lines of demarcation between the activities in the domestic sphere and the public sphere to a considerable degree. Furthermore, the *Hymn to Demeter* promotes the recognition that the two spheres are inextricably intertwined and that each impacts the other and depends upon the existence of the other for the continued sustenance of the individual as well as the community.

To begin with, the conspiracy between Zeus and Hades to abduct Kore for the purpose of marrying her off to the god of the underworld amounts to an alliance between the two gods that has political and public ramifications. However, this alliance, performed as it is in the public sphere and one in which all the powers of patriarchy collude to cement the union between Kore and Hades, also has repercussions in the private sphere: it precipitates Demeter's withdrawal from the public community of the gods and her retreat into the domestic, private sphere of the palace at Eleusis. However, her withdrawal into domesticity—the private world of women—constitutes a political statement against the action of the gods who have deprived her of her daughter (a matter of personal concern). The personal and political are inextricably intertwined.

While in Eleusis, Demeter engages in a private activity, specifically her attempt to immortalize Demophoon. After she is confronted by Metaneira in the performance of this private act, Demeter engages in a series of activities that have ramifications in the public realm: she demands the building of her temple; she initiates a famine that wreaks havoc on humanity and the gods; and she inaugurates the Eleusinian Mysteries, which later became the center for spiritual life for over one thousand years. Similarly, her eventual reunification with her daughter integrates both the private and public arenas. On the domestic level, we have the joyful reunification of a mother and her daughter; on the public level, we have the termination of the famine and the inauguration of the Eleusinian Mysteries.

The *Hymn to Demeter* illustrates the feminist premise that the personal is political. What is personal and private has an impact on what is public and political and vice versa. The two arenas of human activity are insepa-rable. Both are to be respected and both are essential for the sustenance of the individual and the community. A balance is required in which neither realm is promoted as worthy of greater merit than its counterpart. For exam-ple, when Keleos hears of the activities that took place in the private sphere of his own home, he automatically calls for an assembly of the people and engages the city in a public activity: the building of the temple. What emerged in the private, domestic world of female experience is thereby inte-grated into the public, social, and religious fabric of the community at large. Activities in the feminine domain serve as the catalysts to transform the masculine, public domain. Eleusis provides us with an example in which the private, female realm is not hostile to or situated in opposition to the public, male realm. Instead, it is respectfully incorporated into it to the degree that it is difficult to determine at which point one realm ends and the other begins. At Eleusis, the relationship of male/public and female/pri-vate is based on balance, reciprocity, and mutual benefit. Once again, there is not—nor should there be—a hierarchy of values between the public sphere and the private sphere.

The story of Demeter and Persephone also illustrates the importance of gender balance in successfully accomplishing the task of personal trans-formation. As we saw earlier, Demeter is assisted in her journey of personal transformation by a number of individuals, not least of whom are Hekate and Helios. Hekate is the first to come to Demeter's aid; Hekate accompa-nies her as they solicit the assistance of Helios. Helios provides Demeter with information; Helios urges her to reconcile herself to the new circum-stances. As we argued earlier, Hekate and Helios represent polar opposites. The former constellates lunar consciousness (feminine) and the latter con-stellates solar consciousness (masculine). The former provides Demeter with emotional support and guidance; the latter provides her with rational expla-nations and logical outcomes. Because the type of assistance they offer is not mutually exclusive, both Hekate and Helios are essential helpers. They provide Demeter with the assistance she needs as she embarks on her jour-ney of death, renewal, and transformation.

Similarly, Persephone is assisted on her journey in and out of the underworld by a male and female helper: her uncle/spouse, Hades, and her mother, Demeter. As rapist and god of the underworld, Hades is male. But as we argued earlier, Hades is a more complex figure than his male coun-terparts since he moves from adherence to a rigid masculinity that embraces domination and hierarchy to one that comes to embrace many feminine attributes and undertakes many feminine tasks. Demeter experiences a sim-ilar journey but her movement is in the opposite direction. As mother and goddess of agriculture, Demeter is female. But she, too, crosses gender lines by moving from an emotional, unstructured reaction to her daughter's abduction ("feminine") to formulating a plan, strategizing, and pursuing a logical course of action ("masculine"). Both Hades and Demeter cross gender lines and experience transformation by the end of the poem. And as male and female, they assist Persephone as she undertakes her own journey of transformation.

Our journey of death, renewal, and transformation must entail similar assistance from the masculine and feminine attributes embodied by our male or female helpers. The journey to wholeness involves transgendering: moving beyond socially circumscribed gender norms and adopting productive attributes and performing constructive tasks associated with both the masculine and the feminine and so transcending the limitations of an exclusive reliance on either realm.

Finally, like the story of Eve in *Genesis*, the Homeric *Hymn to Demeter* shows us that it is women who will bring about the transformation. The masculinist perspective will not change if left to its own devices. It has to be educated. And, in some cases, it may have to be coerced. Persephone demonstrates that through her influence, Hades' initial misogyny is transformed into an embrace of the feminist paradigm. Demeter demonstrates that even though he was kicking and screaming all the way, Zeus was ultimately coerced into an accommodation of the feminist paradigm. And on a more general level, the activities that transpire in the private, domestic realm of the palace at Eleusis are translated into the public realm through the inauguration of the mysteries—mysteries that will impact private lives as well as the public lives of the communities they serve. And all these transformations came about as a result of feminine perspectives, feminine values, feminine activity, and the feminine sphere of influence.

Feminism is the force that will free us to move beyond hierarchy and oppositional dichotomies. Feminism is the force that will enable us to transcend socially constructed gender norms and cultivate qualities that are conducive to the health of the individual as well as the community—qualities that are free from the taint or bonus of being associated with either gender. Just as Demeter refuses to be ignored and insists on her rights as a mother and as a female in an environment that is hostile to both, feminism refuses to hush up and go away.

Feminism continues to insist on the rights of all people, regardless of their race, gender, ethnicity, age, ability, or sexual orientation to be treated as equals and afforded the same respect and granted the same opportunities in life that have been bestowed on the privileged few who, historically, have had the power to name, define, and assign values. And if there are some folks out there who prefer to live in a system of hierarchy and dominance, like Zeus in the Homeric *Hymn to Demeter*, they will just have to learn to accommodate to the new vision that is based on balance, partnership, collaboration, inclusivity, mutual respect, equality, and symmetry—a vision that is conducive to health, healing, renewal, and happiness.

The *Hymn to Demeter* concludes with the poet asking Demeter and Persephone to grant his song a living that warms the heart. In return, he promises to remember them and a new song as well. It appears as if Demeter and Persephone granted his request. For the Homeric *Hymn to Demeter* has survived the centuries and continues to warm our hearts and inspire us as we journey through the ups and downs, the ins and outs, the underworlds and over-worlds, and the living and dying that constitute the intricate web of our human lives.

One Day in a Life

The myth of Demeter and Persephone provides me with an opportunity to share with my students a very old story that can be empowering as well as transformative. I think it is important to impress upon people of all ages that our ancestors have much to say to us that is meaningful if we only take the time and make the effort to listen and understand. These old stories were told and retold throughout the centuries for a reason—because they have vitality and significance. Their very endurance testifies to their ability to speak to the perennial concerns of humanity. We need to retrieve them from our dusty bookshelves, blow off their cobwebs, open their pages, and allow their words to sing to receptive ears.

In this fast-paced age of technology, it befits us to remember that underneath the zoom and the glitz and the hype and the cyber glory of our modern environment, we harbor many of the same concerns and anxieties that plagued our ancestors throughout the centuries. It profits us well to pause and listen to their stories about coping with grief; moving beyond trauma; maintaining networks of support; learning to provide support; respecting and honoring the diversity within ourselves as well as within others; deriving insight and knowledge from negative experiences; defeating the opposition; and, finally, cultivating a balance in our internal as well as our external environment.

Depending on what stage of life my students are in, when we discuss the story of Demeter and Persephone, some of them will more closely identify with Kore/Persephone and others with Demeter. A story about abduction, betrayal, and loss of innocence has the potential of striking a universal chord in each of us. Its narrative resonates with the experience of sharing a common humanity—regardless of our age, gender, race, or class.

I have been privileged to participate in many memorable discussions with students about this particular myth, but perhaps one of the most poignant conversations I had concerning this myth was with a relatively young female in my Women in Literature class several semesters ago.

It began during class when we were analyzing the story of Kore and Demeter. The discussion followed the usual path: the myth's connection with the agrarian cycle and its association with the patriarchal rape of woman and earth. My students voiced outrage at Hades for abducting and raping his niece; anger at Zeus, her father, for allowing it to happen and turning his back on Kore's anguished plea for help; praise for Demeter who forced the male-centered, male-dominated power structure to acknowledge her loss and return her daughter; and sympathy for the young Kore who had been violated.

"Patriarchy rearing its ugly head, once again," I said, by way of affirming my students' reading of the story. "But let us look at this same story from a different angle," I suggested, trying to disguise my eagerness. And then I asked a question that both bewildered and horrified them: "Can Hades be perceived as a positive figure?" My question was greeted with blank stares and silence. I persisted.

I watched them carefully, trying to gauge their reaction as I looked at the story from the perspective of Kore.

"Kore is a young girl on the cusp of womanhood, tied to her mother's apron string. Perhaps like some of you in here, she is afraid to let go. Afraid to spread her wings. Afraid to cut the umbilical cord. Along comes Hades and chops off the umbilical cord and severs her parasitic connection with mother. In the process, he forcibly thrusts her in the direction of independence, autonomy, and selfhood. Persephone can no longer be mother's little girl, clinging desperately to mother's apron string. The umbilical cord has been severed, and the nature of her relationship with mother has been altered irrevocably. This transformation is signified by her new name, Persephone.

"In Greek mythology, Persephone is depicted as an autonomous queen, powerful in her own right. Her love for Hades and his love for her becomes the stuff of which legends are made. As Persephone, she controls her fate and the fate of all those who enter her domain. Her first emergence from the underworld signifies her altered status. She is no longer the same, innocent child she was before her abduction. However—and fortunately for her—she is absolved of any guilt for achieving the independence and autonomy that can only be achieved upon severing one's dependency on mother. After all, she didn't seek the abduction. She had no knowledge of what was about to happen until she found herself tumbling to the underworld. She was minding her own business, playing with her girlfriends, picking flowers. It's true that she made a conscious decision to pick the narcissus, but she had no prior knowledge of the calamity that would ensue as a consequence of her action. One can almost hear her proclaim her innocence: 'But, mother, how was I to know that he had planted the narcissus on purpose to trap me? Believe me, mother, if I had known, I would never have plucked it. It wasn't my fault; it was all his fault.' Absolved of guilt, she had had her cake—or pomegranate seed—and had eaten it, too.

"Hades, her abductor, emerges as a transformational agent, the guide who helps Kore (and the Kore within us) free herself from the ties that can choke and stunt movement towards autonomy and authentic selfhood. He unleashes our eros—that potential that lies within each one of us that pushes us forward to manifest our inner being. And he performs this service while, at the same time, absolving us of the burden of responsibility that comes with severing our connection with mother and seeking our freedom."

The class was hushed—perhaps a little too hushed. I waited for a few seconds to see if anyone wanted to volunteer any comments or insights. But they all appeared to be waiting for me to continue. So I did.

"If we read the story in the way I have suggested, then maybe the underworld is not such a terrible place after all. True, it is dark, foreboding, and can be terrifying. It is, after all, in the deepest sense, the chthonic realm. No one in his or her right mind would want to go there voluntarily. Hence, we have to be kidnapped, forced into the inner depths against our will. But the underworld is also a place of tremendous growth if—and this is a big if—we use our time in there wisely. True growth can only come from suffering," I remind them.

I try to conceal the quake that invariably accompanies my voice when I speak of the underworld. Possessing an intimate knowledge of the underworld, I am very cognizant of its seductive powers—powers that hold the promise of transformation and growth, but powers that can also be very dangerous. So I attempt to impress upon my students the importance of balance.

"Look," I said. "Have you ever made a decision in your life which you thought would take you in one direction, but it ended up taking you in an entirely different one? If you had known you would end up on the wrong path, you may never have made the decision. But by the time you had figured out that you should have done things differently, that you shouldn't have picked that damned narcissus no matter how enticing it looked, it is already too late. You find yourself plummeting to the underworld, without a clue as to how you are going to get out. You lose some of your innocence, some of your naiveté. You curse yourself; you curse the narcissus; you swear you will never touch another one again as long as you live. You grope around in the dark, trying desperately to find a way out. You feel hopeless and without hope. But then, in the proverbial nick of time, along comes Hades, pointing to the Exit sign and offering you a ride out.

"While you are in the underworld, use your time wisely," I said. "Learn about yourself, about what it means to be you, about how you fit into the world around you, about where you went wrong and where you went right. Learn about what it means to be human. Squeeze every ounce of insight you can from this experience. Such a reprieve from a life on the surface is beneficial, but only if it is temporary. If it becomes permanent and you lose the will or desire to leave, time in the underworld will eventually lead to self-destruction. To death. There's the rub. So while you are there, you have to keep looking for ways out. You have to maintain a delicate balance by reaping the benefits of being in the underworld while simultaneously being ever on the alert for Hades' chariot which will whisk you out of the darkness to Mother, waiting on the surface.

"Believe me, no matter how bleak it seems to you while you are down there, you will get out, but only if you want to. I have no idea how long your stay will last because the time spent in the underworld varies from person to person and from situation to situation within the same person. But if you hold fast, you will emerge, like Persephone, a wiser and more powerful human being. And, if you are lucky, you will have the dubious distinction of experiencing the depths again and again, each time painfully shedding your old skin and birthing yourself anew.

"After you have paid a few visits to the underworld, you will come to look upon it as a fertile, dark time—a sort of incubation period. A liminal phase in your life in which an old self has to die before a new self can be born. And as with all birth and death, pain is intrinsic to the process."

The class period was almost over, so I felt the need to provide some sort of closure. I decided to inject my personal voice. I told them that I wish someone had interpreted the story of Kore in this way to me when I first started paying my respects to the underworld at the ripe old age of 15. I wish someone had reassured me that I would eventually get out of there and that I would be wiser as a result of my ordeal. I wish someone had told me the death and rebirth I experienced was all part of a natural process, one of the many psychological growth spurts that I was to undergo along the rocky road to middle age.

"That is why I am telling you this. I don't know if any of you understand what I am talking about. I don't know if any of you have visited the underworld. Maybe you haven't yet. Maybe you never will. But maybe—just maybe—you will. And if you do, remember Kore. And remember that she emerges with new life. And you will, too. All I can do is tell you her story.

All I can do, ultimately..." and I hesitated a few seconds before completing the sentence, "is to plant the seed." Seeing the obvious connection to the agrarian cycle, the students laughed.

As I was collecting my books to make my way to the next class, one of my students came up to me. She had tears in her eyes and a tremor in her voice. "I wanted you to know," she said, "that I felt as if you were talking only to me. I felt as if you and I were the only ones in the room. I felt as if you could see inside my heart. I felt as if you knew me and knew what I have been going through." Then the tears started to gush. "I didn't want to come to class today," she continued, in between the sobs. "I was thinking of dropping out of school. Nothing here seemed important. But after this, I feel different. And I want to thank you and let you know how much you have touched me."

I felt awkward and humbled—as I always do before such profuse out-pourings of gratitude. So this is what it is all about, I remember thinking to myself. This is what it means to hear the voice on the other side of silence: finding voice and giving voice to another's silences. I thanked her. I offered whatever words of encouragement I could. And then I tried to bring us both back to the solid ground under our feet by reminding her to get her overdue paper in to me as soon as possible.

A few days later, she showed up in my office. Amid sobs, she gushed out her story of being a victim of persistent sexual abuse that began when she was six years old; of how her mother had refused to believe her for years; of how she still harbored residual anger towards her mother because of this; of how she was finally trying to come to terms with her molesta-tion; of how her 13-year-old son was getting into trouble; of how she was worried that he may end up in jail if she didn't do something to help him; of how she had made the heart-wrenching decision to give him up to her estranged husband in the hope that a strong male figure might keep him steered in the right direction; of how her nine-year-old daughter had expressed bitter anger towards her for depriving her of her only sibling; of how she felt her whole life was falling apart, unraveling at the seams.

I listened; I comforted; I tried to reassure. And, as always, I waited for the tears to stop. Eventually, they did. Then I began to tiptoe my way through her underworld, trying to do so with respect and sensitivity. It is always a precarious balancing act for me to suggest professional counseling. On the one hand, I don't want my students to think I am insensitive to their cries for help and am dumping their problems on to someone else; on the other hand, I know I am woefully unequipped to help them because I have not been trained as a counselor. So I try to steer them gently, with compassion and sympathy.

"There is no shame in seeking professional help," I reassured her.

"There are trained professionals who know how to help you navigate your way through this turmoil." Prompted by her willingness to seek assistance, I rushed to my list of agencies and provided her with several different names and phone numbers, followed by brief explanations of their specific areas of expertise. I urged her to call on them, and she assured me she would. She had calmed down considerably by this time. We chatted for a few more minutes and then she got up to leave. I stood up, too. As we embraced in a giant bear hug, she looked me intently in the eye and said, "Thank you for all your help. Thank you for listening." She smiled and walked out of my office.

To this day, I find myself thinking of her every now and then, of how, for at least an instant, she had found a story that resonated with her own experiences in a meaningful way, a vehicle that voiced what was on the other side of her silence. I hope that she has found a Hekate, an Iambe, a Metaneira, her four daughters, and a Rheia in the form of professional counselors and guides who are assisting her in reaping the benefits from her experiences in the underworld while helping her to navigate her way out of there successfully. I hope her voice hasn't been muffled. I hope it is booming loudly and clearly for all to hear. And I hope that like Persephone, she has emerged from her ordeal in the depths a wiser and stronger human being, full of the promise and the hope that are the harbingers of new life.

Notes

Introduction

1. Edith Hamilton, *Mythology: Timeless Tales of Gods and Heroes* (New York: Mentor, 1969).

2. Christine Downing, ed. *The Long Journey Home: Re-Visioning the Myth of Demeter and Persephone for Our Time* (Boston: Shambhala, 1994).

3. Helene P. Foley, trans. and ed. *The Homeric Hymn to Demeter: Translation, Commentary, and Interpretive Essays* (Princeton: Princeton UP, 1994), 2–27.

4. Bettina L. Knapp, *Women, Myth, and the Feminine Principle* (New York: State U of NY P, 1998), xii.

1. The Story

1 Edward F. Edinger, *The Eternal Drama: The Inner Meaning of Greek Mythology* (Boston: Shambhala, 1994), 177.

2. For a fuller discussion of the ritual, see Helene P. Foley, "Background: The Eleusinian Mysteries and Women's Rites for Demeter," in *The Homeric Hymn to Demeter*, trans. and ed. Helene P. Foley, 65–75.

3. Barry B. Powell, *Classical Myth* (Englewood Cliffs: Prentice Hall, 1995), 237.

4. Sarah B. Pomeroy, *Goddesses, Whores, Wives, and Slaves: Women in Classical Antiquity* (New York: Schocken, 1975), 76.

5. Downing, *The Long Journey Home*, 3.

6. Carl Kerenyi, *Eleusis: Archetypal Image of Mother and Daughter*, trans. Ralph Manheim (Princeton: Princeton UP, 1967), 94.

7. Ibid., 105.

8. Deborah Lyons, *Gender and Immortality: Heroines in Ancient Greek Myth and Cult* (Princeton: Princeton UP, 1997), 116.

9. Tanya Wilkinson, *Persephone Returns: Victims, Heroes, and the Journey from the Underworld* (Berkeley: Pagemill, 1996), 26.

10. Edinger, 177.

11. Kerenyi, 146.

12. Ibid., 147.

13. Downing, *The Long Journey Home*, 3.

14. Beatrice Bruteau, "The Unknown Goddess," in *The Goddess Re-Awakening: The Feminine Principle Today*, ed. Shirley Nicholson, (Illinois: Quest, 1989), 68–80.

15. All quotations from the Homeric *Hymn to Demeter* are from the translation by Helene P. Foley in *The Homeric Hymn to Demeter: Translation, Commentary, and Interpretive Essays*.

16. Kerenyi, 15.

17. Ibid., 23.

18. Wilkinson, 217–218.

19. Helene P. Foley, "The 'Theology' of the Mysteries," in *The Homeric Hymn to Demeter: Translation, Commentary, and Interpretive Essays*, trans. and ed. Helene P. Foley, 95.

2. Demeter: Grieving, Retaliation, and Reconciliation

1. Nanci DeBloois, "Rape, Marriage, or Death? Gender Perspectives in the Homeric *Hymn to Demeter*," *Philological Quarterly* 76 (1997): 245–262.

2. Bettina Aptheker, *Tapestries of Life: Women's Work, Women's Consciousness, and the Meaning of Daily Experience* (Amherst: U of Massachusetts P, 1989), 247.

3. Elisabeth Badinter, *The Myth of Motherhood: An Historical View of the Maternal Instinct*, trans. Roger DeGaris (London: Souvenir, 1981), x–xiii.

4. Polly Young-Eisendrath, "Demeter's Folly: Experiencing Loss in Middle Life," in *The Long Journey Home*, ed. Christine Downing, 212.

5. Germaine Greer, *The Change: Women, Aging, and the Menopause* (New York: Alfred A. Knopf, 1992), 236.

6. Paulo Friere, *Pedagogy of the Oppressed*, trans. Myra Bergman Ramos (New York: Continuum, 1990), 49.

7. Kathie Carlson, *Life's Daughter/Death's Bride: Inner Transformations Through the Goddess Demeter/Persephone* (Boston: Shambhala, 1997), 30.

8. Kathryn Allen Rabuzzi, *Motherself: A Mythic Analysis of Motherhood* (Bloomington: Indiana UP, 1988), 25.

9. Henrietta Moore, *Feminism and Anthropology* (Minneapolis: U of Minnesota P, 1990), 29.

10. Stephanie Golden, *Slaying the Mermaid: Women and the Culture of Sacrifice* (New York: Harmony, 1998), 118.

11. Ibid., 119.

12. Carol P. Christ, *Laughter of Aphrodite: Reflections on a Journey to the Goddess* (San Francisco: Harper and Row, 1987), 131.

13. Carlson, 26.

14. Cheryl Exum, *Plotted, Shot, and Painted: Cultural Representations of Biblical Women* (Sheffield: Sheffield Academic P, 1996), 93.

15. Kathie Carlson, *In Her Image: The Unhealed Daughter's Search for Her Mother* (Boston: Shambhala, 1990), 91.

16. Edinger, 41–42.

17. Rabuzzi, 43–59.

18. Wilkinson, 24.

19. Christine Downing, "Persephone in Hades," in *The Long Journey Home*, ed. Christine Downing, 222.

3. Persephone: Moving Beyond Victimization

1. Wilkinson, 28.

2. Shulamith Firestone, *The Dialectic of Sex: The Case for Feminist Revolution* (New York: William Morrow, 1970), 52.

3. Jean Shinoda Bolen, *Goddesses in Older Women: Archetypes in Women Over Fifty, Becoming a Juicy Crone* (New York: Harper Collins, 2001), 13.

4. Mary Daly, *Gyn/Ecology: The Metaethics of Radical Feminism* (Boston: Beacon, 1990), 69.

5. Kim Chernin, *Reinventing Eve: Modern Woman in Search of Herself* (New York: Time, 1987), 134.

6. Gerda Lerner, *The Creation of Patriarchy* (Oxford: Oxford UP, 1986), 151.

7. All quotations from the Bible are taken from *The Jerusalem Bible: Reader's Edition* (New York: Doubleday and Co., Inc., 1968).

8. Lerner, 182.

9. Carol Gilligan, *In a Different Voice: Psychological Theory and Women's Development* 2nd ed. (Cambridge: Harvard UP, 1993), 8.

10. Nancy Chodorow, "Family Structure and Feminine Personality," in *The Homeric Hymn to Demeter: Translation, Commentary, and Interpretive Essays*, trans. and ed. Helene P. Foley, 248.

11. Ibid., 257.

12. Kathie Carlson, *In Her Image*, xi.

13. Vera Bushe, "Cycles of Becoming," in *The Long Journey Home*, ed. Christine Downing, 183.

14. Carlson, *In Her Image*, 120.

15. Ibid., 24.

16. Gilligan, 8.

17. Rabuzzi, 36.

18. Carlson, *In Her Image*, 25.

19. Helen Luke, *Woman, Earth, and Spirit: The Feminine in Symbol and Myth* (New York: Crossroads, 1981), 55–68.

20. Rabuzzi, 106.

21. Esther Harding, *Woman's Mysteries, Ancient and Modern: A Psychological Interpretation of the Feminine Principle as Portrayed in Myth, Story, and Dreams* (New York: Putnam's Sons, 1971), 125.

22. Roberta Seelinger Trites, *Waking Sleeping Beauty: Feminist Voices in Children's Novels* (Iowa: U of Iowa P, 1997), 6.

23. Young-Eisendrath, 215.

24. Judith Lewis Herman, *Trauma and Recovery* (New York: Basic, 1992), 175.

25. Ibid., 155.

26. Ibid., 181.

27. Carolyn Heilbrun, *Writing a Woman's Life* (New York: Ballantine, 1988), 46.

28. Cheryl Sattler, *Teaching to Transcend: Educating Women Against Violence* (Albany: State U of NY P, 2000), 34.

4. A Narcissus, a Veil, and a Pomegranate

1. Janice Delaney, Mary Jane Lupton, and Emily Toth, *The Curse: A Cultural History of Menstruation* (New York: E.P. Dutton, 1976), 159.

2. Lerner, 123–140.

3. Ibid., 135.

4. Ibid., 137–139.

5. Ibid., 138.

6. Clarissa Pinkola Estes, *Women Who Run with Wolves: Myths and Stories of the Wild Woman Archetype* (New York: Ballantine, 1992), 441.

7. Fatima Mernissi, *The Veil and the Male Elite: A Feminist Interpretation of Women's Rights in Islam*, trans. Mary Jo Lakeland (Massachusetts: Addison-Wesley, 1987), 85.

8. Ibid., 101.

9. Ibid., 93.

10. Pinkola Estes, 443.

11. Germaine Greer, *The Change: Women, Aging, and the Menopause* (New York: Alfred Knopf, 1992), 273.

12. Ibid., 279.

13. Nancy Qualls-Corbett, *The Sacred Prostitute: Eternal Aspect of the Feminine* (Toronto: Inner City, 1988), 64.

14. Barbara Smith, "Greece" in *The Feminist Companion to Mythology*, ed. Carolyne Larrington (London: Pandora, 1992), 89.

15. Bruce Lincoln, *Emerging from the Chrysalis: Rituals of Women's Initiation* (New York: Oxford UP, 1991), 85.

16. Marylin Arthur, "Politics and Pomegranates: An Interpretation of the Homeric *Hymn to Demeter*" in *The Homeric Hymn to Demeter: Translation, Commentary, and Interpretive Essays*, trans. and ed. Helene P. Foley, 237.

17. Marina Valcarenghi, *Relationships: Transforming Archetypes* (Maine: York Beach, 1997), xii.

18. Homer. *The Odyssey*, trans. Robert Fitzgerald (New York: Anchor, 1963).

19. Edinger, 109.

20. Lerner, 194.

21. Carlson, *Life's Daughter/Death's Bride*, 112.

22. Harding, 37.

5. Female Mentoring

1. Golden, 249.
2. Sally Helgesen, *The Female Advantage: Women's Ways of Leadership* (New York: Doubleday, 1990), 14.
3. Ibid., 27–28.
4. Ibid., 30.
5. Ibid., 37.
6. Bettina Knapp, *Women, Myth, and the Feminine Principle* (New York: State U of NY P, 1998), xvi.
7. Bolen, *Goddesses in Older Women*, 46.
8. Ibid., 47.
9. Ibid., 60.
10. Audre Lorde, *Sister Outsider: Essays and Speeches* (California: Crossing, 1984), 111.
11. Kerenyi, 39.
12. Powell, 223–235.
13. Bolen, 106.
14. Arthur, 230.
15. Winifred Milius Lubell, *The Metamorphosis of Baubo: Myths of Woman's Sexual Energy* (Nashville: Vanderbilt UP, 1994), xix.
16. Ibid., 79.
17. Ibid., 54.
18. Susan Brownmiller, *Femininity* (New York: Linden, 1984), 166.
19. For a full discussion of de-selfing, see Harriet Goldhor Lerner, *The Dance of Intimacy* (New York: Harper and Row, 1989).
20. Barbara Walker, *The Crone: Woman of Age, Wisdom, and Power* (San Francisco: Harper and Row, 1985), 91.
21. Ibid., 90–92.
22. Carlson, *Life's Daughter/Death's Bride*, 30.
23. Nancy Felson-Rubin and Harriet M. Deal, "Some Functions of the Demophoon Episode in the Homeric *Hymn to Demeter*" in *The Homeric Hymn to Demeter: Translation, Commentary, and Interpretive Essays*, trans. and ed. Helene P. Foley, 196.
24. Gilligan, 104.
25. Wilkinson, 37.
26. Madonna Kolbenschlag, *Kiss Sleeping Beauty Good-bye: Breaking the Spell of Feminine Myths and Models* (New York: Doubleday, 1970), 41.
27. Mary Daly, *Beyond God the Father: Toward a Philosophy of Women's Liberation* (Boston: Beacon, 1973), 50.

6. Zeus and Helios: Male Power and Masculinities

1. Nanci DeBloois, "Rape, Marriage, or Death? Gender Perspectives in the Homeric *Hymn to Demeter*," *Philological Quarterly* 76 (1997): 245–262.
2. Aeschylus, *The Oresteia*, trans. Robert Fagles (New York: Viking Penguin, 1975).

3. Merlin Stone, *When God Was a Woman* (New York: Harcourt Brace Jovanovich, 1976), 32.

4. Ibid., 161–162.

5. Ibid., 161–197.

6. Lerner, 228–229.

7. Riane Eisler, *The Chalice and the Blade: Our History, Our Future* (San Francisco: Harper, 1989), xvii.

8. Ibid., xix.

9. Ibid., 19–21.

10. Ibid., 164.

11. Ibid., 164–169.

12. Golden, 249–250.

13. Ibid., 250.

14. Ibid., 283.

15. Gerda Lerner, *The Creation of Feminist Consciousness: From the Middle Ages to Eighteen-Seventy* (New York: Oxford UP, 1993), 10.

16. Deborah Tannen, *You Just Don't Understand: Women and Men in Conversation* (New York: Ballentine, 1990), 26.

17. Ibid., 28.

18. Aptheker, 44.

19. Harding, 38.

20. Lorde, 74.

21. Bolen, 26.

22. Ibid., 27.

23. Andrea Dworkin, *Woman Hating* (New York: E. P. Dutton and Co., Inc., 1974), 160.

24. Golden, 92.

25. Susan Griffin, *Pornography and Silence: Culture's Revenge Against Nature* (New York: Harper and Row, 1981), 142.

26. Nor Hall, *The Moon and the Virgin: Reflections on the Archetypal Feminine* (New York: Harper and Row, 1980), 5.

27. Aptheker, 253.

28. Lerner, *The Creation of Patriarchy*, 18.

29. R. W. Connell, *Masculinities* (Berkeley: U of California P, 1995), 37.

30. Ibid., 76.

31. Ibid., 68.

32. Ibid., 232.

33. Ibid., 233.

7. The Underworld and Hades: Death, Transformation, and Rebirth

1. Harding, 163.

2. Bolen, 55.

3. Sylvia Brinton Perera, "The Descent of Inanna: Myth and Therapy," in *Feminist Archetypal Theory: Interdisciplinary Re-Visions of Jungian Thought*, eds. Estella Lauter and Carol Schreier Rupprecht (Knoxville: U of Tennessee P, 1985), 166.

4. Chernin, 82.

5. Downing, "Persephone in Hades," 227.

6. Marion Woodman and Elinor Dickson, *Dancing in the Flames: The Dark Goddess in the Transformation of Consciousness* (Boston: Shambhala, 1996), 37.

7. Bolen, xiii.

8. Kathie Carlson, *Life's Daughter/Death's Bride*, 27.

9. Chernin, 16.

10. Sylvia Perera, *Descent to the Goddess: A Way of Initiation for Women* (Canada: Inner City, 1981), 167.

11. Downing, "Persephone in Hades," 230.

12. Valcarenghi, 205.

13. Wilkinson, 35.

14. Valcarenghi, 137.

15. Lorde, 171.

16. Ibid., 171–172.

17. Harding, 75.

18. Bolen, xvi.

19. Downing, "Persephone in Hades," 225.

20. Griffin, 55.

21. Christine Downing, *The Goddess: Mythological Images of the Feminine* (New York: Crossroad, 1981), 11.

22. Rabuzzi, 25.

23. Myra Sadker and David Sadker, *Failing at Fairness: How America's Schools Cheat Girls* (New York: Charles Scribner's Sons, 1994), 1.

24. Ibid., 204–206.

25. Ibid., 220.

26. Carlson, *Life's Daughter/Death's Bride*, 203.

27. Griffin, 1.

28. Ibid., 22.

29. Ibid., 55–57.

30. Ibid., 15, 66.

31. Aaron Kipnis and Elizabeth Herron, *Gender War, Gender Peace: The Quest for Love and Justice Between Men and Women* (New York: William Morrow and Co., Inc., 1994), 25.

32. Barbara McManus, *Classics and Feminism: Gendering the Classics* (New York: Twayne, 1977), 95.

33. Ibid., 107.

8. Rape

1. Elaine Morgan, *The Descent of Woman* (New York: Stein and Day, 1972), 83.

2. Susan Brownmiller, *Against Our Will: Men, Women, and Rape*, (New York: Fawcett Columbine, 1975), 14.

3. Ibid., 254.

4. Ibid., 18.

5. Ibid., 17.

6. Ruth Seifert, "War and Rape: A Preliminary Analysis," in *Mass Rape: The*

War Against Women in Bosnia-Herzegovina, ed. Alexandra Stiglmayer, trans. Marion Faber (Lincoln: U of Nebraska P, 1994), 59.

7. Brownmiller, *Against Our Will*, 38.

8. Lerner, *The Creation of Patriarchy*, 80.

9. Ibid., 80–81.

10. Ibid., 209.

11. Brownmiller, *Against Our Will*, 35.

12. Stone, 66.

13. Elinor Gadon, *The Once and Future Goddess: A Symbol for Our Time* (San Francisco: Harper, 1989), 106.

14. Cynthia Eller, *Living in the Lap of the Goddess: The Feminist Spirituality Movement in America* (New York: Crossroad, 1993), 163.

15. Ibid., 166.

16. Stone, 66.

17. Carlson, *Life's Daughter/Death's Bride*, 3.

18. Lorde, 55.

19. Ibid., 54.

20. Ibid., 54–55

21. Annis Pratt, Barbara White, Andrea Lowenstein, and Mary Wyer, *Archetypal Patterns in Women's Fiction* (Bloomington: Indiana UP, 1981), 24.

22. Lincoln, 78.

23. Wilkinson, 26.

24. Brownmiller, *Against Our Will*, 17.

25. Ibid., 384.

26. Lorde, 41.

27. Athena Devlin, "The Shame of Silence," in *Women: Images and Realities: A Multicultural Anthology*, ed. Amy Kesselman, Lily D. McNair, and Nancy Schniedewind, 2nd ed. (California: Mayfield, 1999), 437–438.

28. Carlson, *Life's Daughter/Death's Bride*, 26.

29. Patricia Berry, "The Rape of Demeter/Persephone and Neurosis," in *The Long Journey Home*, ed. Christine Downing, 202.

The Homeric Hymn to Demeter

Translated by Helene P. Foley

Demeter I begin to sing, the fair-tressed awesome goddess   1
herself and her slim-ankled daughter whom Aidoneus
seized; Zeus, heavy-thundering and mighty-voiced, gave her,
without the consent of Demeter of the bright fruit and golden sword,
as she played with the deep-breasted daughters of Ocean   5
plucking flowers in the lush meadow—roses, crocuses,
and lovely violets, irises and hyacinth and the narcissus,
which Earth grew as a snare for the flower-faced maiden
in order to gratify by Zeus's design the Host-to-Many,
a flower wondrous and bright, awesome for all to see,   10
for the immortals above and for mortals below.
From its root a hundredfold bloom sprang up and smelled
so sweet that the whole vast heaven above
and the whole earth laughed, and the salty swell of the sea.
The girl marveled and stretched out both hands at once   15
to take the lovely toy. The earth with its wide ways yawned
over the Nysian plain; the lord Host-to-Many rose up on her
with his immortal horses, the celebrated son of Kronos;
he snatched the unwilling maid into his golden chariot

and led her off lamenting. She screamed with a shrill voice, 20
calling on her father, the son of Kronos highest and best.
Not one of the immortals or of humankind
heard her voice, nor the olives bright with fruit,
except the daughter of Persaios; tender of heart
she heard it from her cave, Hekate of the delicate veil. 25
And lord Helios, brilliant son of Hyperion, heard
the maid calling her father the son of Kronos. But he sat apart
from the gods, aloof in a temple ringing with prayers,
and received choice offerings from humankind.
Against her will Hades took her by the design of Zeus 30
with his mortal horses—her father's brother,
Commander- and Host-to-Many, the many-named son of Kronos.
So long as the goddess gazed on earth and starry heaven,
on the beams of the sun, she still hoped 35
to see her dear mother and the race of immortal gods.
For so long hope charmed her strong mind despite her distress.
The mountain peaks and the depths of the sea echoed
in response to her divine voice, and her goddess mother heard.
Sharp grief seized her heart, and she tore the veil 40
on her ambrosial hair with her own hands.
She cast a dark cloak on her shoulders
and sped like a bird over dry land and sea,
searching. No one was willing to tell her the truth,
not one of the gods or mortals; 45
no bird of omen came to her as truthful messenger.
Then for nine days divine Deo roamed over the earth,
holding torches ablaze in her hands;
in her grief she did not once taste ambrosia
or nectar sweet-to-drink, nor bathed her skin. 50
But when the tenth Dawn came shining on her,
Hekate met her, holding a torch in her hands,
to give her a message. She spoke as follows:
"Divine Demeter, giver of seasons and glorious gifts,
who of the immortals or mortal men 55
seized Persephone and grieved your heart?
For I heard a voice but did not see with my eyes
who he was. To you I tell at once the whole truth."
Thus Hekate spoke. The daughter of fair-tressed Rheia
said not a word, but rushed off at her side 60
holding torches ablaze in her hands.
They came to Helios, observer of gods and mortals,

and stood before his horses. The most august goddess spoke:
"Helios, respect me as a god does a goddess, if ever
with word or deed I pleased your heart and spirit.   65
The daughter I bore, a sweet offshoot noble in form—
I heard her voice throbbing through the barren air
as if she were suffering violence. But I did not see her with my eyes.
With your rays you look down through the bright air
on the whole of the earth and the sea.   70
Tell me the truth about my child. Have you somewhere
seen who of the gods or mortal men took her
by force from me against her will and went away?"
Thus she spoke and the son of Hyperion replied:
"Daughter of fair-tresssed Rheia, mighty Demeter,   75
you will know the truth. For I greatly revere and pity you
grieving for your slim-ankled daughter. No other
of the gods was to blame but cloud-gathering Zeus,
who gave her to Hades his brother to be called
his fertile wife. With his horses Hades   80
snatched her screaming into the misty gloom.
But, Goddess, give up for good your great lamentation.
You must not nurse in vain insatiable anger.
Among the gods Aidoneus is not an unsuitable bridegroom,
Commander-to-Many and Zeus's own brother of the same stock.   85
As for honor, he got his third at the world's first division
and dwells with those whose rule has fallen to his lot."
He spoke and called to his horses. At his rebuke
they bore the swift chariot lightly, like long-winged birds.
A more terrible and brutal grief seized the heart   90
of Demeter, angry now at the son of Kronos with his dark clouds.
Withdrawing from the assembly of the gods and high Olympus,
she went among the cities and fertile fields of men,
disguising her beauty for a long time. No one of men
nor deep-girt women recognized her when they looked,   95
until she came to the house of skillful Keleos,
the man then ruler of fragrant Eleusis.
There she sat near the road, grief in her heart,
where citizens drew water from the Maiden's Well
in the shade—an olive bush had grown overhead—   100
like a very old woman cut off from childbearing
and the gifts of garland-loving Aphrodite.
Such are the nurses to children of law-giving kinds
and the keepers of stores in their echoing halls.

The daughters of Keleos, son of Eleusis, saw her   105
as they came to fetch water easy-to-draw and bring it
in bronze vessels to their dear father's halls.
Like four goddesses they were in the flower of youth,
Kallidike, Kleisidike, fair Demo, and Kallithoe,
who was the eldest of them all.   110
They did not know her—gods are hard for mortals to recognize.
Standing near her, they spoke winged words.
"Who are you, old woman, of those born long ago?
From where? Why have you left the city and do not
draw near its homes?" Women are there in the shadowy halls,   115
of your age as well as others born younger,
who would care for you both in word and in deed."
They spoke, and the most august goddess replied:
"Dear children, whoever of womankind you are,
greetings. I will tell you my tale. For it is not wrong   120
to tell you the truth now you ask.
Doso's my name, which my honored mother gave me.
On the broad back of the sea I have come now from Crete,
by no wish of my own. By force and necessity pirate men
led me off against my desire. Then they   125
put into Thorikos in their swift ship, where
the women stepped all together onto the mainland,
and the men made a meal by the stern of the ship.
My heart did not crave a heartwarming dinner,
but racing in secret across the dark mainland   130
I escaped from my arrogant masters, lest
they should sell me, as yet unbought, for a price overseas.
Then wandering I came here and know not at all
what this land is and who lives here.
May all the gods who dwell on Olympus   135
give you husbands to marry and children to bear,
such as parents wish for. Now pity me, maidens,
and tell me, dear children, with eager goodwill,
whose house I might come to, a man's
or a woman's, there to do for them gladly
such tasks as are done by an elderly woman.   140
I could nurse well a newborn child, embracing it
in my arms, or watch over a house. I could
spread out the master's bed in a recess
of the well-built chamber and teach women their work."
So spoke the goddess. To her replied at once Kallidike,   145

a maiden unwed, in beauty the best of Keleos' daughters.
"Good mother, we mortals are forced, though it hurt us,
to bear the gifts of the gods; for they are far stronger.
To you I shall explain these things clearly and name
the men to whom great power and honor belong here,   150
who are first of the people and protect with their counsels
and straight judgments the high walls of the city.
There is Triptolemos subtle in mind and Dioklos,
Polyxenos and Eumolpos the blameless,
Dolichos and our own lordly father.   155
And all these have wives to manage their households.
Of these not one at first sight would scorn
your appearance and turn you away from their homes.
They will receive you, for you are indeed godlike.
But if you wish, wait here, until we come to the house   160
of our father and tell Metaneira our deep-girt mother
all these things straight through, in case she might bid
you to come to our house and not search after others'.
For her only son is now nursed in our well-built hall,
a late-born child, much prayed for and cherished.   165
If you might raise him to the threshold of youth,
any woman who saw you would feel envy at once,
such rewards for his rearing our mother will give you."
Thus they spoke and she nodded her head. The girls
carried proudly bright jars filled with water and   170
swiftly they reached the great house of their father.
At once to their mother they told what they saw and heard.
She bade them go quickly to offer a boundless wage.
Just as hinds or heifers in the season of spring
bound through the meadow sated with fodder,   175
so they, lifting the folds of their shimmering robes,
darted down the hollow wagon-track, and their hair
danced on their shoulders like a crocus blossom.
They found the famed goddess near the road
just where they had left her. Then to the house   180
of their father they led her. She, grieved in her heart,
walked behind with veiled head. And her dark robe
swirled around the slender feet of the goddess.
They soon reached the house of god-cherished Keleos,
and went through the portico to the place where   185
their regal mother sat by the pillar of the close-fitted roof,
holding on her lap the child, her young offshoot. To her

they raced. But the goddess stepped on the threshold. Her head
reached the roof and she filled the doorway with divine light.
Reverence, awe, and pale fear seized Metaneira.   190
She gave up her chair and bade the goddess sit down.
But Demeter, bringer of seasons and giver of rich gifts,
did not wish to be seated on the shining seat.
She waited resistant, her lovely eyes cast down,
until knowing Iambe set out a well-built stool   195
for her and cast over it a silvery fleece.
Seated there, the goddess drew the veil before her face.
For a long time she sat voiceless with grief on the stool
and responded to no one with word or gesture.
Unsmiling, tasting neither food nor drink,   200
she sat wasting with desire for her deep-girt daughter,
until knowing Iambe jested with her and
mocking with many a joke moved the holy goddess
to smile and laugh and keep a gracious heart—
Iambe, who later pleased her moods as well.   205
Metaneira offered a cup filled with honey-sweet wine,
but Demeter refused it. It was not right, she said,
for her to drink red wine; then she bid them mix barley
and water with soft mint and give her to drink.
Metaneira made and gave the drink to the goddess as she bid.   210
Almighty Deo received it for the sake of the rite.
Well-girt Metaneira spoke first among them:
"Hail, lady, for I suppose your parents are not lowborn,
but noble. Your eyes are marked by modesty
and grace, even as those of justice-dealing kings.   215
We mortals are forced, though it may hurt us, to bear
the gifts of the gods. For the yoke lies on our necks.
But now you have come here, all that's mine will be yours.
Raise this child for me, whom the gods provided
Late-born and unexpected, much-prayed for by me.   220
If you raise him and he comes to the threshold of youth,
any woman who saw you would feel envy at once,
such rewards for his rearing would I give you."
Rich-crowned Demeter addressed her in turn:
"Hail also to you, lady, may the gods give you blessings.   225
Gladly will I embrace the child as you bid me.
I will raise him, nor do I expect a spell or the Undercutter
to harm him through the negligence of his nurse.
For I know a charm more cutting than the Woodcutter;

I know a strong safeguard against baneful bewitching."   230
So speaking, she took the child to her fragrant breast
with her divine hands. And his mother was glad at heart.
Thus the splendid son of skillful Keleos, Demophoon,
whom well-girt Metaneira bore, she nursed
in the great halls. And he grew like a divinity,   235
eating no food nor sucking [at a mother's breast];
[For daily well-crowned divine] Demeter anointed
him with ambrosia like one born from a god
and breathed sweetly on him, held close to her breast.
At night, she would bury him like a brand in the fire's might,
unknown to his own parents. And great was their wonder   240
as he grew miraculously fast; he was like the gods.
She would have made him ageless and immortal,
if well-girt Metaneira had not in her folly
kept watch at night from her fragrant chamber
and spied. But she shrieked and struck both thighs   245
in fear for her child, much misled in her mind,
and in her grief she spoke winged words.
"Demophoon, my child, the stranger buries you
deep in the fire, causing me woe and bitter cares."
Thus she spoke lamenting. The great goddess heard her.   250
In anger at her, bright-crowned Demeter snatched
from the flames with immortal hands the dear child
Metaneira had borne beyond hope in the halls and,
raging terribly at heart, cast him away from herself to the ground.
At the same time she addressed well-girt Metaneira: 255
"Mortals are ignorant and foolish, unable to foresee
destiny, the good and the bad coming on them.
You are incurably misled by your folly.
Let the god's oath, the implacable water of Styx, be witness,
I would have made your child immortal and ageless   260
forever; I would have given him unfailing honor.
But now he cannot escape death and the death spirits.
Yet unfailing honor will forever be his, because
he lay on my knees and slept in my arms.
In due time as the years come round for him,   265
the sons of Eleusis will continue year after year
to wage war and dread combat against each other.
For I am honored Demeter, the greatest
source of help and joy to mortals and immortals.
But now let all the people build me a great temple   270

with an alter beneath, under the sheer wall
of the city on the rising hill above Kallichoron.
I myself will lay down the rites so that hereafter
performing due rites you may propitiate my spirit."
Thus speaking, the goddess changed her size and appearance,   275
thrusting off old age. Beauty breathed about her and
from her sweet robes a delicious fragrance spread;
a light beamed far out from the goddess's immortal skin,
and her golden hair flowed over her shoulders.
The well-built house flooded with radiance like lightning.   280
She left the halls. At once Metaneira's knees buckled.
For a long time she remained voiceless, forgetting
to pick up her dear only son from the floor.
But his sisters heard his pitiful voice and
leapt from their well-spread beds. Then one took   285
the child in her arms and laid him to her breast.
Another lit the fire; a third rushed on delicate feet
to rouse her mother from her fragrant chamber.
Gathering about the gasping child, they bathed
and embraced him lovingly. Yet his heart was not comforted,   290
for lesser nurses and handmaids held him now.
All night they tried to appease the dread goddess,
shaking with fear. But when dawn appeared,
they explained to wide-ruling Keleos exactly
what the bright-crowned goddess Demeter commanded.   295
Then he called to assembly his innumerable people
and bid them build for fair-tressed Demeter
a rich temple and an altar on the rising hill.
Attentive to his speech, they obeyed at once and did
as he prescribed. It grew as the goddess decreed.   300
But once they finished and ceased their toil,
each went off home. Then golden-haired Demeter
remained sitting apart from all immortals,
wasting with desire for her deep-girt daughter.
For mortals she ordained a terrible and brutal year   305
on the deeply fertile earth. The ground released
no seed, for bright-crowned Demeter kept it buried.
In vain the oxen dragged many curved plows down
the furrows. In vain much white barley fell on the earth.
She would have destroyed the whole mortal race   310
by cruel famine and stolen the glorious honor of gifts
and sacrifices from those having homes on Olympus,

if Zeus had not seen and pondered their plight in his heart.
First he roused golden-winged Iris to summon
fair-tressed Demeter, so lovely in form.   315
Zeus spoke and Iris obeying the dark-clouded
son of Kronos, raced swiftly between heaven and earth.
She came to the citadel of fragrant Eleusis
and found in her temple dark-robed Demeter.
Addressing her, spoke winged words: 320
"Demeter, Zeus, the father, with his unfailing knowledge
bids you join the tribes of immortal gods.
Go and let Zeus's word not remain unfulfilled."
Thus she implored, but Demeter's heart was unmoved.
Then the father sent in turn all the blessed immortals;   325
one by one they kept coming and pleading
and offered her many glorious gifts and whatever
honors she might choose among the immortal gods.
Yet not one could bend the mind and thought
of the raging goddess, who harshly spurned their pleas.   330
Never, she said, would she mount up to fragrant
Olympus nor release the seed from the earth,
until she saw with her eyes her own fair-faced child.
When Zeus, heavy-thundering and mighty-voiced,
heard this, he sent down the Slayer of Argos to Erebos   335
with his golden staff to wheedle Hades with soft words
and lead back holy Persephone from the misty gloom
into the light to join the gods so that her mother
might see her with her eyes and desist from anger.
Hermes did not disobey. At once he left Olympus's height   340
and plunged swiftly into the depths of the earth.
He met lord Hades inside his dwelling,
reclining on a bed with his shy spouse, strongly reluctant
through desire for her mother. [Still she, Demeter,
was brooding on revenge for the deeds of the blessed gods].   345
The strong Slayer of Argos stood near and spoke:
"Dark-haired Hades, ruler of the dead, Father Zeus
bids me lead noble Persephone up from Erebos
to join us, so that her mother might see her with her eyes
and cease from anger and dread wrath against the gods.   350
For she is devising a great scheme to destroy
the helpless race of mortals born on earth,
burying the seed beneath the ground and obliterating
divine honors. Her anger is terrible, nor does she go

among the gods but sits aloof in her fragrant temple,   355
keeping to the rocky citadel of Eleusis."
Thus he spoke and Aidoneus, lord of the dead, smiled
with his brows, nor disobeyed king Zeus's commands.
At once he urged thoughtful Persephone:
"Go, Persephone, to the side of your dark-robed mother,   360
keeping the spirit and temper in your breast benign.
Do not be so sad and angry beyond the rest;
in no way among immortals will I be an unsuitable spouse,
myself a brother of father Zeus. And when you are there,
you will have power over all that lives and moves,   365
and you will possess the greatest honors among the gods.
There will be punishment forevermore for those wrongdoers
who fail to appease your power with sacrifices,
performing proper rites and making due offerings."
Thus he spoke and thoughtful Persephone rejoiced.   370
Eagerly she leapt up for joy. But he gave her to eat
a honey-sweet pomegranate seed, stealthily passing it
around her, lest she once more stay forever
by the side of revered Demeter of the dark robe.
Then Aidoneus commander-to-many yoked   375
his divine horses before the golden chariot.
She mounted the chariot and at her side the strong
Slayer of Argos took the reins and whip in his hands
and dashed from the halls. The horses flew eagerly;
swiftly they completed the long journey; not sea nor   380
river waters, not grassy glens nor mountain peaks
slowed the speed of the immortal horses,
slicing the deep air as they flew above these places.
He brought them to a halt where rich-crowned Demeter
waited before the fragrant temple. With one look she darted   385
like a maenad down a mountain shaded with woods.
On her side Persephone, [seeing] her mother's [radiant face],
[left chariot and horses,]and leapt down to run
[and fall on her neck in passionate embrace].
[While holding her dear child in her arms], her [heart   390
suddenly sensed a trick. Fearful, she] drew back
from [her embrace and at once inquired:]
"My child, tell me, you [did not taste] food [while below?]
Speak out [and hide nothing, so we both may know.]
[For if not], ascending [from miserable Hades],   395
you will dwell with me and your father, the

dark-clouded [son of Kronos], honored by all gods.
But if [you tasted food], retuning beneath [the earth,]
you will stay a third part of the seasons [each year],
but two parts with myself and the other immortals.   400
When the earth blooms in spring with all kinds
of sweet flowers, then from the misty dark you will
rise again, a great marvel to gods and mortal men.
By what guile did the might Host-to-Many deceive you?"
Then radiant Persephone replied to her in turn: 405
"I will tell you the whole truth exactly, Mother.
The Slayer of Argos came to bring fortunate news
from my father, the son of Kronos, and the other gods
and lead me from Erebos so that seeing me with your eyes
you would desist from your anger and dread wrath   410
at the gods. Then I leapt up for joy, but he stealthily
put in my mouth a food honey-sweet, a pomegranate seed,
and compelled me against my will and by force to taste it.
For the rest—how seizing me by the shrewd plan of my father,
Kronos's son, he carried me off into the earth's depths—   415
I shall tell and elaborate all that you ask.
We were all in the beautiful meadow—
Leukippe; Phaino; Elektra; and Ianthe;
Melite; Iache; Rhodeia; and Kallirhoe;
Melibosis; Tyche; and flower-faced Okyrhoe;   420
Khryseis; Ianeira; Akaste; Admete;
Rhodope; Plouto; and lovely Kalypso;
Styx; Ourania; and fair Galaxaura; Pallas,
rouser of battles; and Artemis, sender of arrows—
playing and picking lovely flowers with our hands,   425
soft crocus mixed with irises and hyacinth,
rosebuds and lilies, a marvel to see, and the
narcissus that wide earth bore like a crocus.
As I joyously plucked it, the ground gaped from beneath,
and the mighty lord, Host-to-Many, rose from it   430
and carried me off beneath the earth in his golden chariot
much against my will. And I cried out at the top of my voice.
I speak the whole truth, though I grieve to tell it."
Then all day long, their minds at one, they soothed
each other's heart and soul in many ways,   435
embracing fondly, and their spirits abandoned grief,
as they gave and received joy between them.
Hekate of the delicate veil drew near them

and often caressed the daughter of holy Demeter;
from that time this lady served her as chief attendant.   440
To them Zeus, heavy-thundering and mighty-voiced
sent as mediator fair-tressed Rheia to summon
dark-robed Demeter to the tribes of gods; he promised
to give her what honors she might choose among the gods.
He agreed his daughter would spend one-third   445
of the revolving year in the misty dark and two-thirds
with her mother and the other immortals.
So he spoke and the goddess did not disobey his commands.
She darted swiftly down the peaks of Olympus
and arrived where the Rarian plain, once life-giving   450
udder of earth, now giving no life at all, stretched idle
and utterly leafless. For the white barley was hidden
by the designs of lovely-ankled Demeter. Yet as spring came on,
the field would soon ripple with long ears of grain;
and the rich furrows would grow heavy on the ground   455
with grain to be tied with bands and sheaves.
There she first alighted from the barren air.
Mother and daughter were glad to see each other
and rejoiced at heart. Rheia of the delicate veil then said:
"Come, child, Zeus, heavy-thundering and mighty-voiced,   460
summons you to rejoin the tribes of the gods;
he has offered to give what honors you choose among them.
He agreed that his daughter would spend one-third
of the revolving year in the misty dark, and two-thirds
with her mother and the other immortals.   465
He guaranteed it would be so with a nod of his head.
So come, my child, obey me; do not rage overmuch
and forever at the dark-clouded son of Kronos.
Now make the grain grow fertile for humankind."
So Rheia spoke, and rich-crowned Demeter did not disobey.   470
At once she sent forth fruit from the fertile fields
and the whole wide earth burgeoned with leaves
and flowers. She went to the kings who administer law,
Triptolemos and Diokles, driver of horses, mighty
Eumolpos and Keleos, leader of the people, and revealed   475
the conduct of her rites and taught her Mysteries to all of them,
holy rites that are not to be transgressed, nor pried into,
nor divulged. For a great awe of the gods stops the voice.
Blessed is the mortal on earth who has seen these rites,   480
but the uninitiated who has no share in them never

has the same lot once dead in the dreary darkness.
When the great goddess had founded all her rites,
the goddesses left for Olympus and the assembly of the other gods.
Their they dwell by Zeus delighting-in-thunder, inspiring   485
awe and reverence. Highly blessed is the mortal
on earth whom they graciously favor with love.
For soon they will send to the hearth of his great house
Ploutos, the god giving abundance to mortals.
But come, you goddesses, dwelling in the town of   490
fragrant Eleusis, and seagirt Paros, and rocky Antron,
revered Deo, mighty giver of seasons and glorious gifts,
you and your very fair daughter Persephone,
for my song grant gladly a living that warms the heart.
And I shall remember you and a new song as well.   495

Bibliography

Aeschylus. *The Oresteia.* Trans. Robert Fagles. New York: Viking Penguin, 1975.

Ann, Martha, and Dorothy Myers Imel. *Goddesses in World Mythology: A Biographical Dictionary.* Oxford: Oxford UP, 1993.

Aptheker, Bettina. *Tapestries of Life: Women's Work, Women's Consciousness, and the Meaning of Daily Experience.* Amherst: U of Massachusetts P, 1989.

Arthur, Marylin. "Politics and Pomegranates." *The Homeric Hymn to Demeter: Translation, Commentary, and Interpretive Essays.* Ed. Helene P. Foley. Princeton: Princeton UP, 1994. 212–242.

Austen, Hallie Iglehart. *The Heart of the Goddess: Art, Myth, and Meditations of the World's Sacred Feminine.* Berkeley: Wingbow, 1990.

Badinter, Elisabeth. *The Myth of Motherhood: An Historical View of the Maternal Instinct.* Trans. Roger DeGaris. London: Souvenir, 1981.

Belenky, Mary Field, et al. *Women's Ways of Knowing: Development of Self, Voice, and Mind.* New York: Basic, 1986.

Berry, Patricia. "The Rape of Demeter/Persephone and Neurosis." *The Long Journey Home: Re-Visioning the Myth of Demeter and Persephone for Our Time.* Ed. Christine Downing. Boston: Shambhala, 1994. 197–205.

Bolen, Jean Shinoda. *Goddesses in Every Woman: A New Psychology of Woman.* New York: Harper Colophon, 1984.

_____. *Goddesses in Older Women: Archetypes in Women Over Fifty, Becoming a Juicy Crone.* New York: HarperCollins, 2001.

Brownmiller, Susan. *Against Our Will: Men, Women, and Rape.* New York: Fawcett Columbine, 1975.

_____. *Femininity.* New York: Linden, 1984.

Bruteau, Beatrice. "The Unknown Goddess." *The Goddess Re-Awakening: The Feminine Principle Today.* Ed. Shirley Nicholson. Illinois: Quest, 1989. 68–80.

Burkert, Walter. *Ancient Mystery Cults.* Massachusetts: Harvard UP, 1987.

Bushe, Vera. "Cycles of Becoming." *The Long Journey Home: Re-Visioning the Myth of*

Demeter and Persephone for Our Time. Ed. Christine Downing. Boston: Shambhala, 1994. 173–185.

Campbell, Joseph, and Charles Muses, eds. *In All Her Names: Explorations of the Feminine in Divinity.* San Francisco: HarperCollins, 1991.

_____. *The Masks of God.* 4 Vols. New York: Viking, 1959.

Carlson, Kathie. *In Her Image: The Unhealed Daughter's Search for Her Mother.* Boston: Shambhala, 1990.

_____. *Life's Daughter/Death's Bride: Inner Transformations Through the Goddess Demeter/Persephone.* Boston: Shambhala, 1997.

Chernin, Kim. *Reinventing Eve: Modern Woman in Search of Herself.* New York: Time, 1987.

Chodorow, Nancy. "Family Structure and Feminine Personality." *The Homeric Hymn to Demeter: Translation, Commentary, and Interpretive Essays.* Ed. Helene P. Foley. Princeton: Princeton UP, 1994. 243–265.

Christ, Carol P. *Laughter of Aphrodite: Reflections on a Journey to the Goddess.* San Francisco: Harper and Row, 1987.

Cicero. *The Republic and the Laws.* Trans. Niall Rudd. Oxford: Oxford UP, 1998.

Cleary, Thomas, and Sartaz Aziz. *Twilight Goddess: Spiritual Feminism and Feminine Spirituality.* Boston: Shambhala, 2000.

Cline, Sally, and Dale Spender. *Reflecting Men at Twice Their Natural Size.* New York: Henry Holt and Co., 1987.

Connell, R. W. *Masculinities.* Berkeley: U of California P, 1995.

Daly, Mary. *Beyond God The Father: Toward a Philosophy of Women's Liberation.* Boston: Beacon, 1973.

_____. *Gyn/Ecology: The Metaethics of Radical Feminism.* Boston: Beacon, 1990.

DeBloois, Nanci. "Rape, Marriage, or Death? Gender Perspectives in the Homeric Hymn to Demeter." *Philological Quarterly* 76 (1997): 245–262.

De Castillejo, Irene Claremont. *Knowing Woman: A Feminine Psychology.* Boston: Shambhala, 1997.

Delaney, Janice, Mary Jane Lupton, and Emily Toth. *The Curse: A Cultural History of Menstruation.* New York: E. P. Dutton, 1976.

Devlin, Athena. "The Shame of Silence." *Women: Images and Realities: A Multicultural Anthology.* Ed. Amy Kesselman, Lily D. McNair, and Nancy Schniedewind. 2nd ed. California: Mayfield, 1999. 437–438.

Downing, Christine. *The Goddess: Mythological Images of the Feminine.* New York: Crossroad, 1981.

Downing, Christine, ed. *The Long Journey Home: Re-Visioning the Myth of Demeter and Persephone for Our Time.* Boston: Shambhala, 1994.

Dworkin, Andrea. *Intercourse.* New York: The Free Press, 1987.

_____. *Woman Hating.* New York: E. P. Dutton and Co., Inc., 1974.

Edinger, Edward F. *The Eternal Drama: The Inner Meaning of Greek Mythology.* Boston: Shambhala, 1994.

Eisler, Riane. *The Chalice and the Blade: Our History, Our Future.* San Francisco: Harper, 1989.

Eller, Cynthia. *Living in the Lap of the Goddess: The Feminist Spirituality Movement in America.* New York: Crossroad, 1993.

_____. *The Myth of Matriarchal Prehistory: Why An Invented Past Won't Give Women a Future.* Boston: Beacon, 2000.

Engelsman, Joan Chamberlain. *The Feminine Dimension of the Divine.* Philadelphia: Western Press, 1979.

Estes, Clarissa Pinkola. *Women Who Run with Wolves: Myths and Stories of the Wild Woman Archetype.* New York: Ballantine, 1992.

Exum, Cheryl. *Plotted, Shot, and Painted: Cultural Representations of Biblical Women.* Sheffield: Sheffield Academic P, 1996.

Fallon, Patricia, Melanie A. Katzman, and Susan C. Wooley, eds. *Feminist Perspectives on Eating Disorders.* New York: Guilford, 1994.

Felson-Rubin, Nancy, and Harriet M. Deal. "The Functions of the Demophoon Episode in the Homeric *Hymn to Demeter.*" *The Homeric Hymn to Demeter: Translation, Commentary, and Interpretive Essays.* Ed. Helene P. Foley. Princeton: Princeton UP, 1994. 191–197.

Firestone, Shulamith. *The Dialectic of Sex: The Case for Feminist Revolution.* New York: William Morrow, 1970.

Foley, Helene P., trans. *The Homeric Hymn to Demeter: Translation, Commentary, and Interpretive Essays.* Princeton: Princeton UP, 1994.

_____. "The 'Theology' of The Mysteries." *The Homeric Hymn to Demeter: Translation, Commentary, and Interpretive Essays.* Ed. Helene P. Foley. Princeton: Princeton UP, 1994. 84–97.

Forden, Carie, Anne E. Hunter, and Beverly Birns, eds. *Readings in the Psychology of Women: Dimensions of the Female Experience.* Boston: Allyn and Bacon, 1998.

Frazer, Sir James George. *The Golden Bough: A Study in Magic and Religion.* 3rd ed. 2 vols. New York: St. Martin's, 1996.

Friday, Nancy. *My Mother My Self: The Daughter's Search for Identity.* New York: Dell, 1977.

Friere, Paulo. *Pedagogy of the Oppressed.* Trans. Myra Bergman Ramos. New York: Continuum, 1990.

Gadon, Elinor W. *The Once and Future Goddess: A Symbol for Our Time.* San Francisco: Harper, 1989.

Garland, Robert. *The Greek Way of Death.* New York: Cornell UP, 1985.

Gilligan, Carol. *In a Different Voice: Psychological Theory and Women's Development.* 2nd ed. Cambridge: Harvard UP, 1993.

Gimbutas, Marija. *The Goddesses and Gods of Old Europe: Myths and Cult Images: 6500–3500 B.C.* Berkeley: U of California P, 1982.

_____. *The Language of the Goddess.* London: Thames and Hudson, 1989.

Golden, Stephanie. *Slaying the Mermaid: Women and the Culture of Sacrifice.* New York: Harmony, 1998.

Graves, Robert. *The White Goddess: A Historical Grammar of Poetic Myth.* New York: Farrar, Straus, and Giroux, 1948.

Greer, Germaine. *The Change: Women, Aging, and the Menopause.* New York: Alfred A. Knopf, 1992.

Griffin, Susan. *The Eros of Everyday Life: Essays on Ecology, Gender, and Society.* New York: Anchor, 1995,

_____. *Pornography and Silence: Culture's Revenge Against Nature.* New York: Harper and Row, 1981.

Hall, Nor. *The Moon and the Virgin: Reflections on the Archetypal Feminine.* New York: Harper and Row, 1980.

Hamilton, Edith. *Mythology: Timeless Tales of Gods and Heroes.* New York: Mentor, 1969.

Harding, M. Esther. *The Way of All Women: A Psychological Interpretation.* New York: Harper and Row, 1970.

_____. *Woman's Mysteries, Ancient and Modern: A Psychological Interpretation of the Fem-*

inine Principle as Portrayed in Myth, Story, and Dreams. New York: Putnam's Sons, 1971.

Heilbrun, Carolyn G. *Writing a Woman's Life*. New York: Ballantine, 1988.

Helgeson, Sally. *The Female Advantage: Women's Ways of Leadership*. New York: Doubleday, 1990.

Henderson, Joseph L., and Maud Oakes. *The Wisdom of the Serpent: The Myths of Death, Rebirth, and Resurrection*. Princeton: Princeton UP, 1963.

Herman, Judith Lewis. *Trauma and Recovery*. New York: Basic, 1992.

Homer. *The Odyssey*. Trans. Robert Fitzgerald. New York: Anchor, 1963.

Houston, Jean. *The Hero and the Goddess: The Odyssey as Mystery and Initiation*. New York: Ballantine, 1992.

Hughes, K. Wind and Linda Wolf, eds. *Daughters of the Moon, Sisters of the Sun: Young Women and Mentors on the Transition to Womanhood*. British Columbia: New Society, 1997.

The Jerusalem Bible: Reader's Edition. Gen. Ed. Alexander Jones. New York: Doubleday and Co., Inc., 1968.

Jung, C. G. *Archetypes and the Collective Unconscious*. Trans. R. F. C. Hull. 2nd ed. Bollingen Series XX. Princeton: Princeton UP, 1990.

Kerenyi, Carl. *Eleusis: Archetypal Image of Mother and Daughter*. Trans. Ralph Manheim. Princeton: Princeton UP, 1967.

Kesselman, Amy, Lily D. McNair, and Nancy Schniedewind, eds. *Women: Images and Realities: A Multicultural Anthology*. 2nd ed. California: Mayfield, 1995.

Kipnis, Aaron and Elizabeth Herron. *Gender War, Gender Peace: The Quest for Love and Justice Between Men and Women*. New York: William Morrow and Co., Inc., 1994.

Kirk, G. S. *The Nature of the Greek Myths*. New York: Overlook P, 1975.

Knapp, Bettina L. *Women, Myth, and the Feminine Principle*. New York: State U of NY P, 1998.

_____. *Women in Myth*. New York: State U of NY P, 1997.

Kolbenschlag, Madonna. *Kiss Sleeping Beauty Good-Bye: Breaking the Spell of Feminine Myths and Models*. New York: Doubleday, 1970.

Larrington, Carolyne, ed. *The Feminist Companion to Mythology*. London: Pandora, 1992.

Lauter, Estella, and Carol Schreier Rupprecht. *Feminist Archetypal Theory: Interdisciplinary Re-visions of Jungian Thought*. Knoxville: U of Tennessee P, 1985.

Lerner, Gerda. *The Creation of Feminist Consciousness: From the Middle Ages to Eighteen-Seventy*. New York: Oxford UP, 1993.

_____. *The Creation of Patriarchy*. Oxford: Oxford UP, 1986.

Lerner, Harriet Goldhor. *The Dance of Intimacy*. New York: Harper and Row, 1989.

Lincoln, Bruce. *Emerging from the Chrysalis: Rituals of Women's Initiation*. New York: Oxford UP, 1991.

Long, Asphodel P. *In A Chariot Drawn by Lions: The Search for the Female in Deity*. Freedom: Crossing p, 1993.

Lorde, Audre. *Sister Outsider: Essays and Speeches*. California: Crossing, 1984.

Lubell, Winifred Milius. *The Metamorphosis of Baubo: Myths of Woman's Sexual Energy*. Nashville: Vanderbilt UP, 1994.

Luke, Helen. *Woman, Earth, and Spirit: The Feminine in Symbol and Myth*. New York: Crossroads, 1981.

Lyons, Deborah. *Gender and Immortality: Heroines in Ancient Greek Myth and Cult*. Princeton: Princeton UP, 1997.

Mascetti, Manuela Dunn. *Goddesses: An Illustrated Journey into the Myths, Symbols, and Rituals of the Goddess*. New York: Barnes and Noble, 1998.

McManus, Barbara F. *Classics and Feminism: Gendering the Classics*. New York: Twayne, 1997.

Mernissi, Fatima. *The Veil and the Male Elite: A Feminist Interpretation of Women's Rights in Islam*. Trans. Mary Jo Lakeland. Massachusetts: Addison-Wesley, 1987.

Meyer, Marvin W., ed. *The Ancient Mysteries, A Sourcebook: Sacred Texts of the Mystery Religions of the Ancient and Mediterranean World*. San Francisco: Harper and Row, 1987.

Monaghan, Patricia. *The Book of Goddesses and Heroines*. Minnesota: Llewellyn Publications, 1990.

Moore, Henrietta. *Feminism and Anthropology*. Minneapolis: U of Minnesota P, 1990.

Morgan, Elaine. *The Descent of Woman*. New York: Stein and Day, 1972.

Murdock, Maureen. *The Heroine's Journey*. Boston: Shambhala, 1990.

Nicholson, Shirley. *The Goddess Re-Awakening: The Feminine Principle Today*. Illinois: The Theosophical Publishing House, 1989.

Pagels, Elaine. *Adam, Eve, and the Serpent*. New York: Random House, 1988.

Pater, Walter. *Greek Studies: A Series of Essays*. London, Macmillan, 1908.

Perera, Sylvia Brinton. *Descent to the Goddess: A Way of Initiation for Women*. Canada: Inner City, 1981.

_____. "The Descent of Inanna: Myth and Therapy." *Feminist Archetypal Theory: Interdisciplinary Re-Visions of Jungian Thought*. Eds. Estella Lauter and Carol Schreier Rupprecht. Knoxville: U of Tennessee P, 1985. 137–186.

Pomeroy, Sarah B. *Goddesses, Whores, Wives, and Slaves: Women in Classical Antiquity*. New York: Schocken, 1975.

Powell, Barry B. *Classical Myth*. Englewood Cliffs: Prentice Hall, 1995.

Powers, Meredith A. *The Heroine in Western Literature: The Archetype and Her Reemergence in Modern Prose*. North Carolina: McFarland and Co., Inc., 1991.

Pratt, Annis. *Dancing with Goddesses: Archetypes, Poetry, and Empowerment*. Bloomington: Indiana UP, 1994.

_____, Barbara White, Andrea Lowenstein, and Mary Wyer. *Archetypal Patterns in Women's Fiction*. Bloomington: Indiana UP, 1981.

Qualls-Corbett, Nancy. *The Sacred Prostitute: Eternal Aspect of the Feminine*. Toronto: Inner City, 1988.

Rabuzzi, Kathryn Allen. *Motherself: A Mythic Analysis of Motherhood*. Bloomington: Indiana UP, 1988.

Rich, Adrienne. *Of Woman Born: Motherhood as Experience and Institution*. New York: W. W. Norton and Co., 1986.

Sadker, Myra, and David Sadker. *Failing at Fairness: How America's Schools Cheat Girls*. New York: Charles Scribner's Sons, 1994.

Sattler, Cheryl L. *Teaching to Transcend: Educating Women Against Violence*. Albany: State U of NY P, 2000.

Seifert, Ruth. "War and Rape: A Preliminary Analysis." *Mass Rape: The War Against Women in Bosnia-Herzegovina*. Ed. Alexandra Stiglmayer. Trans. Marion Faber. Lincoln: U of Nebraska P, 1994. 54–73.

Smith, Barbara. "Greece." *The Feminist Companion to Mythology*. Ed. Carolyne Larrington. London: Pandora, 1992. 65–101.

Spretnak, Charlene. *Lost Goddesses of Early Greece: A Collection of Pre-Hellenic Myths*. Boston: Beacon, 1984.

Stone, Merlin. *Ancient Mirrors of Womanhood: A Treasury of Goddess and Heroine Lore from Around the World*. Boston: Beacon P, 1990.

_____. *When God Was a Woman*. New York: Harcourt Brace Jovanovich, 1976.

Tannen, Deborah. *You Just Don't Understand: Women and Men in Conversation.* New York: Ballantine, 1990.

Trites, Roberta Seelinger. *Waking Sleeping Beauty: Feminist Voices in Children's Novels.* Iowa: U of Iowa P, 1997.

Tyrell, William Blake and Frieda S. Brown. *Athenian Myths and Institutions: Words in Action.* New York: Oxford UP, 1991.

Valarenghi, Marina. *Relationships: Transforming Archetypes.* Maine: York Beach, 1997.

Von Franz, Marie-Louise. *The Feminine in Fairy Tales.* Boston: Shambhala, 1972.

_____. *Shadow and Evil in Fairy Tales.* Rev. Ed. Boston: Shambhala, 1995.

Walker, Barbara. *The Crone: Woman of Age, Wisdom, and Power.* San Francisco: Harper and Row, 1985.

_____. *The Woman's Encyclopedia of Myths and Secrets.* San Francisco: HarperCollins, 1983.

Wilkinson, Tanya. *Persephone Returns: Victims, Heroes, and the Journey from the Underworld.* Berkeley: Pagemill, 1996.

Woodman, Marion, and Elinor Dickson. *Dancing in The Flames: The Dark Goddess in the Transformation of Consciousness.* Boston: Shambhala, 1996.

Woodman, Marion, Kate Danson, Mary Hamilton, and Rita Greer Allen. *Leaving My Father's House: A Journey to Conscious Femininity.* Boston: Shambhala, 1993.

Young-Eisendrath, Polly. "Demeter's Folly: Experiencing Loss in Middle Life." Ed. Christine Downing. *The Long Journey Home: Re-Visioning the Myth of Demeter and Persephone for Our Time.* Boston: Shambhala, 1994. 206–218.

Index